D0732616

JESUS CHRIST:

LORD OF THE UNIVERSE, HOPE OF THE WORLD

EDITED BY DAVID M. HOWARD

InterVarsity Press
Downers Grove
Illinois 60515

InterVarsity Press is the book
publishing division of
Inter-Varsity Christian
Fellowship, a student movement
active on campus at hundreds
of universities, colleges
and schools of nursing. For
information about this
dynamic association, write IVCF,
233 Langdon, Madison, WI 53703.
If you're a student, four
chances out of five you'll find
a local IVCF chapter on
your campus.

ISBN 0-87784-763-0
Library of Congress Catalog
Card Number: 74-75454

Printed in the United
States of America

CONTENTS

PREFACE

Jesus Christ: Lord of the Universe, Hope of the World. These words rang out clearly at Urbana 73. During the three years of planning and preparation for the tenth Inter-Varsity Missionary Convention, a strong feeling was building that Urbana 73 must sound a positive note. We wanted the convention to be Christ-centered, to focus on the sovereignty of God and to emphasize the worldwide responsibility of the church. Thus a theme was chosen which combined those elements. The entire program was built with this theme—the ultimate triumph of Jesus Christ —in mind.

While recognizing that missions from the West have had their share of failures and that there is much for which we need to repent, we also recognized that God in his sovereignty is going to complete his work in the world regardless of our failures. Therefore, the focus was on Jesus Christ as Lord of the Universe, the One who said, "I will build my church, and the gates of hell shall not prevail against it."

The speakers for Urbana 73 were chosen after long months of prayer and consideration. In every case we had a strong conviction that this was the person God had chosen to bring this message. Throughout the week as each speaker developed the topic assigned to him, it was evident that God had prepared the way and that this was the word coming from God to us through his servant.

The students at Urbana 73 witnessed several innovations in the program. For the first time a message was given through translation, when a Colombian who speaks no English spoke in Spanish (Gregorio Landero). Also for the first time a woman delivered a major address (Elisabeth Elliot Leitch). Three students (Pius Wakatama from Wheaton College, Donald Curry from the University of Calgary and Russell Weatherspoon from Brooklyn College) brought major addresses. This also constituted a "first" for Urbana conventions.

In addition to the speakers in the plenary sessions, approximately 530 missionaries representing 110 mission boards were present to talk with students personally throughout the day. Ninety workshops were offered, giving the students a wide choice of topics and issues which they could discuss with competent leaders. Also, 1,500 small groups of ten gathered each morning in the dormitories to study an assigned passage of Scripture, which had already been used for quiet time that day. The same groups met each night to share what God was teaching the members and to end the day in prayer.

One indication of how the Spirit of God worked throughout the convention was the response of the students. This was evident in personal conversations, in notes of gratitude written to the convention leadership, in decisions made quietly but firmly. Two tangible evidences of the depth of commitment were the following. When an offering was received for student work around the world, the students responded with a total of $153,000 in cash and $37,000 in pledges. This is undoubtedly the largest student offering ever given for the Lord's work. Also, when world evangelism decision cards were made available to each student, 4,062 of them were turned in at the convention, indicating a commitment either to serve God overseas or to pray and seek God's will actively in terms of missionary outreach. Many more cards continued to come in after the convention.

All of this gave evidence that students at Urbana 73 were responding to Jesus Christ as Lord of their Universe and Hope of their World.

The convention itself is over, but the message goes on. We present this compendium of the addresses with the prayer that it may help the church in our day recognize Jesus Christ as Lord of the Universe and the only Hope of the World.

David M. Howard
Director, Urbana 73

INTRODUCTION: WHY ARE WE HERE?

JOHN W. ALEXANDER

First of all, may I add my words of welcome to those already given. It is a pleasure for me, on behalf of Inter-Varsity in the United States, to welcome you to this convention. It is an added pleasure to extend a welcome as a University of Illinois alumnus, for the U. of Illinois is my alma mater. Little did I realize in the late 1930s when I tramped the sidewalks of this campus as an undergraduate that the day would come when I would return with all of you and be singing the praises of the Lord Jesus Christ on this campus and hear his truth proclaimed in numerous classrooms of these buildings. So, welcome to Urbana.

Now the question: Why are we here?

The basic reason is that the Lord Jesus Christ ordained that we be here. The Bible says that God has a plan for all of human history—and, in terms of time, that plan includes the year 1973. In terms of population, his plan includes us as a group—and you and me as individuals. Let us remind ourselves of how the Bible speaks of this plan in the first chapter of Ephesians:

Blessed be the God and Father of our Lord Jesus Christ, who has blessed us in Christ with every spiritual blessing in the heavenly places, even as he chose us in him before the foundation of the world, that we should be holy and blameless before him. He destined us in love to be his sons through Jesus Christ, according to the purpose of his will. . . . In him we have redemption through his blood, the forgiveness of our trespasses according to the riches of his grace which he lavished upon us. For he has made known to us in all wisdom and insight the mystery of his will, according to his purpose which he set forth in Christ as a plan for the fulness of time, to unite all things in him, things in heaven and things on earth. (Eph. 1:3-10)

In harmony with that Scripture, we believe we are here at this time in this place because the sovereign God of all creation ordained in his great plan that there be this missionary convention—with you and me participating.

Why are *we* here? Because we desire gladly to obey such a God, to be where he wants us to be—and doing what he wants us to do.

Let us pursue this question further: Why has he ordained *that* we be here? And why have we come in obedience to that plan?

May I suggest three reasons:

First, we are here to learn more of what the *Word of God* says about his eternal and unchangeable plans for the world. We want to lay a solid biblical foundation for understanding God's plan for the world. To do that we go directly to the Bible, probing it with all our mind, confident that the Holy Spirit will teach us from God's revealed written Word. For the next four days we will employ numerous means to improve our understanding of Scripture: There will be lectures by biblical scholars, there will be over a thousand small group Bible studies each day and there will be time for us privately to meet Christ and probe the Bible alone.

Second, we are here to learn more about *the world*, the condition of society today, the condition of people in general, and of persons in particular, in order that we can do a more effective job of proclaiming the truth of our Lord Jesus Christ to fellow members of mankind. We need to know more about the contemporary scene if we are to evangelize effectively and then to make disciples of those who respond to Jesus Christ. We will do this by listening to several messages in this Assembly Hall, through participation in numerous seminars and discussion groups, and through countless personal conversations with missionaries whose experiences in diverse parts of the world qualify them to instruct us.

Third, we are here to seek God's will for our *individual lives*. Many of you for months have been looking forward to this convention. You have saved your money. You are investing precious time. Some of you have denied yourselves attractive vacation trips to warmer climates in order to be here. Why have you done this? Because you confidently expect to meet the Lord Jesus Christ in a special way at this convention and to receive guidance about what he has in mind for your future.

You're hungry for him. Some of you have told me you're thirsting for him. And you've come expectantly, anticipating the glorious experience of meeting the Lord himself in a special way.

Registration authorities tell us that this is the largest missionary convention in the history of Inter-Varsity. There are over 14,000 of us enrolled. Surely this is a great thrill, being shoulder-to-shoulder with so many colleagues singing God's praises, studying his Word, learning of his world, seeking his will.

But in one sense it is quite immaterial how many of us are here. More important is whether or not the Lord Jesus Christ is here—and whether we are yielded to his Spirit for accomplishing his purpose. To be sure, we are concerned with the question of why we are here. But beneath that question is the more basic one: Why is *he* here?

We believe that he *is* here—to help you and me increase our understanding of him and his Word, to help you and me learn more about him and his world, to help us receive guidance concerning his plan for our lives and, above all, to help us get closer to him personally.

And now, may I personalize the question and phrase it this way: Why are you here? It may be that for you the turning point in the convention will come right now—at this moment—as you finalize in your mind and soul the basic answer to the question: Why am I here?

I count it a privilege to be associated with people such as you who are so committed to Christ that you will pay the price to participate in this endeavor.

The focus throughout this convention will be on Jesus Christ —who is *the* Lord of the Universe, *the* Hope of the World. May he—our Lord and hope—have preeminence in all that is said and done and thought in every aspect of this missionary convention.

And may each of us receive help from the Spirit of the Living God, who meets each of us at every point of need. May Jesus Christ be praised. That is why we are here.

PART I

LORD OF THE UNIVERSE, HOPE OF THE WORLD

JESUS CHRIST: LORD OF THE UNIVERSE

SAMUEL J. ESCOBAR

In a way, I would prefer not to speak tonight but to join all of you in a celebration of the lordship of Christ, in the happy and joyous recognition that he is the Lord indeed, as his Word proclaims and as we have called upon him to be the Lord of our lives. Rather than analysis, I would prefer a joyful celebration of his lordship, because when a multitude of people gathers as we are gathered, the meaning and value of being together comes only if we recognize that we are gathered in the name of the Lord. And then, what can we do but simply join in telling him that we acknowledge the greatness of his power and the reality of his lordship, that we realize that our language is inadequate to express our worship of his greatness and that we would like to have "a thousand tongues" to sing the glories of our Lord.

But today it will be necessary to argue and to reflect with you upon the fact that Jesus Christ is the Lord of the Universe, for this is a truth that we must rediscover together in all its greatness and in all its relevance. First, because we live in a day in which history has become chaotic. As we watch what is going on around the world, the most unexpected and undreamed of events are happening in different parts of the earth. And we come to feel that there is no way to understand the puzzle of historic developments today.

In the sixties, youth on this continent and round the world—Christian youth also—were carried away in an eagerness to move along with history. It was the decade of student power. Youth these days are back to the interior search, to the flight within. As a student told me in Mexico last July, "We do not care about Marxism and the movement of history any more. We want to experience *inside* power. I want to know how I can have this power." Inner power may be your concern also, rather than the movement of history. Let others care about making history. You want to have command of your own personal history. Is this choosing a better option, or is this giving up in despair? Does Jesus the carpenter, with whom we may want to take our trip inside, care about history and the making of it?

Second, we need in these days to remember that Jesus Christ is the Lord precisely because political and social developments are again producing a trend toward totalitarianism. The number of nations that are living unwillingly under military rule is increasing. The nature of historical dynamics seems to be going from a decade of anarchical emphasis on revolution to a decade in which the pragmatic reality of naked power in order to keep the world running efficiently is being imposed around the globe. Men in very different parts of the world are proclaiming openly, and sometimes acting openly though not stating it, their right to rule society and the lives of other men without any kind of check or control.

In some places and nations people are searching for a Messiah who will lead them to security and safety, to a social order with no flaws and no threat of disorder. It is amazing the number of films and books that have been released recently about Hitler and Mussolini and some of the other totalitarian characters who were the nightmare of men four decades ago. When men want to become lords of other men, or are pushed in that direction, it is

necessary to state once and again that there is only One who is
to be the Lord to whom men give unconditional surrender, that
there is only One who is to be worshiped and praised as the Lord
of men because he is the Lord of the Universe and the Lord of
History.

Third, we need to rediscover the richness of the meaning of
the lordship of Christ because in the Western world, where the
majority of the Christian resources—money, scholarship, men—
are concentrated at the moment, the commitment to the advance
of his kingdom and engagement in the task of taking his presence
and proclaiming his name is being officially abandoned by the
great denominational bodies into which the church is organized.
There is in many quarters a retreat from the missionary field.
Christians in the West have to recover the vision of the Lord who
commanded his followers to take his gospel and make disciples
among the nations, in every sociological stratum as well as in
every geographical dimension. Again we need to become missionary-minded with the mind of Christ. Let us do all the necessary revision and all the criticism of the imperialistic age of missions; let us take into account seriously the new historical developments. But by all means, let us be faithful to our Lord, the Lord
of the Universe, who is sending us to cooperate with him in the
accomplishment of his purpose of making his name known
among men of all races, nations and classes, of creating a new
humanity that does not recognize frontiers, that is gathered from
every corner of the world and spread around the earth.

The Paradox of His Lordship

But to come to terms with the lordship of Christ as we find it in
his Word is to come to terms with a paradoxical reality, because
this Lord comes to us in a most unexpected way. The Lord of the
Universe became Jesus of Nazareth, the humble, poor carpenter,
who was born in a stable, who made himself a servant, the One
for whom there was no great reception committee. As Paul says
in Philippians,

> For the divine nature was his from the first; yet he did not
> think to snatch at equality with God, but made himself noth-
> ing, assuming the nature of a slave. Bearing the human like-

*ness, revealed in human shape, he humbled himself, and in
obedience accepted even death—death on a cross. Therefore
God raised him to the heights and bestowed on him the name
above all names, that at the name of Jesus every knee should
bow—in heaven, on earth, and in the depths—and every
tongue confess, "Jesus Christ is Lord," to the glory of God the
Father. (Phil. 2:6-11)*

I have known many among your generation who have discovered, with joy and amazement, this paradoxical humanity of
our Lord, grasping afresh the meaning of Paul's words. And because of that simplicity they have seen the lordship of Christ in
action through the hands of Mother Theresa among the dying
crowds of Calcutta and through Jean Vanier, a Canadian Christian who works among retarded people in France. And I can tell
you of a man who wants to write a *Life of Jesus* for the Muslims.
He has been to Urbana before, but this time we will miss him because he is living among the people of a Muslim nation in order
to know better what and how to write for them about our Lord.

Have we grasped this paradox of the gospel? How can the
Spirit of God open our eyes, the eyes of the church today, to the
fact that his lordship is seen through men who dare to live for
him among men, yes, even in the corners where no one wants to
be, and to go.

Israel had great expectations about the way God the Lord
would come to visit them, about the way the Messiah, the
anointed one, would come. They associated his coming with
human greatness, understood in social, military and political
terms. They could not understand how this simple man, the son
of Mary and Joseph, the one some of them had seen growing up
in Nazareth, could say he was the one the prophets had announced. As Paul says, this is a mystery, and unless the Spirit of
God opens our eyes we will not be able to accept this paradox or
discover its meaning for us. Can you see?

Another aspect of the paradox of the lordship of Jesus Christ
is that suffering is a part of it. The greatness of the crown is
linked to the suffering of the cross. How difficult it was for Peter
the fisherman to learn this! It was he who made the first clear
theological statement of who Jesus was, linking him to the prom-

ises and the expectations about which the prophets had spoken. It was he to whom it was revealed, not by flesh and blood but by the very Spirit of God. But he would not accept the fact that Jesus the Messiah, the anointed one, the expected one, was going to suffer on the cross—receiving the mockery, injuries and death that other men were going to impose upon him.

How difficult it was for Peter to learn that his Lord was also the suffering Messiah! He said, "No, Lord, this shall never happen to you" (Mt. 16:23). It was only after years of faithful, though not always successful, discipleship that he could say,

What credit is there in fortitude when you have done wrong and are beaten for it? But when you have behaved well and suffer for it, your fortitude is a fine thing in the sight of God. To that you were called, because Christ suffered on your behalf, and thereby left you an example; it is for you to follow in his steps. (1 Peter. 2:20-21)

This paradox is especially difficult to grasp in our age because we live in a civilization that praises success and in which suffering is a sign of defeat. If we have been able to mold nature and the environment in such a way that we avoid not only suffering but even discomfort, if we can make an artificial atmosphere, if we are modifying geography, if we can computerize movements of men so that they will not fail, how can we follow in the steps of a suffering Lord?

The history of the way in which the people of God have participated in his mission, in the accomplishment of his purpose, is a history of triumph and glory, but also a history of sweat, tears and suffering, sometimes to the point of martyrdom. To our century and our civilization belong the curious theories that try to conceive, computerize and program the missionary enterprise in such a way that suffering will always be avoided and success will be guaranteed. Believe me, there are some social classes, some nations, cultures and subcultures, some areas of the world today that will not hear the gospel unless there are Christians ready to follow in the steps of the suffering Lord. I have great respect for those missionaries who refuse to leave difficult territories in search of more "productive" lands. I respect those pastors and congregations who have stayed in the inner city even at

the cost of radically changing their program and their approach
to people. I respect those Christian students who have faithfully
kept a light in hostile campuses when many others have left.
And I know all these come to know true joy even in their suffering.

The Lord of the Harvest knows that the glowing reports of
success in his work have been preceded many times by the anonymous faithfulness of suffering sowers. As the Lord himself said
to the twelve, "That is how the saying comes true: 'One sows,
and another reaps.' I sent you to reap a crop for which you have
not toiled. Others toiled and you have come in for the harvest of
their toil" (Jn. 4:37-38).

This does not mean that we are looking for suffering or that
we have a kind of evangelical masochism. As Peter says, there is
suffering that may come because we have "done wrong." That
is not the suffering associated with the lordship of Christ. It
could be suffering that comes simply because we do not obey his
Word or because we do not take reality seriously. I am speaking
of that other kind of suffering where the cause is obedience to the
Lord and faithfulness to him.

I have a friend, a pastor who spent some years in jail in Cuba.
No reason was given in his case other than his refusal to submit
unconditionally to the regime there. He is now free; he ministers
in a difficult situation in the same country: isolated, confined to
his city, carefully watched. But he has been told by local authorities that to them he is more dangerous than a thousand soldiers
fighting against the regime. And around the world under every
type of regime we have brethren whose faithfulness to the Lord
means suffering with him. Never let the fear of suffering rob you
of the joy of obedience to the Lord's call.

Even when we cannot see immediately the way in which our
suffering is used by God, we can rejoice because Christ is a pioneer of any suffering we may go through. I think this is eloquently put in the second stanza of the hymn that was prepared for
this conference:

Lord of the Universe, Hope of the World,
Lord of the infinite eons of time,
You came among us, lived our brief years,

Tasted our griefs, our aloneness, our fears,
Conquered our death, made eternity ours.

There are times when we do not understand suffering, but the Lord pioneered suffering and death, and because of that he can meet with us.

The third element that makes the lordship of Christ a paradox difficult to grasp is that in our life on earth it is experienced within a tension. Christ is already the Lord who on the cross has defeated the kingdom of evil and darkness. This is what Peter announced to the very people who had participated in his crucifixion: "Let all Israel then accept as certain that God has made this Jesus, whom you crucified, both Lord and Messiah" (Acts 2:36).

This is also what Paul states clearly in the passage of Philippians that we quoted above. Christ is the Lord.

Christ is our Lord and our Savior because when we called upon his name we were in slavery to the reality of sin and evil. We could not save ourselves. No measure of good intention, education, social engineering or psychological adjustment could save us, but only the power of the Holy Spirit by the death and resurrection of Christ. Yes, he is our victorious Savior.

However, his lordship is not entirely visible yet. It is a reality that is still to come. The New Testament speaks in different ways of the moment in which it will come: "the Lord's day," "the day of his coming." In a dramatic way Paul tells us in Romans 8 that just as we experience the eagerness for the arrival of that day, the whole creation is in expectation. We live in this eschatological tension. That is why we see the forces of evil at work, apparently challenging the lordship of Christ.

Professor F. F. Bruce has said it well:

Paul's language about "principalities and powers" or "elemental spirits" may have an archaic prescientific sound today, although the current revival of astrology and magic suggests that a "pre-scientific" world outlook is quite congenial to many of our contemporaries. But at a more serious level man today is unprecedentedly aware of powerful and malignant forces in the universe which he does not hesitate to call "demonic." He feels that they are operating against his wel-

*fare but he is quite unable to master them, whether by indi-
vidual strength or by united action. They may be manifestations of the "dynamism of history," they may be Franken-
stein monsters of his own creation; they may be subliminal
horrors over which he has no conscious control; they may be
aspects of the contemporary climate of opinion or current
trends. He knows himself to be involved in situations from
which his moral sense recoils, but what can he do about them?
If he and his fellows are puppets in the hand of a blind and
unfriendly fate, what difference does it make whether they re-
sist and are crushed immediately or acquiesce and are
crushed a little later?*

*To this mood of frustration and despair Paul still provides
the answer. To be united to Christ by faith is to be liberated
from the thraldom of demonic forces, to enjoy perfect freedom
instead of being the playthings of fate.* [1]

So we are conscious of the reality and the presence of evil
taking over political institutions, human associations, financial
empires or intelligence agencies and making them demonic
forces that crush human beings. But we are not afraid of them.
We are in Christ, and we can demythologize them and advance.
Assured of the final triumph, we can say with Paul,

*There is no God but one. For indeed, if there be so-called
gods, whether in heaven or on earth—as indeed there are many
"gods" and many "lords"—yet for us there is one God, the
Father, from whom all being comes, towards whom we move;
and there is one Lord, Jesus Christ, through whom all things
came to be, and we through him. (1 Cor. 8:4-6)*

The Lord of the Universe

The statement that Christ is the Lord of the Universe has an Old
Testament background. (I am in special debt here to the Latin
American theologian Justo González who teaches at Emory Uni-
versity and who has done a great piece of research on the lord-
ship of Christ and its meaning.[2]) Apostolic writers in the New
Testament articulated gradually the meaning of the lordship of
Christ as they were given the revelation of the great reality of
Jesus Christ. They applied to Jesus the same words that were

used for God, particularly the names which the Greek version of the Old Testament translated *kyrios*, that is, *Lord*. There was a recognition, which is ėlaborated by Paul, especially in Colossians and Ephesians, that Christ is also the creator of the universe and that he is, in the same way in which the Psalms speak about God, the sustainer of the universe.

This truth has not always been grasped or accepted by Christians, and some heresies have tended to deny the lordship of Christ in this sense. The Marcionite heresy in the second century is one of these views which has continually recurred through the history of the church. This heresy begins with the presupposition that the created world, and particularly the material world and the human body, are bad in themselves, base, inferior. It does not recognize that the world in which we live is a creation of God and that God is active in his creation. Marcion in the second century rejected the Old Testament because he saw in it a God who had created a wrong world. He could not be the same Father of whom Jesus spoke. Marcion also found a contradiction between the God of justice in the Old Testament and the God of love in the New.

You can see how these presuppositions take one to the idea of a "spiritual" Jesus Christ, who saves us from this world so that we can forget material realities and only aim to go to heaven as soon as possible. This might sound very spiritual, but it is sheer heresy. Unfortunately, Marcion has many followers in our century, even among people who call themselves evangelical.

It was precisely in order to state truth in face of this type of heresy that what we call the "Creed of the Apostles" was drawn up. It starts with the statement, "I believe in God the Father, almighty, maker of heaven and earth." The term translated *almighty* is the Greek *pantocrator*, which really means the one who is ruling everything. Then the creed states, "and in Jesus his only son, our Lord," stating that Jesus Christ, the Lord in whom we believe, is the Son of God, the creator of heaven and earth.

Creeds are to be repeated and sung but also to be lived. If Jesus Christ is the Lord of the Universe, every aspect of our lives is under his lordship. Our daily activity, yes, even our eating and drinking, has to express his lordship. Is he the Lord of your studies? Is he the Lord of your cultural activity? Is he the Lord of your social affairs?

There is no doubt that the so-called Western world has in its social and institutional life the marks of its heritage of Christian influence. We could trace the way in which Christian individuals and communities who took the lordship of Christ seriously in their academic, social and political life changed the shape of the world, so that we have what we call today the Western world. It is also true, however, that there is a process of deterioration of the Christian heritage and that every day this Western world moves increasingly away from its substratum of Christian influence. We have come to the point where expressing the lordship of Christ in our life, in the way we deal with the daily issues of work, money or relationships is going against the stream. Here we need theological awareness so we can distinguish what is decadent and Western from what is biblical and Christian in every area of life.

The individual and communal efforts to participate in the daily life of our societies under the lordship of Christ demand from us wherever we are, whatever our position, a missionary spirit and vocation. There is a Christian way of approaching your work in college. There is, for instance, a Christian way of understanding history and a Christian attitude toward your study of history textbooks. In some areas like chemistry, the content of our learning may not change because we are Christian, but the use to which we put it will be different.

Some virtues like honesty, punctuality, dependability, consideration of others and accuracy are not only values proclaimed by square, old-fashioned parents and teachers. They are habits that express our surrender to the Lord. And they are very important in missionary work.

There is still much more Christians can do individually and as communities in order to keep a measure of sanity and wholeness in a dying, self-destroying society. We must rediscover the excitement of living out our belief in the lordship of Christ in daily, ordinary life—even if that seems revolutionary. And indeed it is.

Jesus Christ, Lord of History

But to affirm the lordship of Christ is to recognize that in being the Lord of the Universe, he is also the Lord of History. The process of the life of men, nations and communities on this planet is going to come one day to an end, and at that end the purpose of God is going to be accomplished. In the historical processes today, as well as in the historical processes in Christ's day, and in all historical process, there is a purpose of God that cannot be defeated. When the Lord gave his Great Commission to the disciples, he stated the principle that all authority was given to him on earth and in heaven; and upon that principle and on the basis of it, on the basis of his lordship, he committed them, and us, to the task of taking his message to all the world.

It is important to observe what happened in the Roman world. The recognition of Christ as the Lord was the central reason for the Roman persecution against Christians in the second and third centuries. It was because Christians, in spite of social and political pressure, refused to recognize the Roman Caesar as lord of their lives in the ideological dimension in which he demanded it that they were sent to the Circus. They became dangerous to the unity of that civilization and to the dreams of imperial manifest destiny that it had.

In the Roman Empire there was another group of people that, even before the Christians, had stated their recognition of God the Lord as the only one who could have claim to all their loyalty. Those were the Jews. Because of different historical circumstances, they were given special treatment and released from the obligation of worshiping the emperor. But the Jews were a minority, a particular group, kept together by racial and cultural links which were easily detected. They could afford to be different, in part because they were not supposed to have a missionary task. They were not calling men to be like them. Some Gentiles were attracted to them but not many joined them.

Christians, on the other hand, were people from different races—Jews, Greeks, Romans, Africans—and from different classes—masters, slaves, freed—and they were convinced that they had been called by Jesus to proclaim his message to all men. They had a definite missionary existence. And because of that they became dangerous. They were committed to obey the Great Commission of Christ the Lord, whatever the cost and whatever the amount of opposition. They were ready to respect the laws of the Roman state as long as those laws and customs would not be against their loyalty and their unconditional obedience to the Lord Jesus Christ.

To state, then, that Jesus Christ is the Lord of History is also to state the truth that the lordship of Christ is the reason for the missionary task of the church, that the way by which his lordship is affirmed is also the extension of his kingdom—the fact that it becomes a reality evident in the lives of people from all nations, races, colors and classes of the world. This historical and universal dimension of the lordship of Christ becomes the essence of the missionary task: *The church exists for mission!*

Maybe one of the reasons why there has been in our generation a diminishing of interest and passion for accomplishing the great task of proclaiming the lordship of Christ in every corner of this world is that historical developments have shown that the way Christians in past generations conceived the evangelization of the world has not been the way it has happened.

Leslie T. Lyall has expressed this eloquently:

At the historic world-wide missionary conference held in Edinburgh in 1910, in the heyday of Western colonial expansion and before the first of two tragic world wars had shattered the imperial dream, missionary statesmen looked out from their Christian citadel in the West over a pagan world, but a world which their optimism expected soon to become Christian through the influence of Christian colonization in Asia and Africa. (They ignored Latin America, which many of them regarded as already "Christian.")

In Europe and North America the church in the Edwardian era was at the height of its power and popularity. Elsewhere in the world it was considered scarcely to exist! The church therefore clearly saw it to be the white Christian's burden to evangelize "the heathen" and to extend the frontiers of the Christian church worldwide. Many conceived their Christian duty to go further and to include spreading Western or Chris-

tian civilization with the gospel. . . .

Sixty years later the picture is profoundly different. The imperial dream has been finally shattered. Imperialism and colonialism instead of proving to be the allies of evangelism came to be regarded after the Second World War as its enemies. The church in the Third World is today acutely embarrassed by any past association with either and is trying to live down and out-live the commonly-held view that Christianity was in some way a part of the "imperialist plot" to dominate the world–"the spearhead of cultural imperialism."[3]

Shattered dreams! But let us not be discouraged, and let us not jump to easy conclusions. As Lyall himself continues,

Whether with the aid of or in spite of colonial expansion, the Christian church has in these sixty years become a worldwide church. In 1971, as the last resistant strongholds have yielded to the messengers of Christ, the church is a universal reality. Bishop Stephen Neill has expressed it in these words: "It is only rarely possible in the history of the world to speak of anything as being unmistakably new. But in the twentieth century one phenomenon has come into view which is incontestably new–for the first time there is in the world a universal religion and that the Christian religion!"[4]

What happened in other moments of human history has happened again. When the Roman Empire was crumbling, attacked by the barbarians, many felt that it was the end of the Christian mission. It was not the end! Christ became the Lord of many barbarians and his church there enriched the church universal in theology, liturgy and the accomplishment of the missionary task. When with the Reformation Christendom became divided and society revolutionized, many saw that as the end. But out of the Protestant churches eventually came the strength for enormous missionary advances. In our day, the very forces, like nationalism, which seemed to be a threat to the growth of the church in the world have become a dynamic influence in the growth of Christian communities in the so-called Third World. Christ the Lord can use the very forces which are hostile to his church to accomplish his purpose. Because of that, we do not despair even if this civilization in which you and I live is falling apart. What we do is try to be faithful to him. It is his name that we are called to carry and announce, not Western civilization.

And he is carrying out his purpose. When churches which had nice sophisticated theology and organization refused to obey the Lord, his Spirit moved among hundreds of independent agencies that with little more than their Bibles and a stubborn obedience are pioneering the remotest areas. When affluent middle-class churches limit themselves to token expressions of missionary concern, God is using the meager proletarian resources of pentecostals here and abroad to spread his kingdom, behind any curtain or wall. When mammoth ecclesiastical organizations, crippled by their bureaucratic machinery, spend themselves in endless talk about ecclesiastical traffic, the Lord has raised his apostles in the counter culture to show us simple ways of praising him, obeying him, proclaiming him and daring to do things differently. What can the Lord do with us in this moment of history? There is nothing that can stop his purpose.

In Africa, in Asia, in Latin America, we look to the future as the point in history in which our dreams will become a reality. We do not share the mood of despair and the mood of defeat that is now overtaking Christians in the Western world. We believe that God still has many things to accomplish before Christ comes again. The end of this so-called Western civilization might be the beginning of a new historical reality. We want to be part of it under Christ, and we want to count on people like you to join us in whatever capacity!

I must confess I have expectations that the Lord will come soon. I must confess that every day I pray "thy kingdom come," with the hope that all the suffering, injustice, war and misery, and our incomplete and poor grasp of his truth, will be replaced by justice, by peace, by a new creation, by complete knowledge of the truth of God in Christ. But at the same time I cannot say when that is going to happen. I want it to happen today. I want it to happen right now. But there is such a great task ahead! There are millions who have not yet heard the gospel, and I hope that the patience of the Lord will wait until this task is accomplished, till the millions who have not had a chance of hearing once of

Jesus Christ the Lord will have their chance.

Jesus Christ is the Lord of the Universe. Are you a living expression of his lordship in every aspect of your life in your society? Let us commit ourselves into his hands so that wherever we go he will make us a missionary presence. Maybe you have never called Jesus Christ your Lord, and his Word says that we can only call him Lord in the Spirit that is in us.

Jesus Christ is the Lord of History. With him we can only move forward. Under him we can only live in obedience. And this obedience is to go wherever he sends us.

Notes
[1]F. F. Bruce, The Message of the New Testament (Grand Rapids: Eerdmans, 1972), pp. 38-39.
[2]Justo González, Jesucristo es el Señor (Miami: Editor Caribe, 1971).
[3]Leslie T. Lyall, A World to Win (London: Inter-Varsity Press, 1972), pp. 27-28.
[4]Ibid.

JESUS CHRIST AND THE AUTHORITY OF THE WORD OF GOD

JOHN R. W. STOTT*

Authority is a dirty word today, dirty, disliked, even detested. I doubt if any other word arouses more instant aversion among the young and the radical of all kinds. Authority smacks of establishment, of privilege, of oppression, of tyranny. And whether we like it or not, we are witnessing in our day a global revolt against all authority, whether of the family, the college, the bosses, the church, the state or God.

Now the Christian is always in an ambivalent position vis à vis the mood of the world. We have to avoid the two extremes of an uncritical acquiescence and of an equally uncritical rejection. On the one hand, we should respond to the contemporary world with sensitivity—listening, striving to understand and where possible agreeing. On the other hand, we must continue to stand

*Mr. Stott's talk has also been published as a booklet entitled *The Authority of the Bible* (IVP, 25ᶜ).

over against the world, evaluating secular society by our own objective Christian criteria, and where necessary disagreeing, protesting and rejecting. It is not the calling of the church to be a chorus girl or—to use a more biblical metaphor—a reed shaken with the wind.

If we adopt this double stance towards the world, what will happen to the debate about authority? It would be extremely foolish if our immediate reaction were completely negative, and we were to give the whole anti-authority movement a blanket condemnation. For I do not hesitate to say that some of it is responsible, mature and truly Christian. It arises from the Christian doctrine of man and his dignity as a creature made in God's likeness. It protests against the dehumanization of human beings and sets itself against all injustice and discrimination which insult both God the creator and man the creature. It seeks to protect man against exploitation by "the system," "the machine," "the institution." It longs to see men liberated to enjoy their God-given freedom.

It is right, therefore, to detect a grievous misuse of authority when civil rights and freedom of speech are denied to citizens, when a racial or tribal or religious minority is victimized, when an economic system holds people in bondage to materialism or when education is hardly distinguishable from indoctrination. In such situations, when non-Christians protest, Christians should not be ashamed to be associated with the protest. Indeed, we should have initiated it ourselves.

On the other hand, much of today's anti-authority mood is more radical still. Sometimes it is a plea not for the true human liberty which God intends for mankind, but for anarchy (a total abolition of the rule of law) and for an individual human autonomy (every man a law to himself) which God never intended. Christians cannot go along with secularists when they agitate for unlimited permissiveness in social and ethical terms, nor when they foolishly imagine that "free thought" is intellectual freedom or that "free sex" is moral freedom. For Christians are convinced that neither truth nor righteousness is relative, since God has given us (by revelation) absolute standards both of what is true and of what is right. Which brings us straight to our subject:

Jesus Christ and the authority of the Word of God.

Our starting point is the remark attributed to Charles Lamb that "if Shakespeare was to come into this room we should all rise up to meet him, but if *that* Person [Jesus Christ] was to come into it, we should all fall down and try to kiss the hem of his garment." For myself I think we would do more than kiss his clothing. We would surely go on to acknowledge him as our Lord. We would kneel beside Thomas saying "My Lord and my God" and beside Saul of Tarsus saying "Lord, what do you want me to do?"

This is the only possible attitude of mind in which to approach our study of Jesus Christ and the authority of the Word of God, for my theme is that belief in the authority of Scripture and submission to the authority of Scripture are necessary consequences of our submission to the lordship of Jesus. I propose first to expound this theme and then to draw some deductions from it.

Exposition

What is the major reason why evangelical Christians believe that the Bible is God's Word written, inspired by his Spirit and authoritative over their lives? It is certainly not that we take a blindfold leap into the darkness and resolve to believe what we strongly suspect is incredible. Nor is it because the universal church consistently taught this for the first eighteen centuries of its life (though it did, and this long tradition is not to be lightly set aside). Nor is it because God's Word authenticates itself to us as we read it today—by the majesty of its themes, by the unity of its message and by the power of its influence (though it does all this and more). No. The overriding reason for accepting the divine inspiration and authority of Scripture is plain loyalty to Jesus.

We believe in Jesus. We are convinced that he came from heaven and spoke from God. He said so: "No one knows the Father, except the Son," he claimed (Mt. 11:27). Again, "my teaching is not mine, but his who sent me" (Jn. 7:16) and "we speak of what we know and bear witness to what we have seen" (Jn. 3:11). So we are prepared to believe what *he* taught for the simple reason that it is *he* who taught it. Therefore we bring our minds into submission to his mind. We want to conform our thoughts to his thoughts. It is from Jesus that we derive our understanding of God and man, of good and evil, of duty and destiny, of time and eternity, of heaven and hell. Our understanding of *everything* is conditioned by what Jesus taught. And this *everything* means *everything:* It includes his teaching about the Bible. We have no liberty to exclude anything from Jesus' teaching and say "I believe what he taught about *this* but not what he taught about *that*." What possible right have we to be selective? We have no competence to set ourselves up as judges and decide to accept some parts of his teaching while rejecting others. All Jesus' teaching was true. It is the teaching of none other than the Son of God.

What, then, *did* Jesus teach about the Bible? We have to remember, of course, that the Bible consists of two halves, the Old Testament and the New Testament. And the way he endorsed each is different—inevitably so because the New Testament had not yet been written.

The Old Testament

Jesus made several direct statements about the Old Testament's divine origin and permanent validity. He had not come to abolish the law and the prophets, he said in the Sermon on the Mount, but to fulfill them. Indeed, "till heaven and earth pass away, not an iota, not a dot, will pass from the law until all is accomplished" (Mt. 5:17-18; cf. Lk. 16:17). Again, "Scripture cannot be broken" (Jn. 10:35).

To these direct statements we should add the indirect evidence provided by the formulae he used to introduce his Scripture quotations. For example, he prefaced a quotation from Psalm 110 by the expression "David himself said in [that is, inspired by] the Holy Spirit" (Mk. 12:35), and he attributed a statement about marriage written by the author of Genesis to the Creator himself, who in the beginning made man male and female (Mt. 19:4-5).

More impressive than what Jesus *said* about Scripture, however, is the way he personally *used* it. His high view of Scripture as God's written Word is amply illustrated in the important place it occupied in his own life and ministry. He did not just talk about Scripture; he believed it and acted upon it himself. Let me give you three examples. In each there was a potential element of uncertainty, a question or problem. In each he answered the question and resolved the problem by an appeal to Scripture. In each, therefore, his personal submission to Scripture is plainly seen.

The first is the area of *personal duty*. What did the Lord God require of him? What were to be the standards and values by which he would live his life? The devil raised such questions as these with Jesus in the wilderness of Judea, as he had raised them with Adam and Eve in the garden of Eden several millenia previously. The devil tempted Jesus to disobey God, to doubt God and to desert God. But whereas in the garden Eve succumbed to the insinuations of Satan, in the wilderness Jesus resisted them. "Begone Satan!" he cried. Why? "Because it stands written [in Scripture] *'you shall not.'*" The plain prohibitions of Scripture were enough for Jesus. For him what Scripture said God said. There was no place for argument and no room for negotiation. He was determined to obey God his Father, and he knew that in order to do so he must submit to Scripture and do what stands written there.

My second example takes us to the area of *official ministry*. The Gospels do not describe the process by which Jesus came to an understanding of who he was (his identity) and what he had come to do (his role). It seems very probable, however, that it was through meditation in the Old Testament Scriptures. Certainly *before* his public ministry began he knew he was the Son of God, the anointed King, the suffering servant and the glorious Son of man described by different psalms and prophets. Also, he had so fused these different pictures in his mind that he knew he could enter his glory only if he were first to serve, suffer and die. This self-understanding was confirmed to him at his baptism when the Father's voice acclaimed him saying: "You are my beloved Son in whom I am well pleased."

But immediately afterwards the devil precipitated him into a painful identity crisis, challenging him repeatedly in the wilderness—"If you are the Son of God . . . if . . . if . . . if . . ."—attempting to sow in his mind seeds of doubt about his identity and role.

And these temptations continued throughout his ministry. Another crisis came at Caesarea Philippi when Jesus first taught the apostles openly "the Son of man must suffer many things and be rejected and be killed," and Peter rebuked him, "No, Lord. God forbid, Lord! This shall never happen to you" (Mt. 16:22). Immediately Jesus rounded on Peter with the fierce words, "Get behind me, Satan!" He recognized in the words of Peter the voice of the devil. It was the same question of his identity and role.

Peter did it again in the Garden of Gethsemane when he drew his sword and tried to avert the arrest of Jesus. Jesus said to him, "Put your sword back into its place. . . . Do you think I cannot appeal to my Father and he will at once send me more than twelve legions of angels? But how then should the Scriptures be fulfilled, that it must be so?" (Mt. 26:52-54).

This "must" ("the Son of man *must* suffer," "it *must* be so") has only one explanation. It was a necessity laid upon him by Scripture. Scripture revealed to him his messianic role. And he was determined voluntarily to fulfill it, because, as far as he was concerned, what Scripture said God said.

The third area of questioning in which Jesus was involved was that of *public controversy*. Every reader of the Gospels quickly notices how many public debates they include. Regarding him as a particularly wise rabbi, individuals would come to him with their questions. Sometimes they were genuine inquiries like "what must I do to inherit eternal life?" On this occasion Jesus' reply is significant. He responded with a counter-question: "What is written in the law? How do you read?" (Lk. 10:25-26).

Jesus was also drawn into disagreement with the religious authorities, in particular the rival groups known as the Pharisees and the Sadducees. Both criticized him and came to him with their trick questions. The Pharisees complained that his followers did not observe the traditions of the elders in ceremonial matters like washing their hands and their vessels. In his reply Jesus accused them of rejecting the commandment of God and making void the Word of God in order to keep their traditions (Mk. 7:1-13). The Sadducees, on the other hand, who did not believe in survival or resurrection, emphasized the problems an afterlife would create. They asked Jesus what would happen to a poor woman who had seven husbands, one after the other, each of whom she outlived. Whose wife would she be in the resurrection? Would she have one of them (which would mean the other six were out of luck) or none of them (which would be a bit hard all round) or all seven (which somehow does not sound decent)? They thought they could dispose of the doctrine of the resurrection by ridicule. But Jesus said to them, "Is not this why you are wrong, that you know neither the scriptures nor the power of God?" (Mk. 12:18-27).

Thus Jesus' complaint to both religious groups concerned their cavalier treatment of the Word of God. For the Pharisees *added* to Scripture (namely, their traditions) while the Sadducees *subtracted* from Scripture (namely, the supernatural). Neither of them gave Scripture the respect it deserved as God's Word written. Jesus accused the Pharisees of making it void and the Sadducees of being ignorant of it. In both cases he appealed against their teaching to Scripture. He made Scripture the judge.

In each of these three examples—concerning the realms of personal duty, official ministry and public controversy—there was a question, a problem, a dispute. And in each case Jesus turned to Scripture to answer the question, to solve the problem, to settle the dispute. When the devil tempted him, he resisted the temptation with "It stands written." When the apostles rejected the necessity of his sufferings he insisted that the Scriptures must be fulfilled. When the Jewish leaders criticized his teaching, he criticized their treatment of Scripture.

This evidence cannot be gainsaid. Jesus endorsed the Old Testament as the Word of God. Both in his view of Scripture and in his use of Scripture he was entirely and reverently submissive to its authority as to the authority of God's own Word. Now the disciple is not above his teacher, nor is the servant above his lord. How then can we, the disciples of Jesus, possibly have a lower view of Scripture than our teacher himself had? How can we, the servants of Jesus, allow Scripture to occupy a smaller place in our lives than it occupied in the life of our Lord himself?

There are only two possible escape routes from this obligation. The first is to say that Jesus did not know what he was talking about, that the incarnation imprisoned him in the limited mentality of a first-century Palestinian Jew, and that consequently he believed the Old Testament as they did, but that he, like them, was mistaken. The second is to say that Jesus *did* know what he was talking about, that he actually knew Scripture to be unreliable, but that he still affirmed its reliability because his contemporaries did and he did not want to upset them. According to the first explanation, Jesus' erroneous teaching was involuntary (he could not help it); according to the second it was deliberate. These theories portray Jesus as either deceived or a deceiver. They discredit the incarnate Son of God. They are incompatible both with his claims to speak what he knew (Jn. 3:11), to bear witness to the truth and to be the truth (Jn. 18:37; 14:6), and with his known hatred of all hypocrisy and deceit. They are totally unacceptable to anybody who has been led by the Holy Spirit to say "Jesus is Lord" (1 Cor. 12:3). Over against these slanderous speculations we must continue to affirm that Jesus knew what he was teaching, that he meant it, and that what he taught and meant is true.

The New Testament

The argument here is different, but equally compelling. If Jesus endorsed the Old Testament, setting upon it the stamp of his own approval, he also foresaw the writing of the Scriptures of the New Testament, parallel to the Scriptures of the Old Testament. Indeed, he not only foresaw it, he actually intended it, and he deliberately made provision for it by appointing and authorizing his apostles.

Apostle is the title which Jesus himself chose for the Twelve, in order to indicate their role. "He called his disciples," Luke writes, "and chose from them twelve, whom he named apostles" (Lk. 6:13). Mark adds that he appointed them "to be sent out to preach" (Mk. 3:14). The verb *apostello* means to send, and the mission on which he proposed to send them was essentially a teaching and preaching mission.

It is true that the word *apostolos* seems to have been used once in the New Testament to describe every Christian (Jn. 13:16), for Jesus sends us all "into the world" as his ambassadors and we are all called to have some share in the apostolic mission of the church (Jn. 17:18; 20:21). It is also true that the same word *apostolos* is used once or twice in the expression "apostles of the churches" (2 Cor. 8:23; cf. Phil. 2:25), which seems to refer to what we would call "missionaries"—Christians sent on a particular mission by the church (cf. Acts 13:3; 14:14). Nevertheless, the almost universal practice of the New Testament is to restrict the word *apostolos* to the special apostles of Christ, namely, the original twelve, together with a very small number of later additions, notably Paul (cf. Gal. 1:1) and James, the Lord's brother (Gal. 1:19).

There was a double background to the word *apostle*—ancient and contemporary—which helps us to interpret its meaning and understand why Jesus chose it. The ancient background is biblical, namely, the repeated Old Testament use of the verb *to send* in reference to the prophets of God. "Come," said God to Moses, "I will send you to Pharaoh" (Ex. 3:10); and later Moses insisted over against his jealous rivals, "You shall know that the Lord has sent me . . .and that it has not been of my own accord" (Num. 16:28-29). It was even clearer in the case of the great prophets of the seventh and eighth centuries B.C. "Whom shall I send?" God had asked in Isaiah's hearing. "Send me," Isaiah had replied (Is. 6:8). "To all to whom I send you you shall go," he said to Jeremiah (Jer. 1:7), and to Ezekiel: "Son of man, I send you to the people of Israel" (Ezek. 2:3). Several times the word of God came to Jeremiah saying, "I have sent to you all my servants the prophets, sending them persistently" (Jer. 35:15). In each case the "sending" is not a vague dispatch but a specific commission to assume the role of a prophet and to speak God's word to the people. It is evident that when Jesus gave to the Twelve the title *apostles* and *sent* them out to teach, he was likening his apostles to God's prophets and indicating that they were to speak in his name and carry his word to others. The prophets of the Old Testament and apostles of the New Testament were equally organs of divine revelation. As such they are the foundation on which the church is being built (Eph. 2:20; 3:5).

The second background was contemporary. It appears from recent research that *apostolos* is the Greek equivalent of the Aramaic *shaliach*, and that the *shaliach* already had a well-defined meaning as a teacher sent out by the Sanhedrin to instruct the Jews of the Dispersion. As such the *shaliach* carried the authority of those he represented, so that it was said, "the one who is sent is as he who sent him." In the same way Jesus sent out his *apostles* to represent him, to bear his authority and teach in his name, so that he could say of them: "He who receives you receives me" (Mt. 10:40; cf. Jn. 13:20).

Both the prophetic and the rabbinic background throw light on the meaning of the word *apostolos*. The apostle was a specially chosen emissary, the bearer of another and higher authority, the herald of a given message.

When one turns to the New Testament itself and to the New Testament's understanding of the apostles of Jesus, it appears that they were given a threefold equipment for their task, which together render them a unique and irreplaceable group. These three qualifications were their personal commission, their historical experience and their special inspiration.

First, their personal commission. No apostle was self-appointed, or even appointed by another man or men or even by the church. They were all personally chosen, commissioned and authorized by Jesus. This was clear in the case of the Twelve. Out of a much wider constituency of *disciples* Jesus "chose from them twelve, whom he named apostles" (Lk. 6:13). It was equally clear in the case of Paul, although Christ chose him after the ascension. One of the accounts of his conversion which Luke preserves in Acts includes the very words of apostolic commissioning, *ego apostello se,* "I apostle you" or "I make you an apostle" (Acts 26:17). And in his letters Paul not only asserts his apostleship ("Paul an apostle of Christ Jesus by the will of God") but vigorously defends it (for example, in Gal. 1:1, "Paul an apostle —not from men nor through man but through Jesus Christ and God the Father who raised him from the dead").

Second, their historical experience. Again, this is clear in the case of the Twelve. Jesus appointed them, writes Mark, "to be with him and to be sent out to preach" (Mk. 3:14). These two purposes belonged together. They could be sent out to preach only after they had been with him, for their preaching was to be a witness to him, out of their own experience, from what they had seen and heard. "You also are witnesses," Jesus was to say to them later, "because you have been with me from the beginning" (Jn. 15:27). So when the time came for somebody to replace Judas, the essential qualification Peter laid down was that he must "have accompanied us during all the time that the Lord Jesus went in and out among us, beginning from the baptism of John until the day when he was taken up from us," and in particular that he must "become with us a witness to his resurrection" (Acts 1:21-22). Saul of Tarsus seems to have been the last apostle to be appointed. Although he was not one of the Twelve and did not know Jesus during his public ministry, yet he had been granted a resurrection appearance. Without this he could not have been an apostle. "Am I not an apostle?" he cried. "Have I not seen Jesus our Lord?" And again, "Last of all as to one untimely born, he appeared also to me. For I am the least of the apostles" (1 Cor. 9:1; 15:8-9). The same was true of James (1 Cor. 15:7).

Third, the apostles were given a special inspiration of the Holy Spirit. Of course all Christians have received the Holy Spirit to dwell within us, to show Christ to us and make us like Christ, but Jesus promised the apostles an altogether unusual ministry of the Holy Spirit, relating to their teaching ministry. The Spirit would bring to their remembrance all that Jesus had said to them, and he would teach them "many things" which Jesus had not said to them because they had been unable to bear them. In fact, he would guide them into all the truth (Jn. 14: 25-26; 16:12-13). These great promises evidently looked forward to the writing of the Gospels (in which Jesus' teaching was remembered) and of the Epistles (in which Jesus' teaching was supplemented).

In these three ways Jesus made a purposeful preparation for the writing of the New Testament Scriptures. He gave his apostles a personal commission, a historical experience and a special inspiration. Each was a gift of Jesus to them, and each was designed to equip them for their unique role as his apostles.

The next point to notice is that the apostles understood these things. They were conscious of the unique position to which Jesus had appointed them. They exercised the authority which he had given them, and they expected the churches to acknowledge it also. We see this in their letters, which they ordered to be read publicly in the early Christian assemblies, alongside the Old Testament Scriptures (for example, Col. 4:16; 1 Thess. 5:27; Rev. 1:3).

Paul stated that his message was "the word of God" (1 Thess. 2:13) and that the very words in which it was communicated were "not taught by human wisdom but taught by the Spirit" (1 Cor. 2:13). This is a claim not to divine revelation only, but to verbal inspiration. Further, he issued commands and required obedience, for he could say, "What I am writing to you is a command of the Lord" (2 Thess. 3:6-15; 1 Cor. 14:37). When he went to Galatia, they received him "as an angel of God, as Christ Jesus" (Gal. 4:14), that is, as if he were himself God's messenger, God's Christ. He did not rebuke them for this. Far from it. His complaint was not that they formerly regarded him thus, but that now the false teachers had made them less ready to defer to his authority. And he evidently told the Corinthians that Christ was speaking in and through him, for he referred to their desire for proof that this was so (2 Cor. 13:3; cf. v. 10).

Turning to other apostles, Peter identified the good news which he had preached and by which his converts had been born again as "the living and abiding word of God" (1 Pet. 1:22-25). And John declared not only that what he and his fellow apostles proclaimed was what they had seen and heard (1 Jn. 1:1-4), but that this original teaching of the apostles was normative for all times. Consequently, he kept calling his readers back to "what they had heard from the beginning" (1 Jn. 2:7, 24). Indeed, conformity to apostolic teaching and submission to apostolic authority were major tests of whether religious teachers really knew and possessed God themselves (1 Jn. 4:6; 2 Jn. 9-10; 3 Jn. 9-10).

The authority of the apostles, which Jesus gave them and which they self-consciously exercised, was recognized by the early church. The first thing we are told about the newly Spirit-

filled church on the day of Pentecost is "they devoted themselves to the apostles' teaching" (Acts 2:42). Spirit-filled
churches always do. The post-apostolic fathers understood
clearly that the apostles were unique. Clement of Rome wrote to
the Corinthians at the end of the first century: "The apostles received the gospel for us from the Lord Jesus Christ; Jesus Christ
was sent forth from God. So then Christ is from God, and the
apostles are from Christ" (par. 5). At the beginning of the second
century, Ignatius, Bishop of Antioch, wrote to the Romans: "I
do not, as Peter and Paul, issue commandments unto you. They
were apostles; I am but a condemned man" (chap. 4; cf. Trallians,
chap. 3; Magnesians, chap. 13 and Ephesians, chap. 3). Some-
what later (about A.D. 200) Tertullian of North Africa was yet
more explicit: "We Christians are forbidden to introduce anything on our own authority, or to choose what someone else
introduces on his own authority. Our authorities are the Lord's
apostles, and they in their turn choose to introduce nothing on
their own authority. They faithfully passed on to the nations the
the teaching which they had received from Christ" (*Prescrip-
tions against Heretics,* chap. 6).

When the time came to settle the canon of the New Testament
and in particular which books should be excluded, the supreme
question about every question-marked book was whether it possessed apostolic authority. Had it been written by an apostle? If
not, did it carry the imprimatur of apostles in that it came from
their circle and represented their teaching? The test of canon-
icity was apostolicity.

It is tragic in our day to witness the loss of this understanding.
People talk of Paul, Peter, John and the other apostles as if they
were foolish and fallible first-century Christians whose teaching
was nothing but their own opinions and may readily be set aside
if we do not happen to like it. Even biblical scholars are sometimes most irresponsible in their treatment of the apostles.
"That's Paul's view," they say, "or Peter's or John's. But this is
mine. And my view is just as good as theirs, in fact better." But
no. The teaching of the apostles is the teaching of Christ. To receive them is to receive Christ, to reject them is to reject Christ.

Would that we could return to the clear-sighted understanding of the sixteenth-century Reformers on this matter! Here, for example, is Luther: "Jesus . . . subjects the whole world to the apostles, through whom alone it should and must be enlightened. . . . All the people in the world—kings, princes, lords, learned men, wise men, holy men—have to sit down while the apostles stand up, have to let themselves be accused and condemned in their wisdom and sanctity as men who know neither doctrine nor life nor the right relation to God" (*Luther's Works*, Vol. 21, Concordia, 1956, p. 61).

We are ready now to summarize the argument for our acceptance of the whole Bible as God's Word written, uniquely revealed, verbally inspired, supremely authoritative. The argument is easy to grasp, and we think impossible to refute. It concerns the teaching of the Lord Jesus Christ. He endorsed the Old Testament Scriptures. He made provision for the writing of the New Testament Scriptures.

This argument is not circular, as some objectors maintain. They represent us as saying something like this: "We know Scripture is inspired because the divine Lord Jesus said so, and we know the Lord Jesus is divine because the inspired Scripture says so." If that were our position, we would indeed be arguing in a circle. But our critics mistake our reasoning. Our argument is not circular, but linear. We do not begin by assuming the very inspiration of Scripture which we are setting out to prove. On the contrary, we come to the Gospels (which tell the story of Jesus) without any doctrine of Scripture or theory of inspiration at all. We are content merely to take them at their face value as first-century historical documents (which they are), recording the impressions of eyewitnesses. Next, as we read the Gospels, their testimony (through the work of the Holy Spirit) leads us to faith in Jesus as Lord. And then this Lord Jesus, in whom we have come to believe, gives us a doctrine of Scripture (his own doctrine, in fact) which we did not have at the beginning. Thus the argument runs not in a circle (Scripture witnesses to Jesus who witnesses to Scripture) but in a line (historical documents evoke our faith in Jesus, who then gives us a doctrine of Scripture).

The central issue relates therefore, not to the authority of the

Bible, but to the authority of Christ. If he accepted the Old Testament as God's Word, are we going to reject it? If he appointed and authorized his apostles, saying to them, "he who receives you receives me," are we going to reject them? To reject the authority of either the Old Testament or the New Testament is to reject the authority of Christ. It is supremely because we are determined to submit to the authority of Jesus Christ as Lord that we submit to the authority of Scripture.

Deductions

"But," an objector may say, "Does it really matter whether the Bible is completely and infallibly true or not? Isn't the argument rather academic and remote from real life?" No. The question of biblical authority is of immense personal, practical and contemporary relevance. Just how fundamental it is to every Christian's everyday Christianity I hope now to show in a series of four deductions.

First, submission to the authority of Scripture is fundamental to *Christian discipleship*. I am not of course implying by this that nobody who denies the authority of Scripture can be a disciple of Jesus in any sense at all. The facts are otherwise. There are followers of Jesus whose confidence in Scripture is minimal. But I have to add that their Christian discipleship is bound thereby to be impaired.

For what is Christian discipleship? Surely all would be agreed that, at the very least, discipleship includes worship, faith, obedience and hope. Yet each of these ingredients is impossible without a reliable objective revelation from God.

How can we worship God if we do not know his character? Christians are not Athenians. We do not worship "an unknown God" as they did in Athens; we worship "in truth," as Jesus said we must (Jn. 4:24), and we glory in God's "name," his revealed character.

How can we trust God if we do not know his faithfulness? Genuine faith is never irrational. It rests on the reliability of a God who has spoken. The foundation of trust is truth—God's truth and truthfulness.

How can we obey God if we do not know his will? Obedience is impossible if no laws or commandments have been given us to obey.

How can we hope in God if we do not know his promises? Christian hope is not the same as secular optimism. On the contrary, it is a joyful confidence about the future, which is aroused by and rests on specific promises about the return of Christ and the triumph of God.

Thus worship, faith, obedience and hope—four basic ingredients of Christian discipleship—all depend on our knowledge of God. Worship depends on his character, faith on his faithfulness, obedience on his commandments and hope on his promises. And God's character, faithfulness, commandments and promises are all revealed in Scripture. Therefore, Scripture is fundamental to Christian discipleship. If we would grow up into maturity as followers of Jesus, the Word of God will occupy a central place in our lives.

Second, submission to the authority of Scripture is fundamental to *Christian integrity.*

Many would deny this and would even affirm the contrary. They regard the acceptance of biblical infallibility as actually untenable and therefore charge Christians who hold it with a lack of mental integrity, with intellectual obscurantism, schizophrenia or suicide, and with other horrid crimes!

But we plead "not guilty" to these charges and insist that our conviction about Scripture arises from the very integrity which our critics say we lack. For what is *integrity? Integrity* is the quality of an "integrated" person who is at peace and not at war within himself. Instead of a dichotomy between his various beliefs, or between what he believes and how he behaves, there is harmony.

Now one of the foundational and most integrating of all Christian beliefs is the truth that "Jesus is Lord" (for example, Rom. 10:9; 1 Cor. 12:3; Phil. 2:11). A Christian is somebody who not only confesses with his lips that Jesus is Lord, but brings every aspect of his life under the sovereign lordship of Jesus—his opinions, his beliefs, his standards, his values, his ambitions, *everything!*

To us, then, submission to Scripture (for reasons already

given) is part and parcel of this submission to the lordship of Jesus. We cannot accommodate ourselves to the idea of a selective submission—for example, agreeing with Jesus in his doctrine of God but disagreeing with him in his doctrine of Scripture, or obeying his command to love our neighbor but disobeying his command to make disciples. Selective submission is not true submission at all; there is in it a reprehensible element of pride and self-will. This is the reason why Paul refers to false teachers (precisely because they presume not to "agree with the sound words of our Lord Jesus Christ") as "puffed up with conceit" and even as "insubordinate," an adjective he has just used of unruly children (1 Tim. 6:3-4; Tit. 1:6, 10). There is about false (that is, unbiblical) teaching a certain immaturity, arrogance and lack of discipline which arise from a basic unwillingness to submit our minds to the lordship of Christ.

This principle indicates what we should do with biblical problems. In affirming the full inspiration and authority of Scripture we are not by any means denying that there are problems—philosophical, scientific, historical, literary and moral. But then every single Christian doctrine has problems. And we must learn to deal with problems over Scripture exactly as we deal with problems over any other Christian doctrine. The example I like to give is our belief that "God is love," for this is a fundamental part of the Christian creed shared by all Christians of all persuasions. Yet the problems surrounding the doctrine are immense—questions about the origin and continuance of evil, about why the innocent suffer, about the so-called silences of God (for example, unanswered prayers) and the so-called acts of God (that is, natural disasters). What do we do when confronted with such problems? Do we conclude that in order to preserve our intellectual integrity we have to renounce our belief in the love of God? Not at all. We retain our conviction about God's love *in spite of the problems* for the simple and straightforward reason that this is what Jesus taught by word and deed. It is loyalty to Jesus which gives us the true principle of integrity.

It is the same with biblical problems. Of course we should grapple with them. It is no part of Christian responsibility either to pretend they are not there or to ignore them. And as we study them, some will diminish in size or even disappear (many problems which troubled former generations are no longer problems today). Yet some problems will remain. We have to be prepared to live with them, believing that if we had further knowledge they too would be solved. We certainly should not allow the problems to shift us from our conviction regarding Scripture. For our view of Scripture depends on our loyalty to Christ, not on our ability to solve all the problems. As with the love of God, so with the Word of God: We hold this doctrine *in spite of the problems* for the simple and straightforward reason that Jesus taught it and exhibited it. And to believe a Christian doctrine because of the acknowledged lordship of Jesus Christ cannot possibly be dismissed as obscurantism. It is the very opposite. It is Christian humility, Christian sobriety, Christian integrity.

Third, submission to the authority of Scripture is fundamental to *Christian freedom.*

Once again, many imagine that the reverse is true. I have several times used the word *submission*—submission to the authority of Scripture and submission to the lordship of Christ. And to large numbers of our contemporaries *submission* and *freedom* are incompatible. If I am to be free, they say, I must rebel against all authority; to *submit* to any rule (whether intellectual or moral) is to lose my freedom. But those who say such things have not yet grasped the character of true freedom.

True freedom is not absolute. Intellectual freedom, for example, is not the same as free thought. What do you say of the flat-earther who denies that the earth is round? Is he free? Not at all. He is a fool. He is also a prisoner, in bondage to falsehood and fantasy. Again, what do you say of a man who denies the law of gravity and jumps from the top of the Empire State Building? His "freedom" becomes a synonym for suicide.

True intellectual freedom is found not in independence of the truth, but in submission to the truth, whether the truth is scientific or biblical. When the mind submits to the truth, it is set free from falsehood, from the deceits of men and the lies of the devil, from its own subjective insecurity, from the shifting sands of existential experience and from the everchanging fashions of the world. Submission to truth is the true freedom.

Jesus himself clearly taught this. He said that whoever commits sin is the slave of sin and that, in contrast to this bondage, he could set men free. What was this freedom which he promised? "If you continue in my word, you are truly my disciples, and you will know the truth, and the truth will make you free" (Jn. 8:31-36). Freedom is found in discipleship, and discipleship is continuing submission to the Word of Jesus, for the Word of Jesus is the truth. No wonder Paul wrote of his resolve to "take every thought captive to obey Christ" (2 Cor. 10:5).

Fourth, submission to the authority of Scripture is fundamental to *Christian witness.*

The contemporary world is in great confusion and darkness. Men's hearts are failing them for fear. Has the Christian church any word of assurance for modern man's bewilderment, any light for his darkness, any hope for his fear? One of the greatest tragedies of today is that just when the world is becoming more aware of its need, the church is becoming less sure of its mission. And the major reason for the diminishing Christian mission is diminishing confidence in the Christian message.

We Christians should affirm with great confidence that Jesus is the supreme Lord, to whom all authority has been given in heaven and on earth, and that he bids us go and make disciples and teach them all his teaching (Mt. 28:18-19). His commission is that we should proclaim his name as the crucified and risen Savior, and that on the ground of this one and only name forgiveness and new life are available to all who will repent and believe (cf. Lk. 24:44-49). We have no liberty to alter these terms of reference which Christ gave his church in his commission. There is only one gospel. We may neither embellish nor modify nor manipulate it. We are to be the heralds of God's good news. We are charged to lift up our voice with strength, to lift it up without fear and to publish abroad the salvation of God (Is. 40:9; 52:7). Our announcement is given to us; we do not invent it. All we contribute is the voice to make it known, yes, and the life and love which lie behind the voice. In this respect every Christian resembles John the Baptist. For each of us is to be but a voice crying in the world's dry wilderness, bearing witness to Christ, gladly decreasing in ourselves in order that he may increase (Mk. 1:2-3; Jn. 1:6-8, 19-23; 3:30).

So I conclude. I have tried to develop only two great themes about submission to the authority of Scripture. First, that submission to Scripture is part and parcel of our acknowledgement of the lordship of Jesus. Second, that submission to Scripture is fundamental to everyday Christian living, for without it Christian discipleship, Christian integrity, Christian freedom and Christian witness are all seriously damaged if not actually destroyed.

Christ still calls us to take his yoke upon us and learn from him (assuming his yoke is a metaphor for submitting to his teaching authority); he still promises that under his yoke we shall find rest to our souls; for he still assures us both that he himself is gentle and that (unlike all other yokes) *his* yoke is easy and *his* burden is light (Mt. 11:29-30). If you put this to the test, you will find it—as I have—to be true.

JESUS CHRIST AND THE LOSTNESS OF MAN

EDMUND P. CLOWNEY

An old popular song tells it like it was:

> *Don't bank down those inner fires,*
> *Follow out your heart's desires*
> *Until the day comes when they come for you;*
> *Make today a holiday, take tomorrow, too.*
> *You can't take it with you, Jack,*
> *And when you're gone you can't come back,*
> *You are only going–through!*

That's an old song, well before your time. As a matter of fact it was popular in Egypt before 1300 B.C. My version is a bit of a paraphrase. You can find a more literal translation under "A Song of the Harper" in Pritchard's *Ancient Near Eastern Texts*.[1] For more than three millenia men have been drinking to the idea that you only go around once so you had better grab for gusto while you can. But beneath the bravado lurks fear—the fear of death. The "morning after" is bad enough, but what of the night after? Life never escapes that shadow.

From the time of the "Song of the Harper" comes the song of another harper, full of solemn grandeur rather than trivial froth: the song of Moses the man of God, Psalm 90 in the Old Testament. Again we hear of the brevity of human life: "They are as a sleep: in the morning they are like grass which groweth up. In the morning it flourisheth, and groweth up; in the evening it is cut down and withereth" (vv. 5-6).

But Moses sets the brevity of man's life in fearful contrast with God's eternity: "Even from everlasting to everlasting, thou art God . . . a thousand years in thy sight are but as yesterday when it is past, and as a watch in the night" (vv. 2, 4).

Put against God's eternity, our living is only slow dying, and not even *slow* dying at that. Death's shadow flies upon us and blots out today's sunlight with tomorrow's darkness. Life is only a breath, and that breath is a sigh. The Nobel playwright Samuel Beckett takes up Moses' theme in the briefest, strangest and strongest of his plays, entitled *Breath*. It is a play without a hero, without actors, without words. The stage is set with a pile of junk. As the light grows we hear a baby's birth cry, then a long inhalation, followed by a choking exhalation, that ends in a death rattle. Beckett's bitter hope can offer only another birth cry as the stage sinks into darkness. "We bring our years to an end as a sigh" (v. 9). Our life-breath expires in that sigh.

Men try to come to terms with death. Fortified with arguments for immortality, Socrates drinks the hemlock with philosophic calm. Tasting the yet more bitter cup of vengefulness a modern terrorist sows death that he may reap it. A popular Freudian philosopher warns that the fear of death is the morbid fruit of repression. Liberate the body from all repressions, he says, and it will be ready to meet death with no life unlived.[2] The opposite advice is no less ancient (or modern): Mortify the body as the prison of the soul, and hasten the absorption into the cosmic consciousness. But death's head is still visible behind the many masks we make. Even a doctor of thanatology must die.

But if death is the last enemy, it does not come as a stranger. The horror of the death we do not know reaches us in the agony of the life we do know:

I am poured out like water,
And all of my bones are out of joint:
My heart is like wax;
It is melted within me.
My strength is dried up like a potsherd;
And my tongue cleaveth to my jaws;
And thou hast brought me into the dust of death.
(Ps. 22:14-15)

The anguish of the sufferer in the psalm intensifies the sigh of frustration to a roar of agony. Man's misery is quiet despair at best. At worst it is a scream from the depths.

Man the Rebel

Yet all the sufferings of life and the death they foreshadow do not in themselves fill the cup of human misery. The poison in the cup of life is our guilt. Moses mourns, "Thou hast set our iniquities before thee, our secret sins in the light of thy countenance" (Ps. 90:8).

Standing beneath an empty sky, a man can strike a tragic pose as the victim of mortality. He can even pretend to be a hero of the absurd, who gives meaning to life's meaninglessness by an act of will. Albert Camus pictures Sisyphus (doomed in Tartarus) as heroically human precisely because his labor has no meaning. He toils forever to roll a rock up a hill knowing that it will forever roll down again. "There is no fate," says Camus "that cannot be overcome by scorn." Yet the scorn with which a man shakes his fist at the empty sky shows that the sky is not really empty. Man's sense of tragedy betrays him. Man is not a victim but a rebel. He stands before God and stands revealed for what he is—a sinner. God's holiness manifests the enormity of our crimes against our brothers. In his rebellion man can not only sanction but even sanctify his hatreds in tribal or national pride. He can brutalize his women and discard his babies. Hilarion, a traveling businessman of the year 1 B.C., writes a letter to his wife in Egypt: "If by chance you bear a child, if it is a boy, let it be, if it is a girl, cast it out."[3]

It is before the living God that adultery is vile and infanticide murder. The dignity that "humanizes" man is the reflection of his likeness to God—his creation in God's image. By that image God's claim is on every man: He cannot be made a chattel or a pawn without defiance to his Maker.

When Jesus was asked whether Jews should pay taxes to Caesar he asked to see a Roman silver coin, a denarius. One was produced from a questioner's fat purse. "Whose is the image and superscription?" asked Jesus. "Caesar's," was the reply. Jesus' retort is a double-edged sword: "Give to Caesar what is Caesar's, but give to God what is God's" (Mt. 22:15-22).

We need to ponder the kingdom teaching of this Messiah who authorized Roman taxation. But even more we need to ponder the kingdom claim of the other edge of Christ's saying. Who bears the image of God? We do. What do we owe to God? Ourselves. God's image sets God's seal against all exploitation of our fellow man.

But it does much more than this. It forbids us to rob God by withholding ourselves. When the apostle Paul describes the unrighteousness of men, he begins at the beginning—with their ungodliness. They are without excuse, because "knowing God, they glorified him not as God, neither gave thanks; but became vain in their reasonings, and their senseless heart was darkened" (Rom. 1:21).

In strange ways God causes even the wrath of men to praise him. Just as man's tragic sense witnesses to God's creation, so man's rage witnesses to God's righteousness. Try taunting some furious protester with the logic of what he claims to believe. Tell him, "O.K., so there is no God; man is a chemical accident in a random universe. What are a few thousand lives, more or less? What if a bomb suddenly reorganizes the molecules that were for the moment patterned in the form of a little girl. So what? No energy is lost."

When he calls you a fool or a monster, his rage for righteousness bears witness to the God he denies. We measure right and wrong by an absolute standard. We are blind not to see that the imperative of "rightness" points beyond our own desires or the desires of other men anywhere or everywhere. Only before the living God does morality find meaning. All sin is at last sin against God. The most heinous sin is the root of all other sin—

rebellion against God. Because the mind of the flesh is enmity against God, we cannot see our sin as it is. Paul says that our understanding is darkened in the ignorance of hardened hearts (Eph. 4:18). Violence, licentiousness, greed, envy, murder—all the perversity that poisons human society springs from a deeper hate that we disguise and deny. We hate God, and we hate him because he is God: holy, just and good.

It is the measure of our hardening that hating God is made the least of sins, perhaps even a virtue: Promethean courage against an omnipotent tyrant. When God pleads with his rebellious people in the Old Testament, he exhausts the images of broken faith to show how heinous the great sin is. Israel is a vine bearing bitter grapes to the divine vinedresser who has spared no pains in cultivation (Is. 5). God's people is a rebellious son turning against the father who held him in his arms and taught him to walk (Hos. 11). The nation is an adulterous wife requiting a husband's faithful love with shameless harlotry.

We may be filled with rage at callous crimes of selfish violence reported in the newspaper, but we cannot comprehend the the wickedness of violent rebellion against the living God. Yet our judgment is proportionate to our crime. Moses descends to one last level in his psalm of human misery. The tragedy of life is not only the vanity of our days and the sinfulness of our hearts. There is more, for the sinfulness of our hearts is open to the eyes of God: "Thou hast set our iniquities before thee, our secret sins in the light of thy countenance" (Ps. 90:8). Therefore, "we are consumed in thine anger, and in thy wrath are we troubled" (v. 7) . . . "all our days are passed away in thy wrath" (v. 9) . . . "who knoweth the power of thine anger and thy wrath according to the fear that is due unto thee?" (v. 11).

Moses' psalm has its setting in the wilderness where a generation of rebels was doomed to wander until they perished. Refusing to believe that God would give them the Land of Promise they heard God's word of judgment turning them back to the desert. That word echoes in Psalm 90: "Thou turnest man to destruction; and sayest, Return, ye children of men" (v. 3).

Men are not only sinners, they are "children of wrath," subject to the righteous judgment of God. Death comes as a curse, "the wages of sin is death" (Rom. 6:23). "It is appointed unto men once to die, but after this the judgment" (Heb. 9:27).

The apostle Paul in the fifth chapter of Romans is at pains to trace the course of sin in the world to its source. Where death comes, there sin is being judged. The death-knell tolls through the genealogies of Genesis, the first book of the Bible: "and he died . . . and he died . . . and he died." Those who died were judged as sinners. Before the law had been given to Moses, before its precepts could call sin to account, men were guilty and liable to death.

At what point, then, did sin enter, and death through sin? Evidently in the first sin of the first man, Adam. Through one trespass death ruled over many (Rom. 5:19). Paul, of course, presses on to the parallel in salvation. As one act of sin made men guilty, caused sin to be charged against them—for all men sinned in Adam (Rom. 5:12, 18)—so one act of righteousness brought justification and life to the new humanity in Christ.

We may need to review the apostle's reasoning in reverse. As Christians we understand that Christ was our representative who stood in our place as the Head of the new humanity. But we must also recognize the role of the first Adam in relation to the second. The guilt and judgment of Adam's transgression is shared by those who are united to Adam their head by God's creative appointment. All die in Adam because all are guilty in Adam. The sinfulness of all humanity is not a survival of the jungle; it is the result of the Fall. Man's doom stretches back to his initial rebellion and grows with his multiplied iniquity.

Before God's holiness our ruin is complete. We are dead in trespasses and sins (Eph. 2:1). We are by nature children of wrath (Eph. 2:3). It is the heart of man that is "deceitful above all things and exceedingly corrupt" (Jer. 17:9). No, man is not as bad as he can be, for God restrains men from the hellish fury of their own corruption. But no part of man escapes the blight of sin. His mind is at enmity with God, "for it is not subject to the law of God, neither indeed can it be; and they that are in the flesh cannot please God" (Rom. 8:7-8).

And more—man the sinner is in bondage not only to evil but to the Evil One. He is taken captive by the snares of the devil

(2 Tim. 2:26) and walks according to the prince of the powers of the air, the evil spirit that works in the sons of disobedience (Eph. 2:2). Men who were made to be sons of God have become children of the devil, doing the works of their father and doomed to share his judgment (Eph. 2:2; Mt. 25:41, 46; Jn. 8:44).

Man's bondage to evil rolls like a subterranean river of fire through human history. In willful ignorance man fabricates his delusions and destroys himself and his world in the lusts of his idolatries (Eph. 4:18; Rom. 1:28; 6:21, 23). No man can overlook human evil; he may only add to it by condoning as pitiable that which God reveals to be damnable.

The Wrath of God

But God is not mocked. Whatever a man sows he will reap. The biblical teaching about the wrath of God is very different from the mechanical wheel of fate in Eastern religions. God cannot be a detached observer in a spiritual world of cause and effect where actions generate their own inevitable consequences. Nor is God merely a name for the process. The living God is personal: a God who reveals himself to his people as slow to anger and abundant in lovingkindness and truth (Ex. 34:6). The wrath of God is not soon kindled. God is not "vindictive" in our usual sense of the word. Yet God's wrath is the zeal of his own holiness against all sin. "Our God," warns the writer of Hebrews, "is a consuming fire" (Heb. 12:29). Not fate, not the reincarnational process of the wheel of samsara, but the searching knowledge of the living God judges the sinner.

Yet God does employ the fruits of our deeds to judge us. Indeed, he often makes our very sins to become our punishment. As Paul in Romans 1 describes the plunge of the heathen nations into depravity, he shows the justice of God by matching man's abandonment to sin with God's abandonment to judgment. Paul's Greek is more vivid than our translations. Man gave up the glory of the incorruptible God for idols (v. 23); God gave them up in the lusts of their hearts to uncleanness (v. 24). Men gave up the truth of God for a lie (v. 25); God gave them up to vile passions (v. 26). Men gave up the knowledge of God (v. 28), and God gave them up to a reprobate mind (v. 28). Even man's abandonment of natural sexual relations is judged by a divine abandonment to the chains of perversion (vv. 26-27). A man is lost as he rejects God for his own desires. His lostness is his doom as God abandons him to those desires. C. S. Lewis once said that heaven is the place where man says to God, "Thy will be done," and hell is the place where God says to man, "Thy will be done." That is not the whole truth, but it catches the meaning of God's judgment as abandonment.

At last, the justice of God's judgment must be confessed by every sinner. Jean-Paul Sartre's play No Exit has the much-quoted line, "Hell is other people."[4] He pictures a sitting room in hell into which three strangers, one man and two women, are ushered. They are without eyelids; nothing can be changed or forgotten; and since they are already dead, murder or suicide is impossible. Given that setting, the "Hell is other people" line is easy to understand! But the climax of the play is in an earlier line. After bitter conversation has stripped away their pretensions, the "hero," Garcin, is revealed as a coward who had deserted his comrades. Inez, who has savagely torn away Garcin's lies, says, "You are—your life, and nothing else."[5]

"You are—your life, and nothing else." No, you cry. I am not what I have been—I am what I am going to be; I am what I meant to be. In the day of judgment, the gaze before which you will stand naked is not the lidless eyes of another sinner, but the burning eyes of Almighty God. There will be no injustice, only truth; you will be revealed for what you are, and nothing else. "Yea, O Lord God, the Almighty, true and righteous are thy judgments" (Rev. 16:7).

When every knee bows to God in the day of judgment, all rebellion is ended. No sinner will dispute God's sentence. The gnashing of teeth that Scripture describes on the part of those who are forever lost is no longer the gnashing of hatred and defiance, but of anguish and remorse.[6] We who still taste the possibilities of earthly life cannot imagine the meaning of existence without hope where the guilt of past rebellion seals the abiding wrath of God. Michelangelo tried to portray the horror of the lost on the wall of the Sistine Chapel, where the damned sink down behind the altar. Yet neither Christ the Judge nor the doomed who peer out from the candle soot of the centuries are convincing figures. Far worse are the grotesque horrors of Hieronymous Bosch. No, the meaning of judgment must be approached from within, not without. The man who rejects what the Bible teaches about the Last Judgment should stand before God instead of presuming to call God to account. Let him ask, before God, "What do my sins deserve?" The deepest agony of hell itself is the realization that eternal separation from God is what the sinner has demanded and deserved.

The solemn argument of Paul in Romans concludes that all men are under God's wrath because all men deserve it. The nations of the Gentiles are without excuse, for they have forsaken the God they knew. He never left himself without a witness—in the world and in their own hearts. Their very ignorance is of their own making; their false worship of their own devising; and their degrading vices their continuing delight. But when the Gentiles are condemned by self-righteous men who know the law, Paul writes a stronger condemnation. Not the hearers of the law are justified, but the doers. The man who knows the law and disobeys is worse than the man who never knew the law. Paul's conclusion is the verdict of the psalmist: "There is none righteous, no, not one; there is none that understandeth, there is none that seeketh after God. . . . that every mouth may be stopped, and all the world may be brought under the judgment of God" (Rom. 3:10-11, 19b)

Yes, there are mouths today that chatter on, mouths of men excusing themselves and blaming God, or excusing others to overturn the sentence of God. The only remedy is for the man with the mouth to stand before God. If he beholds the Lord, he will cry with Job, "I have heard of thee by the hearing of the ear; but now mine eye seeth thee. Wherefore I abhor myself, and repent in dust and ashes" (Job 42:6).

The Gospel

Yet in describing some of the teaching of the Bible about man's lostness I have been holding back the context in which we learn these things. To consider lostness, death and doom by themselves, we end up splitting Bible verses in half. "The wages of

sin is death"—yes, we must know *that* in the sin explosion of our
times—but how can we stop with "death"? "But the gift of God
is eternal *life* through Jesus Christ our Lord!" (Rom. 6:23).

The Bible reveals God's wrath in the proclamation of the gospel. Why does Paul so insist in Romans that all have sinned and
come short of the glory of God?" (Rom. 3:23). Because he wants
us to know that "God hath shut up all unto disobedience, that
he might have mercy upon all" (Rom. 11:32). See the connection
between the revelation of the righteousness of God in the gospel
(Rom. 1:17) and the revelation of the wrath of God (Rom. 1:18).
The wrath of God is not disclosed simply as a timeless principle of retributive righteousness. God's judgment is proclaimed
as part of the news of God's purpose and work. You hear this in
Paul's preaching in the book of Acts. The message of judgment
calls the nations from walking in their own ways (Acts 14:16),
for now God "commandeth men that they should all everywhere
repent: inasmuch as he hath appointed a day in which he will
judge the world in righteousness by the man whom he hath ordained; whereof he hath given assurance unto all men, in that he
hath raised him from the dead" (Acts 17:30-31).

Even the appointing of a day of judgment shows God's mercy,
for it means that there is time given to the nations to repent. Judgment means hope, for the day of wrath is the day of deliverance
from the oppressor. Only by judgment can there be a new order,
a new world of righteousness. But when a self-righteous people
assumed that the day of the Lord would be all brightness for
them, they were warned that they, too, must face the Judge of all
the earth, who does right (Amos 5:18-20).

How, then, can the preaching of judgment bring hope to sinners? Why need they hear of a new creation delivered from
groaning if they have forfeited all inheritance in it? The unimag-
inable answer of the gospel is that God's absolute righteousness
brings salvation through the outpouring of wrath. God's good
news is Jesus Christ who comes to earth not once but twice. He
will come at last to bring wrath, as the Judge of all the earth. The
coming of God's kingdom in consummation power means the
"revelation of the Lord Jesus from heaven with the angels of his
power in flaming fire, rendering vengeance to them that know

not God, and to them that obey not the gospel of our Lord Jesus; who shall suffer punishment, even eternal destruction from the face of the Lord and the glory of his might" (2 Thess. 1:7-9).

But if that were Christ's only coming, no sinner could be spared. "Who can abide the day of his coming? And who can stand when he appeareth? For he is like a refiner's fire" (Mal. 3:2).

Even John the Baptist, Jesus' forerunner, had difficulty here. He preached the coming of the Messiah to judgment, the Messiah who would baptize with fire and hew down every tree of wickedness. When Jesus wrought miracles of healing rather than signs of wrath, when he opened the eyes of the blind rather than bringing thick darkness, when he raised the dead rather than slaying the wicked, John sent an inquiry from prison—the prison from which the Messiah had not set him free: "Art thou he that cometh, or look we for another?" (Lk. 7:19). Jesus kept John's two disciples with him while he performed more miracles of hope. "Go," he said, "and tell John the things which ye have seen and heard; the blind receive their sight, the lame walk, the lepers are cleansed, and the deaf hear, the dead are raised up, the poor have good tidings preached to them" (v. 22).

Jesus' answer reflects the prophecy of Isaiah 35:5-10, a promise of the blessings of renewal in God's kingdom of salvation. But how could blessing come without judgment? What gospel is there for the poor until their exploiters and oppressors are judged?

Jesus said to John, "Blessed is he whosoever shall find no occasion of stumbling in me" (Lk. 7:23). The answer that John awaited in faith is given to us in the gospel. Jesus came first not to wield the axe of judgment but to bear the stroke of death. Christ, the Judge who must tread the winepress of the wrath of God, Christ himself bears the wrath and drinks the cup from the Father's hand. By his blood we are saved from wrath through faith in him (Rom. 5:9). Christ was made sin for us, bore the curse for us so that we might be made the righteousness of God in him. Only so can God be just and yet be the justifier of him who believes in Christ.

Paul preaches the revealed righteousness of God—righteousness in God's wrath against sin, righteousness as God's gift by grace—righteousness in the first and second coming of Christ. Because God's wrath struck his own Son on Calvary, it is forever past for those who are united to Jesus Christ. The gospel calls men to the cross, where wrath is swallowed up by love, where grace and justice meet.

Is God's Wrath Too Severe?

Is God's wrath too severe, his holiness too intense, his judgment too heavy? After World War II a play in West Berlin made a deep impression on the city. It was *The Sign of Jonah* by Guenter Rutenborn. In a courtroom scene all the actors are found guilty in the evils of the war they have survived, and all transfer the blame to God. God is accused, found guilty and sentenced

> to become a human being, a wanderer on earth, deprived of his rights, homeless, hungry, thirsty. He shall know what it means to die. He himself shall die! And lose a son, and suffer the agonies of fatherhood. And when at last He dies, He shall be disgraced and ridiculed.[7]

God's amazing grace has done more than the most bitter blasphemy could propose. God's wrath has been poured out on earth already, and God himself has borne all its fury.

The Bible itself presents a scene in which God is tempted and accused by his own people. It is the incident of Masseh-Meribah that followed the exodus of Israel from Egypt (Ex. 17). God guides the wilderness march to Rephidim, where there is no water. The people strive with Moses in judicial fashion. They are ready to initiate court-martial proceedings to execute Moses as a traitor who has led the nation into a deathtrap. Moses protests that their case is not just against him but against God. The people are accusing God of unfaithfulness to his covenant promise. The word *Meribah* does not mean merely a controversy. *Meribah* means a law-case. In Micah 6 the prophet uses the term to describe God's law-case against Israel as he summons the mountains and the foundations of the earth to bear witness to his faithfulness.

God is a righteous and just judge. If the people demand a court hearing, a trial will be held. God tells Moses to pass before the assembled people and to call the elders of the people into session. Moses is to take in his hand the rod of judgment, the rod with which he smote the River of Egypt, turning the Nile to blood. In the Pentateuch, the rod is both the symbol and instrument of the infliction of judgment. A guilty man in a controversy was to be beaten with the rod before the face of the judge (Deut. 25:1-3).

But now Moses takes the judicial rod and lifts it to inflict the sentence of judgment. In Isaiah 30 the prophet describes the descent of the rod of God's wrath upon the Assyrian enemy:

For through the voice of the Lord shall the Assyrian be dismayed; with his rod will he smite him. And every stroke of the appointed staff, which the Lord shall lay upon him, shall be with the sound of tabret and harps. (Is. 30:31-32)

Dread fell upon Israel as Moses lifted the rod of God. Upon whom would the wrath of the Lord descend? Here is one of the most amazing verses in the Bible. God says to Moses, "Behold, I will stand before thee there upon the rock in Horeb; and thou shalt smite the rock" (Ex. 17:6).

Nowhere else in the Old Testament does God say that he will stand before a man. God is the Judge. Men come to stand before him. Provision is made for hard judicial cases that can be appealed to the priests, Levites and judge in the place where God will set his name (Deut. 17:8-9).

But here God stands before Moses, the judge with the rod of judgment. God has been accused, and he stands in the prisoner's dock. God is symbolized by the rock on which Moses stands. In the Pentateuch, *Rock* is a name for God: "Ascribe ye greatness unto our God, the Rock, his work is perfect" (Deut. 32:3-4). The psalms that speak of Masseh-Meribah call God *the Rock* (Ps. 95:1, 8; 78:15-17, 35).

God commands Moses to smite the rock. It would be impossible for Moses to smite the Shekinah glory of God. God bears the smiting, and living water flows forth to the people. For this reason John bears witness in his gospel that when the spear was thrust into the side of the crucified Savior there flowed forth blood and water (Jn. 19:34). The Rock in the wilderness was Christ (1 Cor. 10:4) and great was Moses' sin in striking the Rock a second time (Num. 20:10-13).

The mystery of God's mercy foreshadowed in the Old Testament is fulfilled in the New. The measure of God's love shows the reality of his wrath. Do not tell the Father his wrath is too great when he must direct it against his Beloved Son!

How much does the Father love the Son? The Son, who was in the bosom of the Father before the world was . . . the Son, the firstborn, of whom God says, "I will be to him a Father, and he shall be to me a Son" (Heb. 1:5) . . . the Son in whom the Father's heart delights . . . the Son who prays, "Father, glorify thy name!" How much does the Father love the Son at Calvary as he takes the cup and is obedient unto death?

What would God not give for his Son? "For the Father loveth the Son, and hath given all things into his hand" (Jn. 3:35). "For God so loved his only begotten Son that he gave the world that he might not perish . . . !" No, that is not John 3:16! "For God so loved the world, that he gave his only begotten Son, that whosoever believeth in him should not perish but have everlasting life."

In giving his Son, God gives himself, and here is the measure of love.

I cannot understand that. I cannot explain that. Can you? I cannot begin to enter into the mystery of the love of God. But I can say this to you. What do you think it cost the Father to abandon the Son? Abraham took his son Isaac out to the mountain, but Abraham did not have to plunge the knife into his son. The promise was "The Lord will provide." And the Lord did provide. The Father sent the Son, and the Son bore the wrath. And Jesus Christ in the will of the Father hung upon the cross. There upon the cross Jesus Christ cried out, "Eli, Eli, lama Sabachthani": "My God, My God, why hast thou forsaken me?" (Mt. 27:46). In that act, Jesus Christ endured the lostness, the judgment, the doom, the poured-out wrath, because he came to bear that wrath in the place of man.

I know you have doubts. I know you have fears. I know you are bewildered sometimes. And I know you ask why. But oh, my friend, go to the very depths of your doubts and gather them all up; take all your unsolved problems, all the whys that come out

of the anguish of your heart, whys that grow out of major tragedies, whys when you do not understand. Just bring your whys,
your questions, to God.

But come there to stay. Come there to watch Jesus Christ.
Come there to listen while Jesus Christ the God-man in his human nature cries out, "Why?" Then do not say that the Father's
wrath against sin is too much.

"Who knoweth the power of thine anger?" Moses asks in
Psalm 90. We know the answer. Jesus Christ through the power
of the Father knew it, because he bore it. We must proclaim that
the wrath of God is a reality, for God is just and we are vile sinners. But we proclaim God's judgment in the message of the gospel. Praise God. We proclaim it in the message of Jesus Christ.

Do not trifle with Calvary. Paul pleads,

Or despisest thou the riches of his goodness and forbearance
and longsuffering; not knowing that the goodness of God
leadeth thee to repentance? But after thy hardness and im-
penitent heart treasurest up for thyself wrath in the day . . .
when God shall judge the secrets of men, according to my gospel, by Jesus Christ. (Rom. 2:4-5, 16)

No, rather, let the solemnity of God's holy wrath at Calvary
open your eyes to the wonder of his love.

Who know not Love, let him assay
And taste that juice, which on the cross a pike
Did set again abroach; then let him say
    If ever he did taste the like.
Love is that liquor sweet and most divine,
Which my God feels as blood; but I, as wine.[8]

Notes

[1] James B. Pritchard, *Ancient Near Eastern Texts* (Princeton: Princeton University Press, 1950), p. 467.

[2] Norman O. Brown, *Life Against Death* (New York: Vintage Books, 1959), p. 308.

[3] C. K. Barrett, ed., *New Testament Background: Selected Documents* (New York: Macmillan, 1957), p. 38.

[4] Jean-Paul Sartre, *No Exit and Three Other Plays* (New York: Vintage Books, 1949), p. 47.

[5] Ibid., p. 45.

[6] Henri Blocher, "La doctrine du châtiment éternel," *Ichthus*, 32 (April 1973), 8.

[7] Guenter Rutenborn, *The Sign of Jonah* (New York: Thomas Nelson & Sons, 1960), p. 80.

[8] George Herbert, "The Agonie," in *The Works of George Herbert*, ed. F. E. Hutchinson (Oxford: Clarendon Press, 1941), p. 37.

JESUS CHRIST: LORD OF MY LIFE

4

PAUL E. LITTLE

One of the tremendous things about being a Christian is knowing that Jesus Christ is Lord of the Universe. And that is true whether a person believes it or not. One of the great realities of being a Christian is knowing that Jesus Christ is King of Kings and Lord of Lords and ultimately is going to be acknowledged as such. Whenever I am feeling alone and in the minority, I often think of those tremendous words in Philippians 2, where we are told that the Lord Jesus Christ who died for us will be exalted by God the Father and that every knee shall bow and every tongue shall confess that Jesus Christ is Lord to the glory of God the Father. You and I are on the winning side, and we should never lose sight of this; we should live day by day with the long view in mind.

But the question we face now is, Is Jesus Christ Lord of my life? Is he Lord of your life? We have heard a lot in this convention about things "out there." Tonight we want to think about things "in here," because the ultimate impact of this convention will hinge solely on what your response and mine is to what Jesus Christ says to each one of us.

Ever since Mr. Teng said it, I have been thinking about the fact that Jonah professed to know the Lord of the Universe, but he was not willing to have him Lord of his life. Are you like that? Am I like that in any way? How can I know whether I have given my life to Jesus Christ, and how can I know whether he is my Lord?

The Lordship of Christ

In some ways this is very simple. First, we should answer for ourselves the question, Have I ever deliberately and specifically come to Jesus Christ and said, "Lord, here I am, knowing something of what is involved, but realizing your will will continually unfold before me for the rest of my life. Here I am to present to you every dimension of my life. You are my Creator, and you own me as Creator; you have loved me unto death, and you own me by redemption. I give you my life, without reservation."

This is what Paul is talking about in Romans 12:1-2:

I appeal to you therefore, brethren, by the mercies of God, to present your bodies as a living sacrifice, holy and acceptable to God, which is your spiritual worship. Do not be conformed to this world but be transformed by the renewal of your mind, that you may prove what is the will of God, what is good and acceptable and perfect.

Paul is talking about a crisis. We come and deliberately present our bodies as living sacrifices to Jesus Christ. And that crisis leads to a process in which that decision, that commitment, is reaffirmed every day that we live.

Incidentally, I believe this is really what is meant by "being filled with the Spirit." I think we have become complicated about some of the profound simplicities of the Christian life. I am filled with the Spirit if I come to Jesus Christ and give him everything I am and ask him to fill me with himself by his Holy Spirit, to cleanse and use me day by day. If I have given myself to him as best I know how, I can be sure that he has come in and has filled me with his Spirit. If you do not do this daily, you should.

Perhaps, like me, you came to Jesus Christ at an early age, and you did not realize much of the meaning of the lordship of Christ. I became a Christian when I was eight years old. I was raised in a Christian home, for which I am profoundly grateful. My father was a preacher. I heard the Word of God with my oatmeal, and I knew the gospel cold. Fortunately, I was clearly taught that my parents' faith was not enough for me, that God has no grandchildren, that I had to personally put my faith in Jesus Christ.

When I was eight years old, a man in a children's meeting had a series of bells. There were big bells, fat bells, skinny bells. He said, "Look. All these are bells, but one of them doesn't have a clapper. You can't tell by looking at them from the outside which one doesn't. Right?" Right.

"Okay," he said, "that's true of many of you out there. You can't tell by looking at you which one is a Christian and which one isn't. But you know and God knows that you don't have a clapper."

I thought, "Wow, who told him about me?" People used to pat me on the head and say, "My, what a fine boy." And I thought, "Wow, if they'd go through a week with me, they'd get the shock of their lives."

Then he turned the bells up, and we could see inside and see which one did not have a clapper. Then he went on to make the application that we had to trust Christ for ourselves personally, even though others thought we were Christians.

I did not know too much about the lordship of Christ. Perhaps you are just beginning to realize its implications. Our hymns make liars of us all, for often we sing of an experience far beyond our own. Some of us get nervous over that kind of phoniness. I was amused some time ago to read a column by Joe Bayly in which he talked about being in a Christian home and overhearing a four-year-old boy running around the house singing, "Years I spent in vanity and pride." There are a lot of things we know propositionally early in life that do not become vital to us experientially until later, and perhaps for you the lordship of Christ is one of those.

Some Practical Implications

You are now beginning to realize that the lordship of Christ is a double-or-nothing proposition. It involves a great many dimensions of life. Let me just point out a few of them.

It involves the question of career, which is crucial to many of us at this stage of our lives and ambitions. If you were to be asked the question tonight, What are you really living for? how would you answer? One of the ways you can answer is by considering this question: What does your mind turn to in its spare moments? Donald Grey Barnhouse used to say that our minds are like an elastic tape measure. You pull it out, press the button and zing! it goes back in. Where does your mind go when you press the button, when it is not otherwise occupied and it zings? Where does it zing to? Does it zing to the Lord Jesus Christ?

Are you living for enjoyment in a particular way? Are you killing yourself for a material possession, a car maybe? Are you working to establish yourself in a career so then you can serve Jesus Christ? Are you living for marriage? What is it you are living for? Can you say with Paul the apostle "to me to live is Christ"? Maybe you better sit down in the presence of God with a pen and a piece of paper and work that one through.

All of the things I just mentioned are legitimate; but if they are what we are living for, they are illegitimate. As someone has said, "If Jesus Christ is not Lord of all, he is not Lord at all." If Jesus Christ is #2, he is not Lord of our lives.

Does the lordship of Christ affect your behavior in any way? That is another way to answer the question, Is he Lord of my life —not just have I gone through this commitment but does it affect me Tuesday, Wednesday, Thursday, Friday, all the days of the week, in my attitudes and behavior? Have you ever given to him as Lord of your life the question of your relationship with members of the opposite sex? Do you exploit other people in relationships? Or do you commit that area of your life to Jesus Christ?

Have you ever given over to Jesus Christ the question of marriage? This is perhaps the hardest of all because most of us are so committed to the idea that it is unthinkable that we could go through life unmarried. Have you ever said, "Lord, I'm willing to give you my life. Whether you want me married or not is up to you. I'm not going to try to give you any help." A lot of us want to help God along the way. We are sure he needs help, that he has overlooked a few things. We betray a lack of trust in him. Or if we are to be married, have we said, "Lord, will you take over in that area?"

With many Christians, marriage is the last area of holdout more often than any other: "Lord, I'll do anything for you. I'll go anywhere in the world—as long as it's married." Admittedly, some mission boards want you to be married because of the situations into which you would go, and it may be that in some parts of the world whether you are married will be guidance as to whether you go or not. But have you given over that whole question to the Lord?

Has the lordship of Christ had an impact on your attitudes? Are you having hassles with your parents? Is there bitterness and tension? Jesus Christ is Lord of your life whether they are right or wrong. It is a matter of attempting reconciliation, of acknowledging where you have been wrong, of seeking forgiveness and of restoring that relationship and attempting to open communication.

You have problems with other Christians. You are jealous of them, envious of them; you resent them; maybe they have wronged you. If Jesus Christ is Lord of your life, his lordship hits there.

Pius Wakatama pointed out that one of the greatest problems overseas is the superiority complex we Americans so often have. We are often very naive in our whole outlook on life. I once observed an incident in Britain which illustrates the occasional cultural and historical insensitivity of some Americans (and, I suppose, an occasional Canadian). A tourist bus pulled up in Runnymede and the American asked the guide, "What happened here?" The guide said, "This is where the Magna Carta was signed." He said, "Oh, when was that?" The guide answered, "1215." The American looked at his watch and remarked, "Imagine that, Edith. We missed it by twenty minutes." That's funny, but it's not funny when that kind of thing, and many worse things, come out.

None of us like to be the brunt of that kind of thing. I have been living in Europe, and the tremendous amount of anti-American feeling there gets under my skin sometimes. It gets under other people's skins when we who are Americans and Canadians generalize about them in the very same way that we do not appreciate their generalizing about us.

Racism is a tremendous problem in North America, but it is a problem all over the world. Philippinos and Chinese, tribal tensions in Africa, caste in India, black and white relationships in the United States—the sin of man in the area of race relations is worldwide and endemic. We as Christians must judge it and get over it. The lordship of Christ has impact here.

If you want to know something about the depth of the problem in the United States, let me suggest two books: *Crisis in Black and White* by Charles Silberman and *The Autobiography of Malcolm X*. Neither author is a Christian. But if you want to know what the real problems are and to get some of the feeling and the ache and to begin to ask God to help you be part of the solution rather than part of the problem, read these two books. Begin to get to know people across racial barriers, and try to discover ways in which the problem can be solved. All of us have to work through those attitudes that are wrong in the presence of God.

Perhaps for you when it comes to the lordship of Christ the hang-up is the question of foreign service. Mrs. Leitch said something the other day that I have not been able to get out of my mind: "Don't let the image keep you back." You have the image that anybody who is overseas is second-best; he's the kind of guy who couldn't beat his way out of a paperbag, but he'd be great in some jungle somewhere. Forget it. I suspect you have found out in conversation at this convention that the people who really make an impact overseas would make a tremendous impact anywhere in the world.

I was at a Christian college some years ago at a missionary conference. First, we had a public meeting, and then we had a question-and-answer period off in one room at 4:00 in the afternoon. We were overwhelmed with the audience of two that showed up, indicating something about the interest of those students and their general image of and attitude toward missions. We went out for coffee and talked informally about world affairs for an hour. I'll never forget one student, who said, as we walked back across the campus, "Wow! Those missionaries really know what's going on in the world. I learned more in an hour than I have in my course in four months." And I suddenly realized that this was a new thought to him. He did not realize that generally these people who have given their lives know far more about what is going on than many other people. That's not to say there aren't duds among them. What group do you know that doesn't have a dud?

But don't think that the problem and hang-up "nobody wants us" is a general thing. The church overseas does want us if we are the right type of person. The questions of finances, of children, of what would I do—all of these things can be worked through if you are willing to trust the Lord for them.

If you are really thinking seriously about going overseas, be sure to find out all you can about the mission boards you consider, because, if you go that route, you want to be sure you are committed to a group with which you are in total sympathy—with its doctrine and with all of its policies. Dr. Eugene Nida said some years ago from the Urbana platform that the team on which you play is far more important than the stadium in which you play. The group you go with is more important than where you go.

Lord, I'm Willing

The issue beyond all of that is, Will you say this? "Lord, I'm willing to go wherever you want me to go. I'm willing to stay here in America if that's what you want me to do. I'm willing to go overseas. I'm willing to go into the inner city. I'm willing to go out in a rural area where nobody will ever hear of me. I don't care where it is as long as it's the place you want me to be." That is the real issue when it comes to the lordship of Christ.

The problem for most of us is that we tend to think the choice is between doing what we want to do and being happy, and doing what the Lord wants us to do and being miserable. The tragedy is that we have that false conception, for nothing is farther from the truth. God is not a celestial Scrooge who looks down over the balcony of heaven trying to find people who enjoy life and then says, "Cut that out!" The truth of Romans 8:32 has to be burned into the marrow of our souls: "He that spared not his own Son, but delivered him up for us all, how shall he not with him also freely give us all things?" The God who loved you and me enough to die for us when we did not care that much for him is not about to shortchange us when we give him our lives.

God only wants to save us from ourselves, from our own short-sightedness. He knows the end from the beginning. He knows us better than we know ourselves. And he wants to fit our lives into his plan and pattern for time and eternity in a way that he knows will be good for us and make the greatest contribution to his purpose and plan. Dr. Oswald Hoffman of the Lutheran Hour has pointed out, "Having given us the package, will God now deny us the ribbon?"

Robert Munger some years ago wrote a little booklet called *My Heart—Christ's Home*, the story of a man who invited Jesus Christ into his life and thought he could keep him in the living room. But Christ began to wander. The man began to realize that Christ wanted to get into every corner and closet of that house. Are there any rooms you have shut Jesus Christ out of? If you have, make him Lord: Open that door and give the room entirely to him.

The lordship of Christ applies to those of us who are older, too, because not only is it a crisis to which some of us may come, but it is also a process. Sometimes we who are along the road a way and who have talked to others need to be reminded of this. Are you an older Christian who is consumed with disappointment, bitterness, jealousy or failure, perhaps over your children, perhaps over college. What does the lordship of Christ mean to those of us who are older? Let us each think of that in the presence of Jesus Christ.

Guidance

But maybe you know you are committed. There are no areas of holdout. And the question for you is, How can I know what God wants me to do? How do I get guidance?

Do we wait for a liver-shiver? an anonymous letter in the mail? a verse which springs out of the Bible like a hot ingot and strikes us in the eye or the heart? Do we open the Bible at random, as if it were a divine Ouija board, and try to get guidance? How do we in fact know what God wants us to do after we have committed our lives to him?

At Urbana 70 I devoted my whole message to this question (it has been reprinted as a booklet, *Affirming the Will of God*), and I want to summarize some of its major points since this is a crucial problem for every one of us.

First, God's will has two aspects. The first dimension involves those things that are already revealed in the Scriptures. Has it ever struck you that the vast majority of the will of God is already revealed? You want to know what the will of God is for your life? Take the book of James, for instance, and make a list of the commands. That will give you enough to work on for months. As you read the Scripture, crystallize the principles as well as the specific commands about what you are to do and not to do, and you will get a tremendous amount of guidance.

Are any of you thinking about marrying a non-Christian and praying for guidance? Save your breath. God has already spoken monosyllabically on that subject. In 2 Corinthians 6:14 he says that we are not to be unequally yoked together with unbelievers. You don't need to pray about that. God has given you clear guidance already.

Are you praying about whether to be a witness for Jesus Christ? You don't need to pray about it: God wants you to be a witness. Maybe that will be your next step of faith in obedience to the lordship of Christ. Who are the non-Christians you are praying for specifically by name? And who are the people you are attempting to reach for Christ beyond the immediate circle of your friends? Will everybody in your dormitory have had an opportunity to hear of Jesus Christ because you were there this year? Have you thought through how the gospel can be communicated to a significant number of people? That is part of the lordship of Christ and part of knowing what God's will is all about.

Romans 8:29 tells us we are to be conformed to the image of Christ, which takes place as we meditate on who Jesus Christ is and what he wants to do in and through us as we read his Word day by day.

But there is a second dimension of the will of God: those areas of life which are not specifically referred to in Scripture and which vary for each one of us. There is no verse that will tell you, Joe Hammerschlag, whether you're to be married. And there is no verse that says, Mary Jones, you should be a nurse in Jackson, Mississippi, or a teacher in Cambodia. What you're to do, where you're to do it and with whom are dimensions of the will of God that he mediates to us in different ways.

There are several prerequisites for getting guidance in these matters. The first we have already touched on: committing yourself to the will of God sight-unseen, realizing that God is not a divine killjoy and that we can trust ourselves to him with complete confidence. If we are honest enough to admit it, most of us say, "Lord, I'd love to do your will, but would you mind sort of just letting me know what it is? Like, if I could see whether it will be Honolulu or Nome, Alaska, that would be helpful." Of course, without meaning to we are insulting God because we are saying, "God, I don't trust you. I think I know better than you do what would make me happy." As we have already seen, that is a lie of the devil.

Getting on with what we already know to be the will of God is a second prerequisite.

How then does God actually guide? We have already indicated one way, through his Word. Second, he guides us as we pray. How many of you are spending five minutes a day in prayer asking God to show you what his will is in a particular area in which the Bible is not specific?

As we pray, God the Holy Spirit often deepens the conviction and gives us a sense of rightness or wrongness about a particular course of action. This conviction differs from emotion, which is undulant, up-and-down. Conviction deepens day by day. If one day we are going to Japan and the next day we are going to Nigeria and the following day we are going to Argentina and the fourth day we are staying home, all because we happen to meet enthusiastic people from these parts of the world, that is not conviction and that is not the way God guides. Conviction is a deepening constant.

God guides us through circumstances. But again this is only

one piece of the pie. Most of us take that as almost the whole pie: We look at the circumstances and they determine everything. You may be praying about going to graduate school, but if you cannot get into any graduate school in the country, this may be negative guidance that God has something else in mind for you. Circumstances are much more of a guide negatively than they are positively. The fact that you can get into five schools is not necessarily an indication that that is where God wants you. He may want you to do something entirely different because he wants you rather than your training, as George Cowan has pointed out in a helpful booklet, *Your Training or You?* Circumstances are a factor, but they are to be viewed from God's standpoint and with his value system, not simply taken as in themselves totally determinitive.

In the fourth place, God guides through the counsel of friends, those who have been down the road farther than we have, who are equally committed to the will of God, who will really level with us and who know us. This is, I think, one of the most neglected dimensions in guidance today. It is significant, it seems to me, that in Acts 15 we are told, "it seemed good to the Holy Spirit and to us" (Acts 15:28).

I always get a little nervous when people come to me implying that they have a private pipeline to God, using the expression "God led me." Nobody else has gotten any of these vibrations, but they have. Sometimes the direction sounds rather bizarre, but it is very spiritual, you know, to say "God led me." Sometimes that is merely an inversion of self-centeredness, squirting a little spiritual perfume on our decision, and is really not God's guidance at all. Whenever a person uses that expression rather glibly, I always ask, "What makes you think so? Are there any others who sense that this is God's leading?" It is a rare situation when other people who are equally committed to the will of God have no sense in their own spirit that what you suggest is of God. It is true that we sometimes receive bad counsel from friends, but we neglect the counsel of others at our own peril.

When all of these factors coincide—the Word of God (its principles as well as specific commands), the deepening conviction by the Holy Spirit that comes in prayer, the analysis of circumstances from God's point of view and his standard of values, and the counsel of Christian friends—we can be pretty sure we are in the will of God.

Common Mistakes

It is important, however, to avoid some common mistakes in discerning the mind of God. One is to think that if you want to do it, it can't possibly be God's will. I know a girl who determines whether a thing is God's will by how much she loathes it. If she can't stand it, she thinks, "Well, that's proof positive." This again betrays the Scrooge idea of God, as though God is saying, "All right, all right, are you willing to do it, are you willing to do it? C'mon, c'mon."

There are times when there is real struggle in committing ourselves to the will of God, and dying to ourselves is never pleasant. It is exquisitely painful. But there is a paradox, because in that pain comes the deepest satisfaction and joy that can be known this side of heaven. David says in Psalm 37:4, "Delight thyself also in the Lord, and he shall give thee the desires of thine heart." He is not suggesting a dichotomy, not suggesting that if you commit your way to the Lord over here, he will give you the desires of your heart over there—a Cadillac and all this kind of thing. No, he is saying that if you commit your way to the Lord and desire him, he will give you the very desires. That is what Augustine meant when he said, "Love God and do as you please." He was not suggesting spiritual schizophrenia; he was suggesting that if you love God, you will please to do what God wills. That is where real happiness is.

The second mistake to avoid is thinking that to be in the will of God means everything will be moonlight and roses. Sometimes it is after a commitment to the will of God that the bottom seems to fall out of everything. That is what happened to Jairus, you remember (Mk. 5). He asked the Lord to come and heal his daughter, and the Lord said, "I'll come." You can imagine Jairus' spirits zooming. Then our Lord was interrupted by a woman who had been sick for twelve years and could certainly have waited another few hours. While our Lord was talking with her, a servant came and told Jairus, "Don't bother him any longer.

Your daughter is dead." His spirits plunged to the basement. Our Lord's word to him was, "Don't be faithless; only believe."

You may go through tremendous storm—as the disciples did after being told by the Lord to go across the Sea of Galilee (Mk. 4) —in the midst of the will of God. You do not determine whether you are in the will of God by how moonlight-and-roseish everything is. Someone has aptly said, "Never doubt in the darkness what God has shown you in the light."

Third, do not make the mistake of thinking that every decision has to have a subjective confirmation. If God gives you a subjective confirmation, fine. But you may have to make by next Tuesday a basic decision that is going to commit you for a period of time. What do you do? You pray, you talk to your friends, you read the Word of God, you analyze the circumstances. There are four equally valuable ways you can go, you think. What do you do? You decide what you believe is the will of God, trusting that God is going to close the door if that is not it. You say, "Lord, I'm willing to do any of these four that you tell me, or something else if you show me, but you haven't given me any direct guidance so I'm going to go down lane three and trust that you're guiding me."

Then you can go on your way rejoicing without second-guessing yourself for the next ten years, because you realize that God does not play the game of mousetrap. He does not say, "Ahah! You thought that was it. Sorry, back to the start and try over again. You've only got three chances the next time." God does not play games with us. He loves us too much to do that. We can go on our way rejoicing.

Another mistake to avoid is deciding what we are going to do for the Lord. That is a subtle one because it sounds so spiritual: "Lord, I'm going to be a businessman for you. Think of all the money I can kick into that offering three years from now." Or, "Lord, I'm going to be a missionary for you." Fine missionary!

God does not ask us to do that. He invites us with Paul to ask, "Lord, what will you have me to do?" That is the only appropriate response for recruits of the Commander-in-Chief, allowhim the privilege of assigning us in the battle lines.

Finally, we must avoid the mistake of thinking that a call to foreign missions or world evangelism is different from a call to anything else. Many people think that they should just go on doing what they are doing unless God hits them on the head. Many young people approach a missionary conference kind of gritting their teeth. Maybe you have come here thinking, "If I can survive one more Urbana, I'm free and away." You fasten your spiritual seatbelt. You're not going to be swept out of your seat by emotion. And you can go on your way rejoicing, doing what you want, if God doesn't draft you here.

The Lord doesn't draft anybody; he only takes volunteers. And a call to overseas service is no different from a call to anything else. If you are a teacher in Chicago, you have as much need to know that you are called of God to do that as anyone who has ever gone into the ministry or served in Africa. We don't get three points more for doing any particular thing or three points more for being in any particular location. The crucial questions for each one of us are, Where does God want me as an individual? and What does he want me to do?

Perhaps you should begin to move toward overseas service, trusting God to close the doors if he does not want you there. David Howard has asked in Don't Wait for the Macedonians why anyone should seek more specific direction to serve the Lord overseas than he does to serve the Lord in any other capacity or location. It may well be that we should make every effort to go overseas unless God clearly calls us to stay home, rather than the reverse. And as you make the effort and begin to move, God will guide. He can close doors easily, but, as the old story goes, you can't steer a parked car.

Knowing Jesus Christ

Finally, it may be that your problem is that you do not know Jesus Christ in the first place. Maybe you came to this convention thinking you are a Christian, but having met those kids in the Bible studies and mingled with them, you have come to a realization that these people have something you haven't. They seem to know what life is all about. They're going somewhere. They have a joy that does not seem to be completely related to their circumstances. And whatever it is they have, you don't have it. There must be two kinds of Christianity, you say, and I'd like to have what they've got.

It may be that you have come here with a dead orthodoxy. You have given mental assent to the facts for as long as you can remember, but the thing has never lived for you, never been vital; it's a drag, a burden. You have no motivation to witness. You hear about people who enjoy the Christian life, but that has never been your experience. God wants you tonight, in affirming his lordship, to come to him in the first place to receive him as Lord and Savior.

Professor John Scanzoni, a Christian sociology professor at the U. of Indiana, wrote a significant article some years ago entitled "No Faith to Lose." He describes three groups of students that he sees coming every year from evangelical homes and churches to the state university.

The first group are those who simply have an *indoctrination faith*. These are the kids who won all the sword drills back home. You know, they can quote John 3:16 in five languages. In terms of information they have everything, in terms of life, nothing. When they get to the campus, they kick the faith, and everybody back home wrings his hands and says, "Oh, that terrible university! Johnny and Susy have lost their faith." Scanzoni raises the awkward question, Did they lose their saving faith, or did they merely lose an indoctrination faith?

The second group are those who come with a *conformity faith*. These are the kids who do all the right things and don't do all the wrong things. But the only reason they do is because of the external pressure of family and church to conform. Put in an environment for the first time in their lives where they are free to do what they want to do, they shed their faith like a raincoat. And everybody back home wrings his hands and says, "Johnny and Susy have lost their faith." Again, asks Scanzoni, Did they lose saving faith, or did they simply lose a conformity faith?

The third group comes every year with a *commitment faith*. These kids come into the university and hear difficult questions. Not only do they not have the answers—they have never before heard the questions! But they don't junk their faith; they know there must be answers, and they dig them out. They are put in a hostile environment: They face temptations they may not have even known about, let alone faced. But instead of succumbing to the environment, they have an impact on it, like Daniel and his friends when they got the first Fulbright from Jerusalem to Babylon some years ago and really had an impact for God.

Now what makes the difference? The kids in the last group know that to be a Christian is more than giving mental assent to the facts. It is a commitment totally to Jesus Christ as Lord and Savior. They have been born from above by the Holy Spirit. Do you have merely an indoctrination faith? Do you have merely a conformity faith? Or do you know for sure tonight that you have a commitment faith and that you have been born from above?

Some of you are asking, "How do I get what you are talking about? How do I become a Christian as Jesus Christ describes it?" Let me explain as simply and clearly as I know how, in a way that you could explain to another non-Christian, how to step over the line and receive Jesus Christ. One of the clearest statements in the Scripture is John 1:12: "As many as received him to them he gave the power to become the children of God, even to them that believe on his name." There are three operative verbs in that statement: *believe, receive, become.*

It is significant that one of the illustrations the New Testament uses to describe being and becoming a Christian is marriage. No illustration is perfect, but this one helps us to see what is involved.

Suppose you know a fellow or a girl on whom you are absolutely sold. You couldn't believe in that person more if you tried. They have beauty, intelligence, handsomeness, character, ability—everything that is desirable in a member of the opposite sex. They've really got it. Does that make you married to that person? Sad to say, it doesn't. Some of us kind of wish it would. But more is involved than that.

Suppose in addition to your intellectual conviction about this person, you are emotionally involved. You think of the person and you get an all-gone feeling. You try to study, and all you see is a face instead of the book. If you're a girl, you jump three feet when the phone rings. If you're a fellow, you knock down the mailman—and you're not looking for a letter from Mama.

Judging from the irregularity of your heartbeat, you think you must be experiencing that of which the poets have written. Does that make you married? It doesn't.

What else is necessary? A commitment of the will in which you say "I do." You receive that person into your life, and you commit yourself to that person in a relationship. You believe in that person, you receive that person into your life and you become married.

That is exactly how you become a Christian. You come to a conviction that Jesus Christ spoke the truth about himself and about you, that he is the God-man, that he did die for a desperate problem that we have (namely, sin, independent rebellion against God), that he died in our place because he loved us, that he rose from the dead and that he is a living person tonight. You then receive him into your life and become his child.

Someone has said that in becoming a Christian there is something to be believed and someone to be received. That is very true. There are many who simply have an intellectual belief, but they have no life and can't understand why Christianity doesn't mean anything to them. It's like Pepsi-Cola with the fizz out of it or cold mashed potatoes. Yuch! The reason is they have never come to know Jesus Christ.

Becoming a Christian is not rearranging the intellectual furniture and adopting Christian Philosophy 79 as contrasted to Existentialism 13 or Logical Positivism 2 any more than marriage is Philosophy 83 as contrasted to Singlehood 12. Christianity is a relationship. A lot of people are like the fellow who says, "You know, I don't understand why marriage doesn't mean anything to me. I've read twelve books on marriage in the last six months. I've been to half a dozen weddings, but it just doesn't mean anything to me." There's a simple reason—he's not married. Marriage is a relationship. And so it is to be a Christian.

How does one establish the relationship? The clearest statement I know of in the Scripture is in Revelation 3:20. The Lord Jesus Christ likens our lives to a house and says "Behold, I stand at the door and knock; if any one hears my voice and opens the door, I will come in to him and eat with him, and he with me."

Just before I left to come to this conference, at Schloss Mittersill a girl came to me and asked, "How can I become a Christian?"

After explaining what I have just explained to you, I continued, "Suppose someone came to the door of your house and knocked. How would you get the person inside?"

She thought for a minute and replied, "I'd open the door."

"Yes, and then what would you do?"

Her eyes grew wide: "I'd invite the person to come in." You could just see the flash bulb of comprehension going off in her head.

I said, "Precisely, that's how you become a Christian."

Jesus Christ is a living person. He has intellect, emotion and will. He is invisible, but he is more real than I am. If you speak to him, he will respond. He is knocking at the door of your life. He will never gate-crash. But the moment you invite him to come in and commit yourself to him as your Savior and Lord, he will enter your life.

The girl at Schloss Mittersill prayed that night. I gave her the option to go off on her own or to pray with me, and she was so prepared by the Spirit of God that she wanted to do it right there. She received Jesus Christ into her life. In a sense, she said, "I do," and realized that Jesus had done everything necessary for her and for us to be cleansed and forgiven and that all we can do is receive it and respond to him.

One other dimension of marriage is illustrative. If one is going to have a successful marriage, he has to be willing to give up his independence and enter into a consultant relationship about everything in life. You cannot go your own way, ignoring other people, and have a successful marriage. And you cannot receive Jesus Christ as Savior and refuse to have him as Lord. You may have received him years ago and been unaware of his claims of lordship, which you are now beginning to realize, but you cannot continually refuse them and claim to be a Christian.

Again, that is nothing to be afraid of. It is tremendous to think that the Creator of the Universe has promised to be our Guide, our Shepherd, our Friend. But realize that when you come to Jesus Christ, it is a double-or-nothing proposition, and you have to be willing for him to change you. You have to be willing to repudiate what you know is wrong in your life and what he shows you is wrong. He will give you the strength to change and to break habits that you have been unable to break. But you must be willing for him to live his life through you and to begin to call the shots from here on in.

Where Are You?

Where are you on the spectrum?

Are you one who came to Christ early in life but who is just now beginning to realize the implications of the lordship of Christ? Is God speaking to you to give him your life totally and completely without reservation, though you do not know the specifics of God's will?

Are you one who has committed your life and is asking, "Lord, show me clearly what the next steps are?" Ask him to show you some next steps of faith and obedience, which he will.

Or are you one who has never come into the family of God? For you, Jesus Christ is knocking at the door of your life. He wants to come in, and he will if you invite him.

I would like to suggest that at this moment, whatever your situation and wherever on the spectrum you are, you respond to the Lord Jesus Christ privately in your own heart. If you have never made him Lord of your life, right now in the simplicity of your own words tell him. If you have committed yourself to him and made him Lord, lay hold of him in some further dimension. If there is something that God has spoken to you about today, some area of lordship that he wants to claim, give it to him. Some of us need to accept ourselves and our background and circumstances, and acknowledge God's lordship in that—that nothing has happened in our lives up to this point by accident and that nothing will in the future.

If you have not yet come into the family of God, let me suggest you pray something like this: "Lord Jesus Christ, I do believe that you are the Son of God and the Lord of the Universe. I do believe that you died in my place for my sin and rebellion and that you rose from the dead. Today I am asking you to come into my life as my Lord and Master and Savior. Thank you for what you have done." God will hear you when you pray.

Let us respond to whatever he may be saying to us: "Lord,

maybe you're in my life, but in case you're not, this day I am inviting you into my life as Savior and Lord." From here on in you can have the joy that comes with knowing that you are in the family of God.

JESUS CHRIST: HOPE OF THE WORLD

5

SAMUEL H. MOFFETT

I spent two years once in communist China. I couldn't get out.
Day and night it was dinned into me that the hope of the world is
Mao Tse-tung. A large part of the communist world believes it.
Then suddenly I was arrested, given a kind of people's trial,
found guilty of embezzlement and thrown out of China. What a
joy to be back in the free world. But a niece of mine, who ought
to know because she had just graduated from college, soon told
me that there is absolutely no hope for the world anymore. She
had been reading ecology. Now that, too, is false, but a large part
of the free world believes it. So I have most of the world against
me, I am afraid, when I say to you that there is hope for the world,
and that hope is in no other name, in nothing else, but Jesus
Christ. I have that on the authority of the Word of God.

Trace *hope* through the Scriptures, as I have done, and it will
soon be abundantly clear to you that "Jesus Christ: Hope of the
World" is more than a slogan. It is the theme of the whole Bible.

From the Old Testament's "Why art thou cast down, O my soul?
... Hope thou in God" (Ps. 42:5) to the New Testament's "Christ
in you, the hope of glory" (Col. 1:27); from the *symbols* of hope,
the "*anchor* of the soul" (Heb. 6:19) and the "*helmet* of the hope
of salvation" (1 Thess. 5:8), to the *signs* of hope—the sign of the
rainbow in the book of Genesis and the signs of his coming again
in the book of Revelation—from beginning to end the Bible is
flooded with the iridescent light of the Christian's hope.

So my heart was warmed by the encouragements of the promises of God. Then Johan, a young German student, dropped in to
see me. I had known him five years ago as a high-school exchange student in Korea. Now he has graduated from college and
has taken a job in Berlin as a high-school teacher. But before he
began teaching he wanted to see Korea again, so he came back
and we talked. He is a little apprehensive about his job. He is not
a practicing Christian. He wants to get married. "But no children," he said firmly, and he went on to tell me why. "I don't
want to bring any children into a world like this," he said. And
he spoke of wickedness and corruption, pollution and despair,
and loss of human hope in a way that put a chill into me.

In the face of his loss of hope, and all the good reasons he has
for losing hope, how realistic are my reasons for holding on to
hope? It is not enough to stand up and shout, "Jesus Christ is the
Hope of the World." It is not enough for Christians to peer out
hopefully at this incredibly bad world through our happy little
stained-glass church windows and delude ourselves into thinking that our pretty colors will make the world all right. If Jesus
Christ *is* going to be the hope of the world, we have to begin with
the world as it really is, and hope as it really is, and Jesus Christ
as he really is. Slogans are not enough. The words have got to
focus on things believably real, or we remain as self-deluded as a
Red Guard in China with his communist chants and his Chairman Mao.

So to avoid dreams, wishful thinking and a bad headache or
worse when we wake up, let us stay as close as possible to things
as they are, and let me make three simple observations about
Christian hope:

First, if we begin with the world as it is, we must admit with

Johan that there really is not much hope left. There never is, without Christ.

Second, let me point out that to be realistic, hope must reckon with *all* of reality—not just the cramping facts of a dismal present. *Jesus Christ gives us a hope with a future.*

Finally, I must remind you of your part in this hope. If Christ is the Hope of the World, and not just a little private hope for you and me, we must get out into the world with that hope. *Christ gives us hope with a mission.*

The World as It Is: Hopeless

Begin, then, with the world as it is—pretty hopeless. What Dante once wrote over the entrance of hell could be written today over the whole world: "Abandon hope, all you who enter here." That is how Johan seemed to feel. That is why he wanted no children. God gave us a paradise, and we have made it a hell.

The physical facts alone are enough to terrify the imagination. The human race is running out of heat, out of food, out of water— out of just about everything, in fact, but people. The oil crisis is only the latest, and far from the most serious, in a whole series of shocks that have tumbled man out of all his early twentieth-century dreams of inevitable progress. A man who works for one of the largest oil companies in the world told me that even if the earth were a hollow globe and were completely filled with oil— which, of course, it isn't—even then, at the present rate of increasing consumption, we would be completely out of oil in less than seventy years, that is, by the year 2040.

Even before that, by 1990, they say, the United States may be facing a more alarming shortage. We may run out of food. It seems impossible, I know. America has been the wonder of the world, feeding itself with more than enough to eat yet using only about 7% of its population in agricultural production. Most of the world puts 50% of its people on the land, and still cannot feed the rest. But now even America may be coming to the end of the food boom. Without intensive food research, says Dr. Parks, president of Iowa State, in twenty years America, too, will be hungry, just like all the rest of the world. And the worst shortage of all may still be yet to come—water. The world's water table, its reserves of fresh water, are steadily and dangerously draining away. Deserts are eating again into the green earth. In North Africa alone, along the Sahara, millions may die in 1974.

What happened to the bright new world we thought we were building a generation or two ago? The scientists and the poets promised us that progress was "the distinctive mark of man" (Browning). We are the most knowledgeable generation in the history of the world. Is this all that we can do with our vaunted technology, build another Tower of Babel boobytrapped on every rising level with nuclear weapons capable of annihilating all mankind? We have wasted the good earth the Lord has given us, polluted his clear air, fouled the streams and brooks so badly that fish turn belly up and die. Our cities are a stink and a disgrace. In Tokyo, authorities have begun to warn the Japanese that if things go on as they are, in another twelve years they will be able to collect the garbage only once every three months.[1]

Let me jolt you with one last deadly statistic. John Hannah, outgoing administrator of our government's Agency for International Development (AID), says that one-half of all the children born into the world this year will never live to see their sixth birthday.[2]

Look at the world as it really is, and, if you look only at the world, don't babble about hope. It reminds me of Auden's somber lines on human despair:

The glacier knocks in the cupboard
The desert sighs in the bed,
And the crack in the teacup opens
A lane to the land of the dead.[3]

"No children," says my German friend. Not in this kind of world.

Now strangely enough, considering the fact that we are talking about Christian hope, the Bible does not directly dispel such pessimism. It holds out no great hope for this earth as such. "The earth shall perish," says the Old Testament (Ps. 102:25-26). It will be "burned up," adds the New (2 Pet. 3:10).

Some years ago the German theologian Professor Edmund Schlink of Heidelberg University shocked an ecumenical conference which had gathered to consider the same optimistic theme which is ours tonight, "Jesus Christ, the Hope of the World." He said,

> If in our thinking about this subject we place the emphasis on the preservation of this threatened world, we shall miss the point. If we expect Christ to ensure this world so that men may continue undisturbed their pursuit of liberty, may carry on their business, and seek an improvement in their standard of living, then Christ is not the hope of the world, but rather the end of all the world's hopes.[4]

In the Bible, he went on to point out, the coming of Christ as the hope of the world means also the end of the world as we know it now.

The World with Christ: Hope with a Future

If the world is as hopeless as it looks, and if, on top of that, the Bible says it is doomed, what do we mean when we say, "Jesus Christ is the Hope of the World"? To understand that, we must ask what Christians mean by hope, and how it is connected with Jesus Christ.

When people tell me that my Christian hope is unrealistic, I tell them that the trouble is not with my hope, but with their reality. Their reality is too small. They are so petrified by the present that they forget the past and the future. They are so busy looking at the world that they never look up to see God. Of course, in that kind of a world there is no hope. But one of the most important lessons in the whole Bible is that hope is not confined to any one point in space or time. It is tied to a person, Jesus Christ, and it is forever. "Jesus Christ is the same yesterday and today and forever" (Heb. 13:8).

Things do look rather bad these days. But they have been worse. If you have given up hope because today is so bad, look back about 1900 years. The darkest day the world has ever known was not Watergate, My Lai or Hiroshima. It was the day Gentiles and Jews took the Hope of the World, Jesus Christ, and stripped him, beat him and killed him on a cross. The dead shuddered and hell broke loose, and for one agonizing instant, a moment never to be repeated, the whole human race was utterly and completely, God-forsakenly lost. "My God, my God, why have you forsaken me?" came a cry from the cross, from Christ, the second Adam.

But God took that most hopeless of all days and made it the hinge of history, not its end. He is always doing the happily unexpected. Unlike human history, which always seems to turn out bad just when it begins to look good, God's salvation history is at its best when things look worst.

Look at the depressing story of man's hopes. It reads like a bad joke, one of those "That's good, no that's bad" jokes. Centuries ago the Chinese discovered a new source of energy, gunpowder. That's good. No, that's bad. Gunpowder kills people. A few hundred years later the Americans discovered a new source of energy, oil. That's good. Oil goesn't kill people. No, that's bad. It pollutes, it kills the world, and besides, we're running out of it. Well, here's good news anyway: We now have an ever better source of energy, nuclear fission. No, even that is bad. It kills people faster than gunpowder and pollutes more lethally than oil.

There is nothing wrong, of course, with man's discoveries—the more the better. And there is nothing wrong with each new hope as such, except that this kind of hope is anchored to man and not to God; and man without God takes each new shining discovered hope and turns it into an engine of his own destruction. That is his curse. Man's hope lies in the fact that God does just the opposite. He takes the worst and uses it to save. He took death, the ultimate instrument of man's destruction, and conquered it, defused it. He raised Jesus Christ from the dead and the disciples saw him, and even doubting Thomas touched him and at last believed. He who was dead lives, and that makes Jesus Christ the Hope of the World. He gives us a future to live for, not just a present to die in.

The real trouble with the world is not that it is running out of physical resources, but that it is running out of hope. And it is running out of hope because it puts its hope in the wrong thing, in physical resources, for example, which is not where hope belongs. Did you hear Mrs. Meir's rather wry remark some weeks ago: "Our forefather Moses led our people for forty years through the wilderness, and then settled in the only part of the

Middle East without any oil." But Moses was absolutely right. He followed God. It was not oil that made Canaan the Promised Land, not even milk and honey—but the *promise*, God's promise that in Abraham should all the world be blessed. He gave Israel a hope, and the Hope of Israel has made that tiny nation indestructible. It refuses to die.

By contrast, too much of our part of the world has given up hope and seems all too ready to die. Part of the reason, I think, is that the most popular philosophy of our time takes away the future, takes away hope, and thereby takes away the human will to live. "Only the now is real," says the secular existentialist. But if that is so, as the more honest existentialists like Camus admit, there is really no purpose in going on living. Think clearly, he urges, and do "not hope any more."[5] I respect his integrity, but I am not attracted by his squirrel-cage philosophy. It leads to surrender, to suicide, to death.

They say that about 500,000 people, half a million, will try to commit suicide in the United States in 1974, and the U.S. is not even in the top ten of the "suicide countries." It ranks seventeenth.[6] What's worse, people don't even care any more. When the 500th suicide leaped off the Golden Gate Bridge earlier this year, San Francisco newspapers asked their readers if the city should put up a better guard rail. Readers wrote in seven to one against it. It would spoil the view! That is what happens when only the now is real.

I prefer the radical realism of the Christian faith. It does not deny the present. It faces it. It faces all the despairing realities of the now with hope because it sees them in the balancing perspective of the equally true realities of the past and the future. Hope begins with what God did that day on Calvary 1900 years ago, and it never ends. Hope is eternal. Hope is life forever for them that believe. Hope is the promise that he will come again. However the world may end—and let's not pretend to know more about that than the Bible unambiguously teaches—it ends with Christ's victory *for* man, and not with man's annihilation *of* man. It ends with hope, and that is not an end.

O God, our help in ages past,
Our hope for years to come,

Our shelter from the stormy blast,
And our eternal home.

The World and Christ and You: Hope with a Mission

But I must make one final, important point. When some Christians sing that great hymn, the 110th Psalm, they manage to miss one of the key points about Christian hope, namely, that hope carries with it a mission. It is not just a bomb shelter, a safe and future home. It is all that, yes, but more. If as Christians all we have to say is, "There's no hope for the world, and the sooner you are out of it the better. So die and receive the hope laid up for you in heaven"—if that is our gospel, it deserves all the scorn that the communists heap upon it with their caricature, "Pie in the sky by-and-by."

God sent hope into the world not by taking Christians out, but by sending the missionary in, his Son. Jesus is the Hope of the World not simply because he calls us to glory. He is the Hope of the World because he left that glory and became hungry with the hungry to feed them, and weak with the sick to heal them, and condemned with the oppressed to overcome for them.

"To the poor," said Gandhi, "God can only appear as bread and butter." But isn't that precisely how God *did* appear? He came in the flesh, and he said, "I am bread." True, he went on to explain to his disciples the spiritual truth that he is the bread of life, but it was not eternal life he divided that day among the multitudes by Galilee. It was bread. Don't take the meat and the wheat out of the Christian hope.

If food is short, the Christian agriculturalist had better join the search for another miracle grain like the Philippine and Pakistan rice that raised food production five times over and gave Asia the beginning of what is called the "green revolution." Christ fed the multitudes. If you are a physicist, why should it be beneath you as a Christian to get out and look for oil or for alternative sources of energy? One of God's forgotten miracles had to do with oil. Look up the miracle of the olive oil in 2 Kings 4.

To get closer home, if you are a comfortable white, you had better get a little uncomfortable about racial injustice, or don't make the mistake of going as a missionary to Africa. Racism is a sin, one of the deadliest—or have you forgotten that the parable of the Good Samaritan is not just a sweet little story about helping people who get beaten up by thieves? It is a blast against the sin of racism—Jews against Samaritans. But incidentally, if I may speak for a moment as an Asian, if you are a comfortable black you had better get uncomfortable about black discrimination against Asians in Africa. No race has any corner on racism. "All have sinned, and fall short of the glory of God."

Let me put the needle in once more. If you are an American, black or white or yellow or brown, you had better ask yourself as a Christian whether it is quite right for a country with only 6% of the world's population to seize for itself 35% of the whole world's annual production. Ron Seaton of India tells me that if the rest of the world used up materials at the rate the United States does, we would devour six times as much as the world can even produce in a year. It is a sad comment on the free world that we are better at producing wealth but the communists are better at distributing it. One part of the missionary calling in our time may well be a voluntary reduction of our overinflated standard of living, so that those who have never had enough may finally get their fair share. They can, you know. That is part of our hope.

Edward Rogers, in his book *Poverty on a Small Planet*, makes a convincing case for the hope that even with the way we have wasted them the world *can* provide the raw materials and the energy to give its ever-increasing population a decent standard of living. But he adds, "Whether the standard is attained or not depends on the will of man, not on the niggardliness of Nature."[7] I wish he had not stopped there. If it depends on the will of man, we are still back in the squirrel cage. We will botch it up. We always have.

Remember Auden's poem about the crack in the teacup widening and a "lane to the land of the dead"? Its title is "We'd rather be ruined than changed." Auden was a Christian. He saw men choosing ruin, but he knew that man can also choose to be changed. The change is Christ. And that, too, makes him the Hope of the World. He changes people, and people can change the world—physically, not just spiritually.

Some people remember Antioch only as the church where the evangelistic world mission began. I like to remember that in church history it is also famous as the church with a changed heart—a heart for social action. Its welfare program supported 3,000 widows; it had relief for the unemployed, a daily bread line and even a used-clothes department.

Two weeks ago I attended services in the greatest missionary church I know, the Youngnak Presbyterian Church in Seoul. Twenty-six years ago it had twenty-seven members, a handful of bedraggled refugees from North Korea. Today more than ten thousand people almost fight their way to get into the church every Sunday. They have to relay the service over closed-circuit TV to the overflow crowds. They even have instantaneous translation into English with earphones for heathen American tourists who wander in, wondering what all the action is about. They support forty evangelists to carry the gospel to unreached villages. They have sent missionaries to Thailand and Formosa and even as far away as Ethiopia. It is no accident that they also have orphanages, widows' homes, an employment service, family counseling and even a used-clothes offering like Antioch. No part of the life of the people is beyond the heart concern of that missionary church. When occasion demands, it has even been known to talk back to the Korean government.

But—and let me stress the *but*—let's not distort the gospel the other way either. That church calls itself the Youngnak Church, which, in Korean, means the Church of Everlasting Joy. It does not call itself the Church of Full Employment. It knows that the greater dimensions of the Christian hope are not temporal, but eternal. Our hope is the hope of salvation.

For the Christian church to settle for any lesser hope, whether by technological advance or by social action, is a betrayal of the faith and no ultimate service to the human race. Finding enough food, water and oil, or even justice, to keep this world going and saying that that is enough is like throwing a life preserver to a man who has fallen overboard from an ocean liner, but not bothering to stop and pick him up. It may keep him from drowning, but he will still die from the wind or the sun or the sharks. This is not to say that it is no part of the rescue to throw him the life preserver. It is. It may be the only thing that keeps him alive to be rescued. But what finally counts is picking him up and taking him aboard. So with our mission. Anything less than salvation from sin and incorporation into the family of God, his church, is what Jacques Ellul would call "the false presence of the Kingdom." There is a deeper hunger than the physical, a hunger and a thirst that only Christ can satisfy. Social action is not evangelism, and as a substitute for evangelism it is a temptation of the devil. "Turn these stones into bread." And Jesus said, "No. Man does not live by bread alone" (Mt. 4:3-4).

When the world is dying as inexorably and far more permanently from lack of the "living bread" as from all its other hungers combined, and when that makes world evangelism the greatest missionary challenge of all, why is it that so many Christians are saying that the day of the missionary is past?

Some people rationalize it: "We've already done our part. We sent the missionaries. They've established the church. There's a church now in every corner of the globe—an African church in Africa, Indonesian in Indonesia, Korean in Korea. They'll finish the task. Our part is over." So they turn on the TV.

Others just throw up their hands: "The whole thing is hopeless. The missionary has failed. Look at what happened. It's been almost 200 years since William Carey exploded the modern missionary movement around the world, and what are the results? There are more non-Christians in the world today than when we started."

Now which way do you want it? You cannot have it both ways. Is it because we have succeeded or because we have failed that we do not need the foreign missionary any more? Logically speaking, in both arguments the premise is true but the conclusion is false. We have succeeded and we have failed, but this world still needs the missionary, and, praise God, the Lord of Hope and the Lord of the Harvest still sends them out.

What are the facts? Is it true that because we have been so successful at putting the church in every land that those lands now no longer need outsiders like us as missionaries? That's not biblical; it's not historical; it's not even kind. In Christ there are no outsiders. To think so is racist. Christ's body is international.

There was a church in Rome, but Paul the missionary went to Rome. There was a church already in England, but Augustine went to Canterbury, and he changed the whole history of Christianity in England. To argue against sending outsiders to places where the church already exists is like saying to Inter-Varsity, "There is already a church in Massachusetts so keep out of Harvard."

But in some ways my primary objection is that it is not practical. The decision to be a foreign missionary, which is what I am talking about, is not a spiritual decision at all. Of course, to the Christian, all decisions are, in a way, spiritual. But my spiritual decision, the release of my own ambitions, telling the Lord I was ready to go, sent me to North Dakota. Going overseas, going to China—there was nothing spiritual about that. It was a purely practical, common-sense decision. Where would I be most useful? Where was I most needed? Looking at the world as a practical Christian, other things being equal, and remembering that the field is people not geography, shouldn't somebody go where there are fewer Christians and more people than where there are less people and more Christians? Remember Bill Borden's illustration, ten people carrying a log, nine at the little end and one staggering at the heavy end. If you want to help, to which end do you go? That is not a spiritual decision.

What about the other objection: We have already failed? There are more non-Christians today than when we started. Again, that is partly true. The log is getting heavier all the time, more non-Christians in the world every year. And if by *failure* you mean we have not converted the world, we have failed. But that is not our mission. We don't convert, the Lord does. Our task is evangelism, which is just telling the hopeless, all the hopeless, that there is hope and who the hope is. It's an equal opportunity program, not spiritual social security. But we are not very equal about it. Most of the world lives in Asia and Africa, and we still keep 80% of the world's Christians right here in the West. I am speaking statistically, of course. Only God knows where the Christians really are. Latin America has deceived itself into thinking it is 90% Christian, and you people in North America and Europe are just as bad. Asia, by contrast—more than half of all the world's people—is even statistically only 2% Christian. There is our real failure.

But there is nothing hopeless about it. For one thing, we could send more missionaries not less to where most of the non-Christians are, that is, overseas to Asia and Africa. That would take away some of the inequity. We could send them to where the opportunities are, to Korea, to Indonesia. There is nothing unChristian about success. It is perfectly biblical to go where the harvests are white. We could also send some to where the greatest needs are most unmet. Ralph Winter of Fuller Seminary points out in the *Evangelical Missions Quarterly* that most of the world's non-Christians are still in three immense, virtually un-penetrated blocks of people: the Chinese, the Muslims and the Hindus.[8] Just those three blocks number about two billion people, about half the world, and only 5% of the world's 50,000 Protestant missionaries are trying to reach them.

Yes, we have failed. But who says we are beaten? There are signs of miracle and breakthrough everywhere. If you are really discouraged, come to Korea. I will show you a church growing so fast that it doubles the number of Christians every ten years, growing four times as fast as the general population. Talk about the caricature of the missionary treading the burning sands, converting a cannibal now and then—my work as missionary takes me to an office on the eighth floor of the Christian Center Building just off the subway in one of the ten largest cities in the world, a city which has 1,500 Protestant churches. Whole new battalions of missionaries are arising from there. If you North Americans do not get around to the unfinished task, the Koreans will.

There are 3,000 missionaries from the Third World, according to one count, who are already in the work, and no one can tell them it won't work. They're not listening. They have heard the Lord Jesus Christ, the Lord of the Universe, the Hope of the World, and he says "Behold I have set before thee an open door, and no man can close it."

Look at Africa. Ten years ago they told us we were losing Africa to the Muslims. Today we know that it is not the Muslims but the Christians who are sweeping that continent. David

Barrett tells us that Africa is not just the 17% Christian we thought it was, but 40% Christian and growing so fast, thanks to the amazing indigenous spread of African Christianity. By the year 2000 Africa will have 350 million Christians, which is more Christians than there are people in Africa today.[9] Don't you believe the mission has failed—it is just beginning!

Even this wonderful explosion of the faith, however, is not what makes Jesus the Hope of the World. It was not in Korea where everything is going so wonderfully that I learned my most indelible lesson in hope. It was in China, where things are most hopeless.

As I said, I was arrested, charged with embezzlement, thrown out of the country. When they told me to get out, they said I could take $100 in American money. So I rushed home but could not find $100 in American money. I had signed a letter—they had made me sign it—that by permission I was taking $100 in American money out of the country, and all I could find was $97. In my upset condition I began to think it was all a deep communist plot. Somehow they knew I had only $97 so they made me sign a letter that I was taking $100. It was not true, but it worried me, and I was worried all the way to the station, all the way to Shanghai, all the way to Canton.

On the way to the station, two missionaries with the China Inland Mission, Mr. and Mrs. Guinness, came to me and made a request, "Won't you take our son with you when you go? We can't get out; we don't know if we'll ever get out, but we want him to; and he doesn't need any letter of permission."

I replied, "Yes, we'll take Oswald." So he came along.

All the way I began worrying more and more about the missing three dollars. I was waiting for them to seize me, search me and accuse me—"You bribed your way out. Where's the missing three dollars?"—and throw me back into jail. We arrived in Canton. They went through our bags and our luggage, and then they began on our bodies.

Oswald came up and asked, "Are they going to examine me like that?"

I said, "Yes, Oswald, but what difference does it make? They're looking for American money, and you don't have any."

"But I have some American money."

"How much do you have?"

"I have three dollars."

Now don't misunderstand me. I don't believe in God because of any measly three-dollar miracle. My hope does not depend on that kind of intervention by God. What of others who were not able to get out? If there was no such miracle, is there no hope for them? Theirs is a far greater miracle, the miracle of faith and trust and hope even when God's answer is No. My kind is for the weak, and at that point I was weak indeed. I think the good Lord must have looked down and said, "I can't let a missionary of mine stumble out of China like that, tired and discouraged and almost on the verge of nervous collapse." So he chose to minister to my weakness and used a very little thing to remind me that he is still God, and he was still there.

That is the ultimate ground of all hope. Jesus is Lord of the Universe and Hope of the World. Reverse the phrases. He is the Hope of the World precisely because he is Lord of the Universe. If you know that, you will not need little miracles like mine. You will be able to say with David Livingstone, "Without him not one step. With him—anywhere!" He is our hope.

Notes

[1]*Korea Times,* November 1, 1973.

[2]Quoted in *Korea Times,* September 30, 1973.

[3]Quoted in *Time,* October 8, 1973, pp. 113-14.

[4]Quoted in *The Evanston Report* (New York: Harpers, 1955), p. 20.

[5]Quoted in Jurgen Moltmann, *Theology of Hope* (New York: Harper & Row, 1967), p. 23.

[6]*Newsweek,* October 29, 1973, p. 41.

[7]Edward Rogers, *Poverty on a Small Planet* (New York: Macmillan, 1965), p. 75.

[8]Ralph Winter, "Seeing the Task Graphically," *Evangelical Missions Quarterly,* January 1974.

[9]David Barrett, "A.D. 2000: 350 Million Christians in Africa," *International Review of Missions,* January 1970.

PART II

BEING A
MISSIONARY
IN THE 1970s

EVANGELISM AND SOCIAL CONCERN

GREGORIO LANDERO

I was once invited to a church to help solve some problems. A few minutes after I had arrived the pastor's wife said to me, "Brother, come and eat." Of course, I was hungry, having traveled all morning. I pulled up to the table and saw an egg and two pieces of manioc root, which was fine with me because I am accustomed to eating that. I bowed my head to give thanks to God. When I opened my eyes, I saw five children standing around the table with their hands on their hips. "Have you already eaten?" I asked them. Their mother answered, "Don't worry about them, brother. I'll get them something."

I bowed by head again and began to pray. Do you think I could eat that meal? No. I divided the food among those children, and again I bowed my head to pray, saying, "Lord, what would you do with this family right now?" I could not contain myself.

Then the woman said, "Brother Landero, the problem you have been invited to this church to help solve is my fault. The problem is I never attend any of the church services. But the brethren just don't understand my situation. Do you think it's right for me to attend church in these clothes, which are the only ones I have?" She had two knots tied in her dress as repairs. This moved my heart deeply. I began to think and to study the situation of the churches and my Christian brethren.

Plagued by Poverty

I soon realized that most of the people who had come to know the Lord were poor people who had been lifted out of sin, vice, immorality and sickness, but still were plagued and outraged by poverty. Some of them migrate into the jungles looking for a way to eke out their daily bread. Others leave their homes and go off to seek work in Venezuela, a neighboring country. Many pastors remain without work, without salary, with families and without hope. Many of them lose their vision for the pastorate.

Those who could survive in this situation continued to suffer great calamities. They complained to me with extreme sadness: "Brother, what can we do? Help us." And I asked myself, "What would Jesus do for these people? Is it that they lack teaching on stewardship? Or do they lack a total commitment to the Lord?" I began to hold short courses on stewardship and emphasized the need for complete consecration.

The brethren were rejoicing and weeping for joy, but this was not the solution. Then I realized that total stewardship of a Christian's life has to do with every aspect of his life, both spiritual and physical.

Shortly, guerrilla warfare broke out in that section of the country, and many of the brethren migrated into the cities and nearby towns. Widows and orphans came to the Lord, but they continued to seek help for their physical needs. How could I help them? I meditated and studied the Bible more and prayed to the Lord, that he would illuminate my mind and help them.

I read Matthew 14:16, where Jesus was dividing up the bread among 5,000 people. I realized that Jesus said, "Give you them to eat." I could not understand this. I began to send letters to missionaries, asking them how they could help us. I received from them some money, medicine and clothing. Project Hope was a great help to us. When I had gotten all I could, I began to distribute it to many who needed it. This was a great blessing, but it was not the solution either.

The Example of Jesus

Every moment I was getting letters saying, "Brother Landero, help us. We're living in terrible situations." So every day I studied and meditated more in the Scriptures on the life of Jesus Christ. I noticed that Jesus did not only forgive people's sins. He did not just teach them the Word of God, the way of the truth of Christ; he *also* healed the sick and gave bread to the hungry. During this period of meditation and Bible study, I stopped for a while in Matthew:

> *Now when Jesus heard this, he withdrew from them in a boat to a lonely place apart. . . . As he went ashore he saw a great throng; and he had compassion on them, and healed their sick. When it was evening, the disciples came to him and said, "This is a lonely place, and the day is now over; send the crowds away to go into the villages and buy food for themselves." Jesus said, "They need not go away; you give them something to eat." They said to him, "We have only five loaves here and two fish." And he said, "Bring them here to me." Then he ordered the crowds to sit down on the grass; and taking the five loaves and the two fish he looked up to heaven, and blessed, and broke and gave the loaves to the disciples, and the disciples gave them to the crowds. And they all ate and were satisfied. And they took up twelve baskets full of the broken pieces left over. And those who ate were about five thousand men, besides women and children.* (Mt. 14:13-21)

I noticed in this passage seven things:

1. The multitudes followed Jesus—the sick, the diseased and the hungry.

2. Jesus was full of compassion. He healed everybody, of every kind of sickness they had.

3. In another Gospel it says that he taught them from the morning.

4. He solved the problem of hunger.

5. The disciples were worried about the people.

6. The disciples offered Jesus some possible solutions—that the crowds should be dismissed, that the people should solve their own problems—and some excuses—they lacked money, they were tired, they had very little. This demonstrates human justice and human thoughts; the disciples believed that in this way they would escape their own duty. But Jesus said to them, "You give them something to eat." Hallelujah!

7. Jesus commanded, "Bring to me what little you have [here we could think of our talents, money or whatever we might have], organize them and I'll do the miracle." This is something precious to me.

This is the example we find in the life of our Lord Jesus Christ, that we might follow in his footsteps. This is a necessity in Latin America.

This story should teach us something: It is one thing to sit with the Pharisees, scribes, priests and doctors of the law in Jerusalem, but it is quite another to be out in the arid, dry country in the heat of the day sitting on hard rocks by the side of the sea listening to Jesus—sitting before the hungry, thirsty, unclothed, sick multitude, who are without shelter and without hope; ready to forget the tiredness, the privileges of the feasts in Jerusalem, the friends and relatives; prepared to serve the sick, naked, hungry, confused multitudes. Nations, cities, villages, families and individuals are living today with great needs. I pray that God will send disciples from this conference to save multitudes that want to follow Jesus, not treating them as beggars, not serving them as orphans, but as co-inheritors of the kingdom of God, as participants in the body and blood of our Lord Jesus Christ.

The Example of the Early Church

In Acts 2 we see how the Holy Spirit was spilled out over the church. And the apostles were filled with optimism because of the power that they had received, so that they seemed able to dominate all the difficulties.

Here we can make another list, of values and capacities they received: (1) power to testify (which is very important), (2) power to heal (God works today as he did before), (3) power to govern, (4) abundant love, (5) complete submission to doctrine and (6) courage and faith. (The Pharisee's persecution did not bother them. The church went right on growing.) But later the economic problem began to face them and this put the brakes on the growth of the church and the apostolic freedom to testify. It caused the death of Ananias and Sapphira. Crisis and murmurings of the Greeks against the Hebrews grew worse because of the discrimination that existed between the two groups, all because of the economic problems.

This was a difficult situation for the apostles. They could not continue without straightening out the problem, but they themselves took the initiative to solve these economic matters, not the government nor agronomy institutes nor food distribution centers. They did not say, "We are apostles and we can't get ourselves involved in problems like this." No. They considered the economic matters so important that they did not leave these responsibilities to just any person, but they chose extraordinary people to handle these problems, listing specific requirements for this work. They considered teaching to be precious, but the administration for the whole man was necessary.

What can we learn from this? First, we must be careful as disciples of Christ that nothing interfere with the preaching of the Word of God. Second, daily administration of needs is a holy obligation among the saints to a humanity which is waiting. Third, the human race cannot get along just on spiritual ministry; we must minister to the material needs also, that which is necessary for daily life.

The Association for United Action
We have experienced these things in our own flesh, and the success which God has given us in evangelism is fantastic. But in some sense we have felt hindered in being able to continue preaching by the cries of woe coming from those who are hungry and without clothing. From this, the Association for United Action (Associacion Accion Unida) was started, a group of capable professional people, whom God has chosen to help the needy, instructing them about their relationship with God

and also their duty to work.

Here is a small illustration. It is said there are two electrical currents—one positive, the other negative. But it is the two of them together that give light to any bulb. Imagine a person who does not know that both wires are necessary. He plugs in one wire, hoping that the light will come on, but nothing happens. So he takes out this one and puts in the other, with the idea of getting light, and again nothing happens. He says, "I hear that one is negative, the other positive. Which is the positive one? Neither one gives any light." Then somebody tells him, "Put the two of them together." He puts the two wires together and the light comes right on. His problem is solved. This is what is happening in our work. We have learned that the spiritual work is positive and that the social work is negative, that is, something secondary; but these two things are indispensable in the life of any person. Spirit, life, all of our personality—this is the way God has made us for this world.

For example: There were two organized groups that had dismissed their pastors because they could not support them. Then the two groups got together to support one pastor, but they had such difficulty meeting their budget that they agreed to dismiss this pastor. Two of them attended a short course where we were speaking on "The Church and the Economic Problem." They returned with joy to their church and said, "Now God has given us the solution. It is not necessary for us to leave this place. Let's invite Brother Landero so that he can orient us."

I paid them a visit and spoke on total stewardship in the Christian life. They began a work plan suggested by an agronomist, and the result has been a shout of praise to God and a reorganization of the church. The crops are abundant, and the people themselves have taken charge of the evangelization, with joy and enthusiasm. This is the way our God works.

Listen to me, brethren. The work of our Lord Jesus Christ is for the whole world, and problems of this type are universal problems. You are a very important person in this world. It is logical that you should serve the Lord in any part of it. This is the mission that God has placed into our hands, that we should be lights and channels for the salvation of this world.

SELF-SUPPORTING WITNESS OVERSEAS

7

J. CHRISTY WILSON

In Central Asia, I met a young man who was completely out of context. At first I thought he was a Jewish rabbi. He was wearing a black hat and a suit with hooks instead of buttons. He told me he was a Mennonite from Ohio and was teaching English in a government high school in Swat near Kashmir. He mentioned how he and his wife had been able to have Swati students in their home and had studied the Bible with these who had never seen the Christian Scriptures before. Knowing that Swat was a state closed to missionary work, I asked him how he had been able to get in. He said, "I never heard of the place before. I applied under a Fulbright to teach English in Germany, and they sent me to Swat!"

This is an example of an amazing phenomenon which the Holy Spirit has brought about in our day. God revealed to Daniel that in the end times travel and education would be vastly increased (Dan. 12:4). This is certainly true today in spite of the fuel shortage, as many millions are traveling all over planet earth and are making it a "global village." But, evangelistically speaking, this worldwide communication explosion can be the providential factor in completing Christ's commission.

A Christian engineer several years ago taught at a secular university abroad in a country where missionaries were not allowed. Besides doing a top-notch job in his profession, he led some of his students to Christ, discipled them in their faith, conducted prayer meetings and Bible studies in his home and with his family took an active part in the local church for internationals. He also was able to give away over half of his salary to help support missionaries and Christian projects around the world.

We thank God that there are more missionaries serving abroad today than ever before. Nevertheless, government figures show that for every one missionary from the United States and Canada there are over a hundred others from North America living around the world in commercial, professional, technical and governmental capacities. This affords a fantastic potential for supplementing and supporting the missionary forces in the evangelization of the world.

The Biblical Basis of Self-Supporting Witness
In 1 Corinthians 9, we have the apostle Paul's justification for this type of service. He had been accused of not being a bona fide apostle because he was self-supporting. He answers this by saying he could have received support from the churches, even as the other apostles like the Lord's brothers and Peter along with their wives had done. But he had chosen to be self-supporting to make the gospel free so he could "win the more" for Christ. As Paul testified to the Ephesian elders, "These hands have ministered to my own needs and to the men who were with me" (Acts 20:34). He also wrote to the Thessalonian Christians, "With labor and hardship we kept working night and day so that we might not be a burden to any of you; not because we do not have the right to this, but in order to offer ourselves as a model for you, that you might follow our example" (2 Thess. 3:8-9).

Many of the "cloud of witnesses" in the Old Testament were also self-supporting. Abraham was a cattle raiser, Isaac a farmer,

Jacob a roving rancher, Joseph a national administrator, Moses a sheepherder, Joshua a military commander, Ruth a gleaner, David an emperor, Amos a fruit gatherer, Daniel a prime minister, Queen Esther a ruler and Nehemiah a governor. Also in the New Testament, Luke was a doctor, Barnabas a landowner, Cornelius an officer, Priscilla, Aquila and Paul tentmakers, Lydia a seller of purple dye and Zenas a lawyer. Even our Lord, though he was God, humbled himself to become a self-supporting carpenter (Mk. 6:3). But he also set his seal of approval on full-time missionary work since during his ministry he was supported by his friends: "Certain women . . . and many others . . . ministered unto him of their substance" (Lk. 8:2-3).

The Historical Basis of Self-Supporting Witness

Recent scholarship has shown that one of the main motives for the explorations of Marco Polo and Christopher Columbus was evangelization, incomplete as their idea of this may have been. William Carey, the father of the modern missionary movement, supported himself and others in his mission by running an indigo factory as well as being a salaried professor of Sanskrit at the University of Calcutta. He wrote, "We have ever held it to be an essential principle in the conduct of missions that, whenever it is practicable, missionaries should support themselves in whole or in part through their own exertions."[1] Because Henry Martyn was not allowed to go to India as a missionary, he went out as a chaplain for the East India Company. Robert Morrison, who translated the Bible into Chinese, also supported himself by being an interpreter for a trading company. Many do not realize that David Livingstone became a consul for the British government in Africa and pictures often show him wearing the hat of his office.

Sir Herbert Edwardes, who in the last century was the general in charge of the Khyber Pass area of the Northwest Frontier, was firstly a "soldier of Jesus Christ." He invited missionaries to enter that previously closed area. When another officer challenged him, saying this was sure to result in trouble, he answered, "I far more fear disobeying my Lord's explicit command than I fear trouble among the local people." And because of his faith and courage, this area today is dotted with little Christian churches.

Captain Janes, an American self-supporting witness teaching in Japan, led many of his students to Christ, establishing the Kumamoto Band which made a great impact on the emerging church in that land.[2]

Or again, Miss Jenny de Mayer, an amazing Russian Christian, went into Siberia and Central Asia as a Red Cross nurse, witnessing for her Lord and distributing Scriptures in these unreached areas.

Employing this method of self-support, Muslims have spread Islam mainly through their traders and government administrators so that today their adherents number over half a billion, which is more than twice the population of North America. Mormons and Jehovah's Witnesses have lay missionaries by the thousands through whom they are spreading their teachings. Why should others use this method so effectively while evangelical believers neglect it?

In 1951, my wife and I followed other Christian teachers to the closed country of Afghanistan and worked as "tentmakers." Before signing my contract to teach English, I told the Afghan ambassador in Washington that I was also a Christian minister. He said that this would be quite all right since most of their teachers were Muslim priests and therefore it would be good to have a Christian priest also teaching their young people. It has been exciting but hard work. And since receiving the invitation a year ago to come to Urbana, work with the blind that my wife, Betty, was engaged in has been closed, the only church building on neutral Afghan soil has been demolished and we as well as others have been asked to leave the country. But we thank God that the new government is much more favorable and that the living church of Jesus Christ has been planted there even as our Lord promised, "I will build my church, and the gates of hell shall not prevail against it" (Mt. 16:18).

The Practical Basis of Self-Supporting Witness

You who are Christian students can carry on one of the most strategic ministries there is as you study in institutions all over the world and witness for Christ. What an opportunity you have among international students at home and abroad! After the first IVCF-FMF missionary convention, I went to Scotland to study. It proved one of the greatest privileges of my life to work and witness with other young people there. I met a lonely Chinese Christian student in Edinburgh with whom I studied the Bible once a week. He was Philip Teng, who has been teaching us "The Biblical Basis of Missions." You cannot tell what God can do through those whom you encourage and love for Jesus' sake.

If the trend continues, next summer there will be more Christian young people helping on the mission fields of the world than all of us here at Urbana put together. And most will be paying their own way. What a wonderful opportunity not only for witness and service, but also for cross-cultural experience. This was not possible until recently. It took my parents three months travel to get to their mission field in Iran in 1919, or six months for the round trip. You could not spend a summer helping there then. But now you can make the trip by jet in a matter of hours.

Today there are also hundreds of churches around the world caring for the swelling crowds of internationalists. These need evangelical pastors. A classmate of mine in seminary told the Lord that he would be willing to take a church anywhere, provided it was in the United States. He candidated in different ones but could not find out where the Lord wanted him. Finally, as he was riding on public transportation in his home city of Boston, he was so miserable that he told the Lord that he would even go overseas if that were his will. Immediately a wonderful peace came over his heart, and he knew for the first time that God wanted him to take a church in his home city of Boston. Christ is either Lord of all, or he is not Lord at all. Until we are ready to go anywhere, we are not ready to go anywhere.

I have met committed Christians overseas in international business positions, in secretarial jobs, in medical work as doctors and nurses, in military service, in assistance programs, in teaching positions, in student research projects, in diplomatic service and in United Nations missions. A Christian petroleum engineer I know not only holds an important oil company posi-

tion in the Middle East but also preaches and leads a Bill Goth-
ard type seminar on the side. Interestingly enough, his oil company has not boycotted the West. If Christians do not take advan-
tage of these opportunities, others will who can be of more harm
than help to God's work. A heavy drinking American in Afghanistan was shocked by his Muslim neighbor who informed him
that he had become a Christian. He said, "What do you mean
you've become a Christian?" The Afghan man answered, "I
drink whiskey now like you do. Do you have any you can give
me?" To him becoming a Christian was leaving the prohibition
of Islam and indulging like this foreigner, since this was all he
had seen of Christianity. It breaks your heart to meet people who
have never heard the good news about Jesus Christ but who have
learned to swear in his name from secular internationals.

Dedicated Christian tourists can also be wonderfully used
overseas. One friend, an electronics engineer, on a world tour
led two of his guides to Christ. I know another Christian couple
who after retirement have lived abroad on social security and
have led many to the Lord. Today as never before we are seeing
men and women catching the vision of the truth that "every
Christian is a missionary" not only at home but also abroad.

We, however, must recognize real difficulties and limitations
in this type of self-supporting service. The agency for which one
is working may seek to curtail one's testimony. But this is true of
secular employment at home, too. Furthermore, as Ted Ward
pointed out at the last Urbana convention, this kind of service
requires one to be a missionary on an "overtime" basis. But you
can also witness while you work by letting Christ communicate
through your life as well as your lips. A former Inter-Varsity
staff worker and her husband are now self-supporting witnesses
in Latin America. She was recently asked by a national woman
why she was different from other foreigners. This gave her a marvelous opportunity to share Christ and explain the difference
he makes.

As preparation for self-supporting witness, cross-cultural
orientation can be of great value. Forward-looking mission agencies give this to their candidates, but often those going as "tentmakers" must arrange for this on their own initiative. Language

learning is extremely vital, too, and therefore courses in linguistics are also helpful. Studies in the art of successful "overseasmanship" bring out the need for cultural empathy, professional quality, political savvy, organizational ability, real humility instead of an attitude of superiority and adaptability in facing clashes of personality.

The Spiritual Basis of Self-Supporting Witness

Bible training as well as reading of missionary biography and history on your own or in missions courses is also helpful. Learning to lead a person to Christ is a must because if you cannot do it at home, you probably will not be able to do it abroad.

Another essential is to have effective prayer support. Regular missionaries usually enjoy this because people who give also often pray. But those who go in self-supporting capacities must enlist prayer support from friends, fellowships and churches. Paul as a "tentmaker" repeatedly wrote to New Testament churches asking for prayer. More and more mission boards are starting field partner or lay missionary programs whereby they assist self-supporting witnesses in placement, orientation and prayer backing as well as linking them with missionaries and national Christians on the field.

There are also definite advantages to self-supporting witness abroad. A Christian businessman working in Tehran told me he finds many receptive to what he has to say about Christ since they realize he is "not paid to witness." Also, "tentmakers" can go practically anywhere in the world—even into Red China, Russia and many Muslim areas which are off limits for missionaries.

But I can hear someone say, "With the great needs at home, why bother about the rest of the world?" Bill Borden used to answer this by saying, "If you saw ten men carrying a log, and nine were on one end and one on the other, and you wanted to help, to which end would you go?" Dr. Ralph Winter in his booklet *Seeing the Task Graphically*, points out that while the number of non-Christians in Africa and Asia has more than doubled since 1900, the number of people who call themselves Christian has multiplied thriteen times.[3] But the task still remaining is tremendous. According to statistics in 1965 quoted by the same author, three out of four in the West called themselves Christians, one out of four in Africa and only one out of twenty-five bore the name of Christ in Asia, a continent which today has over half the population of the world.[4] If every creature is to be evangelized in our time, it must be through self-supporting as well as regular missionaries. This tentmaking type of service should in no way detract from the fact that many more full-time missionaries are desperately needed around the world; but "tentmakers" can provide much help and encouragement, as self-supporting witnesses and those wholly supported by other Christians work in fellowship.

Difficult as world evangelization is, our Lord has promised us success. He said, "You shall receive power after the Holy Spirit has come upon you and *you shall be witnesses unto me . . . unto the uttermost part of the earth*" (Acts 1:8). Or as Adoniram Judson Gordon has said, "It is not a matter of bringing the world to Christ; it is a matter of taking Christ to the world."

I was once on an airplane in Afghanistan. Our seat belts were fastened, the door was shut and we seemed ready for takeoff. Then, as I looked out of the window, I noticed a man running toward the plane. I thought he must be a late passenger and wondered whether they would let him on. He started knocking on the door of the plane. The steward looked at his watch and it was time for takeoff so he was not going to open the door. But the man knocked louder and louder, so the steward went back and opened the door a crack to see who it was. To our amazement, it was our pilot! We had locked the pilot out of the plane. The stairs had already been taken away so they had to reach down and lift him up by his arms. He then walked up the aisle to the cockpit, and we took off.

When this happened, I thought how much like our lives this is. We may think we are in the right place and that everything is set for our trip through life. But is the Pilot in charge, or have we left him out? Jesus said, "Behold, I stand at the door and knock; if any one hears my voice and opens the door, I will come in" (Rev. 3:20). Will you right now make Christ the Pilot of your life, turning over the controls to him that he may direct you in the perfect plan he has for you personally? For as the Scriptures say, "The world passes away, and the lust thereof, but he [or she] who does the will of God abides forever" (1 Jn. 2:17).

Notes

[1]Sir Kenneth Grubb. *The Need for Non-Professional Missionaries*, (London: World Dominion Press, 1931), p. 11.

[2]S. Herbert Kane, *Winds of Change in the Christian Mission* (Chicago: Moody Press, 1973), p. 118.

[3]Ralph Winter, *Seeing the Task Graphically* (Pasadena: William Carey Library, 1973), pp. 3, 15.

[4]This statistic of 1 in 25 in Asia calling themselves Christians includes the Philippines as well as other islands in the Pacific. This, therefore, brings the number of Christians to a higher percentage than would be found if only the continent of Asia were considered. Thus Dr. Samuel Moffett's statement that less than 2% of Asia call themselves Christian deals with the continent rather than with the Pacific Islands as well.

THE PLACE OF WOMEN IN WORLD MISSIONS

ELISABETH ELLIOT LEITCH

About fourteen years ago I had the great good fortune to meet an unforgettable character whose biography is entitled *The Small Woman* and whose life story was told, after a fashion, in a movie called *The Inn of the Sixth Happiness*. She was Gladys Aylward. To hear this diminutive creature of four feet eleven inches, dressed as a Chinese, tell her own story in a stentorian voice was a stunning experience. I remember how she took the microphone and with no preliminary nonsense whatever thundered forth, "I should like to read just one verse. 'And Jehovah God spoke to Abram and he said, "Get out!" ' " She told us the story of Abraham's faith and his move into an unknown land. Then she said, "And one day, in a little flat in London, Jehovah God spoke to a Cockney parlor maid and he said, 'Get out!' 'Where do you want me to go, Lord?' I said, and he said, 'To China.' " So Gladys Aylward went to China. And what a story that was—a train across Europe and Russia, a frying pan strapped to the outside of her suitcase, an angel's guidance in the dead of night onto a forbidden ship, a breathtaking saga of one woman's obedience to the call of God.

Some twenty-six centuries earlier the call of God came to a much more likely prospect than a parlor maid—he was the descendant of priests—and in a much more likely place than the city of London, Anathoth in the land of Benjamin. Isn't it easier to believe that the word of the Lord might come to somebody in Anathoth than in London? or in Urbana? The man was Jeremiah, appointed a prophet of the nations, but he was reluctant to accept the appointment. "Ah, Lord God," he groaned, "Behold, I do not know how to speak, for I am only a youth." But the Lord said to him "Do not say, 'I am only a youth'; for to all to whom I send you you shall go, and whatever I command you you shall speak. Be not afraid of them, for I am with you" (Jer. 1:6-8).

God's call frequently brings surprise and dismay, and a protest that one is not qualified. Jeremiah hoped he might get out of it by reminding Almighty God (in case Almighty God had not noticed) that he was too young. Gladys Aylward did not strike me as timid, but she might have called God's attention to her limitations: She too was young, she was poor, she had no education, she was no good at anything but dusting, and she was a *woman*. In the case of both prophet and parlor maid, however, the issue was identical. The issue was obedience. Questions of intellect and experience, of age and sex, were quite beside the point. God said *Do this* and they did it.

Women in Mission

What is the place of women in world mission? Jesus said, "*You* [and the word means all of you, male and female] are my witnesses. *You* are the salt of the earth. *You* are the light of the world." And there have been countless thousands who, without reference to where they came from or what they knew or who they were, have believed that Jesus meant exactly what he said and have set themselves to follow.

Today strident female voices are raised, shrilly and ad nauseam, to remind us that women are equal with men. But such a question has never even arisen in connection with the history of Christian missions. In fact, for many years, far from being excluded, women constituted the majority of foreign missionaries.

Missionary, of course, is a term which does not occur in the Bible. I like the word *witness,* and it is a good, biblical word meaning someone who has seen something. The Virgin Mary saw an angel and heard his word and committed herself irretrievably when she said, "Behold, I am the handmaid of the Lord" (Lk. 1:38). This decision meant sacrifice—the giving up of her reputation and, for all she knew then, of her marriage and her own cherished plans. "Be it unto me according to thy word." She knew the word was from God, and she put her life on the line because of it. The thing God was asking her to do, let us not forget, was a thing that only a woman could do. Imagine Joseph or the angel protesting about equal opportunity!

The early history of the church mentions other women who witnessed—by ministering to Christ during his earthly work, cooking for him, probably, making a bed, providing clothes and washing them—women who were willing and glad to do whatever he needed to have done. (And some of you women who despise that sort of work—would you be willing to do it if it were for him? "Inasmuch as ye have done it unto one of the least of these my brethren," Jesus said, "ye have done it unto me.") There was Priscilla, coadjutor of the apostle Paul. There was a business woman named Lydia, who opened her heart to what was said and then opened her home to those who said it. There must have been thousands of women like these who did what lay in their power to do because with all their hearts they wanted to do it. They had seen something, they had heard a word, they knew their responsibility.

In the conversion of the Teutonic peoples women played an important role. Clovis, King of the Franks in the fifth century, made the mistake of marrying a Christian princess, Clotilda, from Burgundy, and through her was eventually baptized. According to the Venerable Bede's account, King Ethelbert of Kent made the same mistake in the next century, and his queen, Bertha, persuaded him to allow a monk named Augustine to settle in Canterbury and within a year ten thousand Saxons were converted.

One of the earliest of those who were actually called missionaries was Gertrude Ras Egede, a Danish woman who, although
violently opposed to her husband's going to Greenland to try to
find the remnants of the church which had been lost for several
centuries, soon saw that her rebellion against him was in reality
opposition to God. She repented and went with her husband to
what turned out to be a far cry from the "Green Land" they had
expected. It was frigid, God-forsaken wasteland where Gertrude
Ras Egede died after fifteen years of hard work (generally called
"labor" if a missionary does it. We all know that missionaries
don't go, they "go forth;" they don't walk, they "tread the burning sands;" they don't die, they "lay down their lives." But the
work gets done even if it is sentimentalized!).

Women in the United States began to swing into action for the
cause of world missions in the beginning of the nineteenth century. There was a Boston Female Society for Missionary Purposes founded in 1800, and a Miss Mary Well founded what was
called the Cent Society in 1802 "for females who are disposed to
contribute their mite towards so noble a design as diffusion of
the gospel light among the shades of darkness and superstition."
There was a Fuel Society which paid for coal for young semi-
narians, a Boston Fragment Society which provided clothes
for indigent mothers and their babies. By 1812, Massachusetts
and Connecticut swarmed with what were called "female missionary societies," and by 1816 three Baptist wives, supported
by these societies, were en route to Ceylon as missionaries. "If
not deceived in our motives," one of them wrote, "we have been
induced to leave our beloved friends and native shores to cross
the tempestuous deep, from love to Christ and the souls which
He died to purchase. And now we are ready, waiting with the
humble hope of being employed, in His own time and way, in
building up His kingdom."

I was surprised to learn that the Civil War strongly affected
the progress of women in missions. It was an educative force in
America, for through it women were driven to organize because of their patriotism and their pity for the fighting men. In
the ten years following the War scores of organizations, including many new missionary societies, were launched.

The nineteenth-century mind boggled at the idea of sending a single woman to a foreign field. A few widows were accepted, having supposedly profited by the guidance of husbands and therefore being more knowledgeable and dependable than single women could be expected to be. The first single women on record who was sent to a foreign land was one Betsy Stockton, and she was a black.

Of Eleanor Macomber of Burma it was said, "No husband helped her decide the momentous question, and when she resolved, it was to go *alone*. With none to share her thousand cares and anxieties, with no heart to keep time with the wild beatings of her own, she, a friendless woman, crossed the deep dark ocean, and on soil never trodden by the feet of Christian men, erected the banner of the Cross." This is typical of the sentimental view of missionaries which makes most of us cringe. This description was written by a man, but don't let the phrases "weak, defenseless woman" and "the wild beatings of her heart" blur the single fact of Eleanor Macomber's action. Don't stay home because you don't like the *image*. True faith is action. Faith cometh by hearing, and results in *doing*.

To prove that women have had an important role in world missions, I could go on listing what women have done. There were Mary Slessor of Calabar, Lottie Moon of China, Amy Carmichael of India, Rosalind Goforth of China, Malla Moe of Africa, of whom it was said that although she could not preach like Peter nor pray like Paul she told thousands of the love of Jesus. And besides these names there have surely been tens of thousands of nameless nuns and other anonymous women who have done what God sent them to do—and they have done it without the tub-thumping of modern egalitarian movements. They had a place and they knew they had it because Scripture says they have.

A Christian's Responsibility

You read in your Bible study booklets this morning from Romans 12: "All members do not have the same function." There is nothing interchangeable about the sexes, and there is nothing interchangeable about Christians. God has given gifts that *differ*. They differ *according to the grace given to us*. You and I, whether we are men or women, have nothing to do with the choice of the gift. We have everything to do with the use of the gift.

There are diversities of operations, but the same Spirit. There are varieties of personalities, but all are made in the image of God. As a woman I find clear guidance in Scripture about my position in church and home. I find no exemption from the obligations of commitment and obedience.

The sphere of my obligations has certainly varied from time to time and from place to place. I started my missionary work as a single woman with three other single women. There was no church, there were no believers, and there were no male missionaries. Later I was a wife and had to rearrange certain priorities in accordance with what I understood to be my job as a wife, as a coworker with my husband in the field and later as a mother.

When my husband was killed by Indians, I found myself in some indefinable positions. There wasn't one missionary man left in Ecuador who spoke the jungle Quichua language. There was no one to teach the young Quichua believers, no one to lead the church, no one but women to carry on where five missionary men had left off. The door to the Auca tribe had slammed shut for those men and was, to our astonishment, opened to two women. It didn't look to me like a woman's job. But God's categories are not always ours. I had to shuffle my categories many times during my last eight years of missionary work. Since coming back to the States I've done it again. I've had a career of sorts, I've been a wife and housewife once more, and again I'm a widow.

But it is the same faithful Lord who calls me by name and never loses track of my goings and reminds me in a still, small voice, "Ye are my witnesses, that ye might know and believe me, and understand that I am he." (Is. 43:10). There is our primary responsibility: *to know him*. I can't be a witness unless I've seen something, unless I know what it is I am to testify to.

And it is the Lord of the Universe who calls you—you women, you men—and offers you today a place in his program. Your education or lack of it, your tastes and prejudices and fears and ambitions, your age or sex or color or height or marital status or income bracket are all things which may be offered to God, after you have presented your bodies as a living sacrifice. And God knows exactly what to do with them. They are not obstacles if you hand them over.

Be still and know that he is God. Sit in silence and wonder and expectancy, and never doubt that the Lord of your life has his own way of getting through to you to let you know the specifics of his will. And if you know that you have seen something, you can add your voice to the host of witnesses like G. K. Chesterton, who, in his reply to the historical query of why Christianity was accepted, answers for millions of others: "Because it fits the lock; because it is like life. We are Christians not because we worship a key but because we have passed a door and felt the wind that is the trumpet of liberty blow over the land of the living."

SPIRITUAL QUALIFICATIONS FOR OVERSEAS SERVICE

BILL
THOMAS

Much of what I have to say regarding spiritual qualifications for missions will apply to those of you who are planning to work at home as well as to those who are considering overseas ministries. For as Dick Hillis of Overseas Crusade has often said, "Every heart without Christ is a mission field; every heart with Christ is a missionary."

Assurance

The first spiritual qualification for overseas service is the assurance that you have come into a right relationship with Jesus Christ as Savior and Lord. I meet a lot of people who tell me that they have accepted or invited Jesus into their lives, but on pursuing the conversation it becomes clear that they have accepted Jesus as a good teacher or a good example to follow or even as one who has brought them satisfaction. But the sin question in their lives has never been dealt with. Do you know Jesus as the One who has freed you from the penalty and guilt of sin and as the One who has first place in your life? This is the foundation for developing an effective ministry. Jesus was once asked by the crowds: "What can we do in order to do God's works?" Jesus answered, "This is the work God wants you to do: believe in the One he sent" (Jn. 6:28-29). Unless Jesus' saving power is a reality in your own life, you will not be able to speak convincingly about him to others. For you can no more give out what you don't possess than you can come back from where you haven't been.

The Fullness of the Holy Spirit

A second qualification is learning to walk in the fullness of the Holy Spirit. We are not filled with the Spirit once and for all. The Bible says that we are to "be being filled with the Spirit" (Eph. 5:18). And we are to walk in his fullness. According to Acts 10:38, Jesus himself carried out his earthly ministry in the power of the Holy Spirit. Before his ascension he commanded his disciples to stay in Jerusalem until they were clothed with power from above. Why did he give this command? Because he wanted his followers to carry on his ministry of preaching, teaching, helping and healing. As we walk in the Spirit, he endows us with his gifts which he distributes according to his own will. He also produces his fruit in our lives: love, peace, patience, kindness, goodness, faithfulness, humility and self-control. You may ask, "How does one learn to walk in the fullness of the Spirit?" I would suggest at least three ways:

1. Regular study of and meditation in the Word of God.

2. Spending time each day in prayer—and this prayer time must be characterized by praise, confession, repentance and thanksgiving, as well as by petitions. As you pray, the Holy Spirit will aid you in your prayers.

3. By being obedient in the daily routine of life. The Bible says: "God gives the Holy Spirit to those who obey him" (Acts 5:32). It is much more difficult to be obedient in the small every-day details of life than in what we consider to be the big things. Yet life is made up mostly of small things.

Commitment

A third qualification is commitment to God, to the task and to each other. Be committed to God. If you are not irrevocably committed to God, there is the danger of being swayed by popular opinion or of being swept along by the tide of social pressure. In 1 Samuel 15, we read the story of King Saul, whom God sent to destroy the Amalekites and to leave nothing alive. After the battle, the prophet Samuel comes to find out whether or not Saul has obeyed God's command. Saul says to Samuel, "Blessed are you of the Lord; I have carried out the command of the Lord." But Samuel says, "What then is the bleating of the sheep in my ears, and the lowing of the oxen which I hear?" Saul then explains that the people rushed upon the spoil and kept the best sheep and oxen. After telling Saul that God has rejected him from being king because of his disobedience, Saul says to Samuel, "I have sinned; I have indeed transgressed the command of the Lord and your words, because I feared the people, and listened to their voice." Be committed to God.

To be committed to God is to be committed to his standards of truth and righteousness, which are applicable to all peoples. In an age when humanism abounds, when men and dictatorial governments make themselves the measure of all things, this commitment to God is extremely hard and dangerous. Are you prepared to pay the price of such a commitment? To be fully committed to God may bring you into conflict with your family and friends, especially when it comes to loving and caring for people of whom they disapprove. But Jesus said,

> Do not think I have come to bring peace to the world; no, I did not come to bring peace, but a sword. I came to set sons against their fathers, daughters against their mothers, daughters-in-law against their mothers-in-law; a man's worst enemies will be the members of his own family. Whoever loves his father or mother more than me is not worthy of me. Whoever loves his son or daughter more than me is not worthy of me. Whoever does not take up his cross and follow in my steps is not worthy of me. (Mt. 10:34-38)

Your commitment will involve your being willing to take your share of suffering as a good soldier of Jesus Christ.

To be committed to God is to believe him, to take him at his word in every situation. It is relatively easy to believe God for something in the future or for something about which you are not too deeply concerned. But to believe God *now*, to rely on him to undertake in a situation about which you are deeply concerned, is not so easy. To learn this kind of trust, however, is to save oneself a lot of worry, anxiety and fear. You can believe God, you can take him at his word when he says he loves you and be fully convinced that his will is best for your life.

Be committed to the task of bearing fruit. Whatever may be your profession—whether it is medicine, education, engineering, politics, economics, social welfare or church ministry —your main task must be that of bringing others to Jesus Christ. In many parts of the world, you may not be able to practice your profession just the way you want to. The man whose first love is engineering and who ends up in an area where he has to wait several weeks for supplies only to find that when they arrive they are not just what he ordered could find himself very frustrated. Then too, what if, after many years of study, you become physically incapacitated? If your first love is your profession, you could have a mental and emotional breakdown. But if your top priority is bearing fruit, that is, of introducing others to Christ, you are on solid ground.

Jesus expects every branch of his to bear fruit. To bear this fruit requires patience. Before I went to Zaire, someone said to me, "There are five things you will need for working there— patience, patience, patience, patience and more patience." And how right they were! In my present job as traveling secretary for the University Bible groups in Belgium and France, I have found that much patience is also needed. It takes time to establish good contacts, to break down walls of suspicion, prejudice and hate. And when few people around you share your vision and burden for making Christ known, this can be frustrating! You must have a lot of love and perseverance if you are not to give up. To bear fruit, you will need to learn to trust the Holy Spirit to bring conviction of sin, righteousness and judgment to the heart of the hearer. Your part is to present the message by word and deed, sincerely, lovingly and as authoritatively as possible. As Campus Crusade puts it, "To share Jesus Christ in the power of the Holy Spirit, and to leave the results to God."

Commit yourself to the task of making Christ known.

Be committed to each other. No man is an island; no man stands alone. God has called you into a community; he has called you to be a part of his body. As such, you can function effectively only through the body. In principle, you should already be experiencing this "body-life" in your I-V groups.

Being committed to each other should make for a healthier prayer life. When you have been praying and pleading with God for days and weeks, and it seems like heaven has gone on strike against you, and you begin to sink into the deep mire of despair, you will need the encouragement and strength of the body-life. As others tell of how their prayers *have* been answered, your faith will be revived.

Being committed to each other should make for more emotional and psychological stability. Of all places where you should really be able to be yourself, it is within the Christian community, within the body. How often, when someone asks you how you are feeling, do you give the traditional answer, "I'm fine"?—when in fact you are really hurting. God wants you to be honest and open with him and with each other. Don't be afraid to admit your weaknesses. For you are still under construction. Christ isn't through with your life. This does not mean that you are to go to the other extreme and become a chronic complainer, or that you are to cease to bear your own burdens. But your brothers and sisters *are* there to help you bear your overloads.

Being committed to each other should make you willing to learn from others. The learning process requires humility and a willingness to admit that you may be wrong. A person who always seeks to justify himself never learns anything. When you go to work in another culture, you are there to contribute, but you are also there to learn. During my pastorate in Kinshasa, my deacons would sometimes say to me, "There are many things about our culture that you don't understand. Here is how we see this situation." Although I was their pastor, I was also their pupil. And it was only after many months of grassroots contacts, that I began to feel what they felt. Intellectually, I understood some of their problems, but I didn't feel them.

A Forgiving Spirit

A fourth qualification is a forgiving spirit toward those who have wronged you. Don't go out with a chip on your shoulder, looking only at the dark side of life. Hebrews 12:15 says, "Be careful that no one become like a bitter plant, that grows up and troubles many with its poison." I know that such admonition is hard for a person who has been born in adverse circumstances and who has had to struggle up the rough side of the mountain. But all over the world there are those who have to struggle. So you are not the only one. The Bible says, "Do not let evil defeat you; instead conquer evil with good" (Rom. 12:21). Evil and hatred destroy the one who hates and seeks revenge. When a man is full of bitterness and resentment, he can't eat or sleep properly, and he trusts nobody. Such attitudes are self-destructive. You might ask, "How does one keep out this root of bitterness?" I would suggest three ways:

1. Remember what you were like in God's sight before coming to him and that, even now, you are only a sinner saved by grace.

2. Try to do something for the person who has wronged you. Neutrality is no good. You must conquer the evil with acts of love. In fact, you must go on the offensive, and not wait until the person has mistreated you nor wait while he remains indifferent to you.

3. For every one look that you take at yourself and at your circumstances, take seven looks at Jesus Christ. The Scripture says, "Let us keep our eyes fixed on Jesus, on whom our faith depends from beginning to end" (Heb. 12:2). Keeping our eyes on him enables us to endure suffering like a good soldier. And God has chosen to use suffering as one of the means of conforming us to the image of his Son. The Bible says that Christ learned obedience through what he suffered. Between Christ and glory stood the cross. He chose to return to heaven not around the cross, but via the cross. Likewise you must be willing to take up your cross of rejection and follow him.

Praising God in All Circumstances

A fifth qualification is learning to praise God in all circumstances. It is easy to rejoice and to praise the Lord when the sun is shining, but God wants you to praise him also when the dark clouds roll in, because he is still the Almighty God. The Bible says, "In all circumstances give thanks; for this is the will of God in Christ Jesus for you" (1 Thess. 5:18). God's will is that your life should be lived in an atmosphere of joy and praise. There is strength in praise. The Bible says that Abraham grew strong in his faith, as he gave praise to God. Paul and Silas found renewed strength in a Philippian jail as they sang hymns to God. Many a Christian martyr has gone triumphantly to his death strengthened by songs of praise. Many a slave has been able to endure the lashes of the master's whip because of the inner strength released by songs of praise. There will be times in your life when it appears that your case is hopeless—times of illness, financial crisis and vocational bewilderment. At such times, praise the Lord!

The Perspective of Eternity

Finally, learn to keep the perspective of eternity. The time will come when you will give your all to heal a sick body, only to have the patient return to the same self-destructive way of life. And you will wonder, "Is it worth it?" There will be times when you will wear yourself out to bring knowledge to ignorant minds only to have many of the students use this knowledge for selfish gain, and you will ask, "Is it worth it?" Or there may be times when you give yourself to much prayer, teaching and preaching, and see the beginnings of a solid work, and then destructive forces will move in and almost destroy the work; and you will ask, "Is it worth it?" The time could come when at the height of your career you or your loved one is struck down by cancer, leukemia, cerebral palsy or some other dread disease; you and many around you will ask, "Is it worth it?"

In times like these you will need to have the perspective of eternity: Christ is coming back. Concerning suffering and the destruction of the body, you will have to be able to say with Paul:

So we do not lose heart. Though our outer nature is wasting away, our inner nature is being renewed every day. For this slight momentary affliction is preparing for us an eternal weight of glory beyond all comparison, because we look not to the things that are seen, but to the things that are unseen; for the things that are seen are transient, but the things that are unseen are eternal. For we know that if the earthly tent we live in is destroyed, we have a building from God, a house not made with hands, eternal in the heavens. (2 Cor. 4:16–5:1)

Regarding your service of love: When Christ returns, you will see how all fits together, both the apparent successes and the apparent failures. Having served the Lord with all your heart, mind and strength, you will hear him say, "Well done, good and faithful servant. You have been faithful over a few things; I will make you ruler over many things. Enter into the joy of your Lord" (Mt. 25:21).

Keep this perspective of eternity. May God bless you as you work together with him!

CULTURAL AND SOCIAL QUALIFICATIONS FOR OVERSEAS SERVICE

PIUS WAKATAMA

In countries of the Third World, missions were exceptionally successful in their task of evangelism and church planting. The Third World church has been founded so well upon the Rock that I am able to say, without fear of contradiction, that in many of our countries today the work would continue to grow without the presence of foreign missionaries. Under the tutelage of the Holy Spirit the church of Jesus Christ has become indigenous in these areas where a few decades ago the light of the gospel was unknown.

Because of the apparent growth of national churches, some Christians in both the Third World and the sending countries are saying that the era of foreign missions is over. They say that the time has come for missionaries and missions to withdraw from many parts of the Third World so that the national churches may find their own identity without hindrance.

This kind of thinking, I feel, is in error. Until the Lord comes, missions and missionaries will be needed not only in the Third World but in the Western countries as well.

There is, however, a need now to see missions in a different light. Because the primary task of church planting has been accomplished, many mission organizations will need to restructure to meet the new needs of indigenous churches. Those which are not amenable to restructuring may have to disappear from the scene entirely.

Along with this restructuring they will also need to recruit missionaries with new tools who will be better equipped to assist the indigenous churches in their growth. The Third World needs a new breed of missionaries—men and women with unique spiritual, social and cultural qualifications.

Qualifications: Academic Training

In the past almost any committed Christian could go overseas as a missionary without undergoing specialized training. These saints gave of themselves in service to the Lord and the result is that today millions who lived in darkness are now in the Light.

Even though the missionaries did such a superb job in church planting and education they also made some errors. There was a general failure to relate Christianity to the different cultures to which they ministered. In presenting the gospel they failed to extract its essence from their own culture. The task of making disciples for Jesus Christ was often confused with that of "civilizing the primitive and savage tribes." There was a tendency to regard all things traditional as pagan and most things Western as Christian.

Much of the missionaries' negative attitude toward other cultures was a result of ethnocentrism. He looked on other cultures as aberrations and his own as the norm. A factor which contributed to this is that many Americans refer to their country as a "Christian nation" and the Third World as "heathen countries." The error in this kind of thinking is self-evident.

In most cases ethnocentrism is the result of a limited educational background. It is born of sheer ignorance of the nature, meaning and function of culture. After working closely with missionaries for over fifteen years, I have observed that the broader a person's educational background the more apt he or she is to accept and see values in other cultures. I, therefore, feel that we have reached the time when, except for special cases, a liberal arts degree and/or theological training at the same level should be the minimum requirement for going overseas as a missionary.

In his book *Frontiers in Mission Strategy* (Moody Press, 1971), Peter Wagner differs with this kind of thinking. He feels that missionaries with educational backgrounds similar to the nationals to whom they minister will be best able to communicate effectively. He says, "That a college degree measurably helps communicate with a semi-literate peasant is a questionable assumption" (p. 61).

I feel Wagner needs either to clarify his statement or to rethink this subject because a good liberal arts background is a must for anybody who is seriously going into cross-cultural and cross-racial communication. I must insist, both on the authority of experts on cross-cultural communications and biculturalism as well as on the overwhelming expressed opinion of national leaders, that this assertion is pitifully inadequate.

I feel that this kind of thinking has been responsible for the sense of almost pathological self-contentment that is evident in missions today. It can also discourage further preparation toward good and effective Christian leadership.

Much damage has been done to traditional social structures by ignorant missionaries who have come in and sometimes needlessly disrupted social systems, in introducing Christianity, without replacing them with appropriate functional equivalents.

Today many Christian colleges have become sensitive to the need to articulate communication across cultures. They are offering courses in biculturalism, cross-cultural communications, social psychology, anthropology of religions and many others.

People with a grasp of the behavioral sciences, coupled with deep compassion, are the kind of missionaries we need in the Third World today. Mission organizations should require these vital subjects as prerequisites for all missionary candidates.

Missionaries home on furlough should also be encouraged to take these courses before returning to their foreign fields.

Missionaries thus trained not only are able to witness more effectively to people of other cultures, but are better able to assist them in thinking out their faith in reference to their own cultural environments, thus formulating biblical theologies which are expressed in indigenous thought-forms and familiar terminology.

It is a fact that the new generation in the Third World is very degree conscious. The words of one with a few letters after his name are paid much attention and his leadership is often respected without regard to his race. A college degree will, therefore, be an invaluable asset to the missionary's ministry. The years of discipline and preparation behind those few letters may also make the difference between a communication that gets across and one that is badly blocked despite good intentions.

Qualifications: Professional Training
In the Third World life is changing rapidly from traditional rural patterns to highly complex urban and industrial ones. Many countries, therefore, view the Western missionary in terms of his potential contribution to the development of the country. Credentials are strictly scrutinized, and those without qualifications to make them assets to the young nations are often refused visas. Those who can offer services which enhance the material and physical well-being of the people often find open doors.

I feel that the idea of self-supporting missionaries (presented so well by J. Christy Wilson in his essay) is worthy of serious consideration. Many countries which will not accept Christian mission organizations will welcome Christian teachers, doctors, engineers, scientists and technological experts of all kinds without restricting them from sharing their faith as individuals.

Many of our churches are very poor even though we are sitting on vast amounts of untapped natural resources. We need men and women with experience in business, agriculture and the trades who will get next to our laymen and share these skills with them. The success of these laymen will mean more money in the churches. This will in turn give the church a much-needed sense of pride, independence and responsibility because it will not be depending entirely on Western gifts for its ministries and projects.

Involvement

The missionary life is a demanding life. It calls for total involvement. It is not a life of idyllic and exotic adventures, as some often imagine. It makes massive spiritual, mental, psychological and physical demands which can only be born by power from on high. This is why spiritual qualifications are most important.

In the light of the fact that a missionary's work calls for total involvement, experience in such involvement becomes a necessary qualification. One must have a background of being involved first of all in one's church, then in the social and cultural life of one's community, and finally with other cultures and subcultures. This experience is vital and will in many cases determine the success or failure of a missionary.

Involvement in the Church. After I had spoken in a church in this country, a lady came up to me and told me that she had always wanted to go to Africa as a missionary but had not been able to go because of family responsibilities. When I inquired about what she was now doing she said, "Oh, nothing much." I hope she was only being modest. Otherwise I would thank the Lord for not opening the way for her to go to Africa, for she would have done "nothing much" there.

One does not become a missionary upon arriving in a foreign land. A true missionary is first of all a missionary at home. Before the Holy Spirit said to the church at Antioch "Set apart for me Barnabas and Paul" (Acts 13:2), they were already involved in missions.

It is amazing how many people think that they will be able to win Africans, Indians or Japanese to Christ when at home they have not been able to lead any of their fellow countrymen to a saving knowledge of Jesus Christ. Unfortunately, some have gone without this experience, and, after several years on the field, their fruit, in terms of winning people into the kingdom, is not very significant.

Involvement in personal witnessing and in the life of one's church is an indispensable qualification for missionary work overseas. It is an indication that one has the gift and essential qualities of a missionary. Such involvement will give a person experience in church work and also expose him to group dynamics, interpersonal relationships and problems that he will likely meet on the mission field.

Involvement in Culture. The most repeated accusation leveled at missionaries today is that they fail to appreciate the cultures of people to whom they minister. There is much validity in this accusation. Because of the ethnocentrism which I touched upon earlier and a sense of superiority, some missionaries denigrate the cultures among which they work.

However, not all lack of cultural appreciation on the part of missionaries can be attributed to ethnocentrism. Much of it is the result of ignorance of the foreign culture because they have not cared to be really involved in the social and cultural lives of the communities to which they minister. Because of this ignorance, they have in their minds a concept of non-Western cultures which is the popular and negative stereotype.

Lack of cultural appreciation can be traced to a missionary's own home background. As a child he grew up in a Christian family. All his friends and close associates were Christians. When he left home, he went to a Christian college or Bible institute. After graduation he left for a foreign country as a missionary.

There was nothing in this missionary's background to prepare him for ministry in a foreign culture. He was not even prepared to work at home because he did not understand or appreciate his own culture. He was raised in an exclusive evangelical subculture, which itself is often ignorantly critical of the mainstream.

On the field this type of missionary usually is happy in the mission compound where he has built a kind of "cultural ghetto" which has nothing to do with the so-called pagan culture outside.

To ignore the cultural mainstream is obviously to retard one's ministry. One cannot witness to people outside of their own cultural context. The very nature of the gospel does not lend itself to this kind of narrowness because the gospel has to do with all aspects of life, as Brother Landero has so aptly demonstrated.

Because a lack of appreciation of foreign cultures comes from one's home background, a necessary qualification for missionary work is therefore a love and appreciation of one's own culture demonstrated by involvement in it. A Christian who has a lively interest in history, economics, politics, music, art and literature will appreciate the same things in other cultures. If he cherishes his own social values and institutions, he will be more likely to respect those of others.

The multicultural nature of the United States makes it an ideal training ground for the missionary who will be communicating across cultural barriers. It offers unlimited opportunities for involvement with different cultures and subcultures, which will give invaluable experience on the foreign field.

This kind of involvement is of itself necessary for the Christian because the Lord said, "Go ye into all the world." The concept of *world* here goes beyond geographical areas. It includes cultural areas, too.

I have difficulty believing the sincerity of a man who has no concern at all for Afro-Americans, Chicanos, Indians and Chinese here in America but who will cross oceans to love these same people in other parts of the world. The English say, "Charity begins at home."

Attitudinal Qualifications
Of all the factors which have contributed to church-mission tension in the Third World, poor attitudes have played the most prominent part. If you talk to national church leaders and ask them to state things they feel missionaries have done wrong, you will discover that most of the things they point out will be those that stem directly from missionaries' attitudes.

There are definite attitudinal qualifications a missionary needs to gain credibility among nationals. Many missionaries went out without many of the qualifications I mentioned earlier but achieved a great amount of success because they had attitudes which endeared them to the national people.

From personal experience, I pick out two attitudes that need special attention. One is racial attitudes and the other is the superiority complex.

Racial Attitudes. It is unfortunate but true that many who are going overseas as missionaries do not have acceptable qualifications as far as their racial attitudes are concerned. I could tell you of several incidents of blatant racism by missionaries, but I will not belabor the point.

If you are seriously considering missions, it is important that you examine your own presuppositions regarding other races and ask the Lord to give you an attitude worthy of a child of God.

Any mission organization which is still sending white-only teams to work in predominately non-white situations is doing harm to the cause of Christ. Christian teams going to proclaim Christ from this country should reflect the multiracial nature of the body of Christ.

Attitude of Superiority. I can work with missionaries who have all kinds of shortcomings insofar as understanding my culture is concerned because I realize that they were not born in it. I do not understand American culture even though I have lived in this country for three years. However, I find it hard to tolerate a missionary with a superior, condescending and overbearing attitude. I have to ask for special grace from the Lord. This is indeed true of most nationals.

In missions this spirit of superiority comes out in these ways:

1. A paternalistic attitude that views mature nationals as being like children who need to be constantly supervised.

2. A lack of faith in the ability of nationals to take responsibility, especially where money is involved.

3. Looking on national Christians as assisting missionaries and not as serving God in their own right. The majority of missionary presentations I have seen in this country only highlight the role of the missionary. The role of the national is always that of helper, recipient or assistant. It is rarely that of equal coworker in Christ.

Identification

The key social qualification for a missionary is a willingness and ability to identify with the people he will minister to. Without this identification effective communication will not take place.

By identification I am not saying that the missionary must "go native." An attempt to be like the nationals in all things will only be superficial and will be rejected. They may even think that the missionary is making a caricature of their culture.

True identification comes from accepting the national culture as it is without putting a value judgment on it. Accepting the culture and respecting it will help you to learn it and then be in a position to work for the change of certain aspects of it which may not be in conformity with the teaching of Scripture. Nationals will consider your point of view seriously if they know that you respect and understand their ways.

There are two main areas through which a missionary can identify with nationals. The first is language. This may seem so obvious as not to deserve mention, but you would be surprised at how many missionaries stop studying the language seriously soon after the required language school. The result is that their communication is bad.

At the same time there are many who should be commended. They become students of our languages and subsequently lay for us superb foundations for indigenous written literatures. Because of this command of language, they are able to communicate effectively and are also readily accepted by the people.

The second area of identification is that of human relationships. A missionary must cultivate genuine human relationships with the people among whom he lives and works. He and his family should promote informal social interaction with both Christian and non-Christian nationals on a personal level. He should constantly keep in mind the fact that one is accepted in proportion to his own acceptance of others.

In order to identify, the missionary must have a personality. He must project himself as a person and not his role as a missionary. He must be recognized as a fellow human rather than as the foreigner who carries a black book and is always asking people, "Are you saved?"

Identification often entails exposing one's weakness and vulnerability. Instead of always telling nationals, "I am praying for you," he should learn to ask, "Will you pray for me?" When people know you need them they are more apt to accept you. Real relationships are reciprocal.

A strong stomach is also a necessary qualification. I know of a missionary who gained many national friends because he really enjoyed the local delicacy of green caterpillars. On the other hand, the missionary lady who became hysterical because her children ate fried white ants in an African home did not have the proper social qualifications.

Conclusion

In conclusion I would like to point out that it is good to read biographies of great missionaries of the past for inspiration. I do that myself. However, we must keep in mind that demands of their world were very different from the demands of our world today.

My prayer is that many of you will leave this great convention with a new determination to go and meet the social and cultural qualifications of a missionary, as the Spirit guides and enables you, so that you will be able with power to communicate Jesus Christ—Lord of the Universe and Hope of the World.

WHAT
IF I
DON'T
GO
OVERSEAS?

DONALD J.
CURRY

What if I feel it is the Lord's will for me to remain in Canada?
What are the implications of such a choice, and what then is my
responsibility as a student or graduate in the world missionary
outreach of the church? I should like to share with you my views
as a student on this question and my own personal search for an
answer.

Considering what might lie ahead after graduation from medical school, and more specifically where I should go, I rebelled
against the idea of staying and working in Canada. There the options open for my future seemed limited. I felt I could almost pre-
dict what would happen: marriage to the right girl, owning a nice
home in suburbia, holding down a good, respectable job and
being a fine, upstanding member of the community—just like a
thousand other people. I would, of course attend church regular-
ly on Sunday morning and be faithful in supporting it with my
tithe (no more, no less). As I neared the end of my university

career, I could gradually see myself slipping into the philosophy of life where security is the prime goal and into a comfortable life with all the amenities that our Western culture provides. I desperately wished to avoid this trap which seemed the almost inevitable result of remaining in Canada.

Working in a Developing Country

Contemplating alternatives I thought about the possibility of working in a developing country. Here I felt the attraction of the unknown, a chance to do something different and unique, a chance to escape the subtle pressures and expectations of our society and live my own life. Thus when the opportunity arose last summer to spend a twelve-week elective working in a small, 110-bed hospital in rural India, I jumped at the chance. Here I would get firsthand experience on what working overseas was like, and I hoped through what I learned I would be able to come to a more concrete decision on my future.

I can still vividly recall the heat and the humidity of India as I experienced it on my arrival. The subtle fragrance of jasmine and the other not-so-subtle smells, the extreme poverty and the fantastic wealth, all served to initiate me into this land of contrasts. My experience in India working and living with others of an entirely different background than my own opened my eyes in many areas. I realized that we from the so-called civilized West have much to learn from a culture and an approach to life that is thousands of years older than our own. Working in a mission hospital and involvement in its day-to-day problems and affairs altered previously held conceptions of missionaries and mission work.

I gradually grew to know both Indians and Canadians working in this situation and was forced to reconsider the difference I thought living in a developing country would automatically make. Despite our varied cultural backgrounds, what we had in common as people was far greater than our differences. In rural India just as much as in urban Canada lay the potential for living a dull, humdrum Christian life, one dictated by the norms of the society. Living in a different setting and working in a different culture would not necessarily guarantee me an answer to this problem; I could not escape the question by running away from it. I must be able to answer the question of how to live a stimulating and challenging Christian life within the bounds of our Western culture, and I must consider the resulting implications for my role in the missionary outreach of the church.

The Parable of the Talents

Thinking over this question on my return, I came upon Jesus' parable of the talents (Mt. 25:14-30). Here is the story of the master of a household who, before leaving on a journey, called his three servants together and handed his property over to them to manage. You will remember that the one given five talents and the one given three both wisely invested and doubled their original sums. The servant given one talent, however, was afraid to invest for fear of losing it; he knew his master to be a hard man so he buried his talent in the ground. When the master returned, he congratulated the two servants who had invested their talents wisely and gave them more responsibility as well as inviting them to share in his rejoicing. The servant who buried the talent was chastised; his one talent was taken away; and he was thrown out of the household to weep over his stupidity. In this parable Christ was speaking to me: I was one of the servants. Three things struck me as I considered the analogy.

The first was that I have been given talents to invest, whether I feel particularly gifted or not; all three servants were given something. I cannot use the excuse that in Jesus Christ's Great Commission I have nothing to offer so I will sit on the sidelines and let my pastor or the missionaries my church sends out do the work. If I have made a commitment to Jesus Christ, I have been given a role to play; I have been given a talent to invest for his glory.

Luke relates that the early church appointed seven men both practically and spiritually minded to be responsible for the accounts and the distribution of food (Acts 6:1-7). This was done so that the twelve could devote themselves wholeheartedly to prayer and the ministry of the Word. The result was that the work of God gained more and more ground, and the number of new disciples greatly increased. Here we have seven men appointed to what seems a menial, nonspectacular job, taking care of the food distribution, yet one which was essential for the effective outreach of the early church.

We often have too narrow a definition of what our talents can be and forget that whether a talent in preaching puts us on the front line or a talent in serving others places us more in the background, all are necessary in the mission of the modern church. As students we must remember that the person in charge of preparing the food for an Inter-Varsity function is no less vital than the main speaker. We as Christians are one body and need the contributions of each member if we are truly to be effective in spreading the good news. Whether we are students or ministers, file clerks or missionaries working overseas, we all have been given talents to invest and, just like the three servants, we all will be held responsible when our master returns for how we invested them.

Second, I noticed that faithful investment and not ability was rewarded; both servants that invested were given similar rewards. The Lord is not calling me to be successful in this world, though this may come, but to be faithful. So often I judge the success or failure of my investment by the false worldly standard and not by the spiritual measure. I often judge the success of my Christian life by how many people come to a function, how well an activity I helped plan was enjoyed or how many people I had a chance to share my faith with this week. This means I am often discouraged that more is not happening, that I am not turning the world upside-down as the early disciples did, that many days seem complete wipeouts as far as my contribution to the furtherment of the kingdom of God.

I must remember that the Lord judges success from a different viewpoint than the world. His eyes often see things to which our human eyes are blind. I must also remember my main purpose here on earth is to worship God and seek to deepen my relationship with him; he will provide the increase. This does not mean that we as Christians do not strive to obey his commands and share our faith with others, but it does mean we do not let ourselves get up tight if the results are not always obvious to our human eyesight.

Gambling

Third, it seems from the parable that the surest way to lose everything is not to invest, not to risk what I have been given. The first two servants invested their talents by doing business. By doing so they were taking the chance of losing what they had been given by the master, for such is the nature of investment. The third servant thought he would play it safe and not run the risk of losing; yet in the end, because he failed to risk, he lost all. I wondered how this concept of gambling as brought out in the parable, that is, of risking something of value on the outcome of an event, applied to my question of how to escape the predictable, nonexciting life that I saw so many churchgoing Christians living today. As a Christian, what does it mean practically to risk as the first two servants did?

I think one thing it means is allowing yourself to get into stretching experiences. By this I mean situations where you do not feel entirely secure in your ability to control the outcome. It might involve taking responsibility for the I-V booktable, even if you are not sure you can answer all the questions that will be thrown at you. It might mean taking a leadership position as Moses did when you have never spoken to a large group before and feel insecure in this capacity. Or it might mean accepting a position after graduation that seems a little big for your capabilities, but into which you feel the Lord is leading you. Often the question we first ask when considering a position is, "Will I feel secure in my ability to handle anything that I might come up against?" instead of "Does the Lord want me to serve him here?" We are so afraid of getting into water over our heads; yet it is only in stretching our own resources to the limit that we can find what our capabilities and talents are, and it is only in taking ourselves to the limit of our own ability that we can truly experience the infinite resources of the Lord.

Another practical example is gambling financially, and I don't mean on the horses. When did you last sit down and ask the Lord what he wants you to do this summer or after graduation, and then allow him to take care of your monetary needs for the next year? I find myself worrying about my financial state and then limiting the course my future will take to situations where I will feel financially secure, instead of allowing myself to get out on a limb and trust the Lord to take care of this area of my life.

Another important question is, How many of us as students are contributing financially to the world missionary effort despite our poor monetary status? The first IVCF staff member sent to North America from Britain, Howard Guinness, was supported by students who sold their sports equipment and books and did without in order to buy him a ticket to Toronto. It wasn't that no one else could have supported him, but that they desired to follow through in a practical way their concern for fellow students. I think that even in our present era of material wealth we students feel that we will start supporting missions after we graduate and are making all that money we hear about. Yet often we have much more than those British students who made a real sacrifice for a situation about which they were concerned.

Now is the time to invest in the kingdom of God, for it is vital for us to remember that patterns set in the university are often patterns we live by the rest of our lives. Unless we are willing to risk financially now, the chances are good that we never will. By worldly standards we may be judged as fools for not worrying more about our material security, yet as Paul writes in 1 Corinthians, "God's foolishness is wiser than men, and his weakness is stronger than men. . . . God has chosen what the world calls foolish to shame the wise; he has chosen what the world calls weak to shame the strong" (1 Cor. 1:25, 27). If we are willing to invest in his kingdom and risk some of our material possessions and security, we stand to gain far more than we could ever imagine.

Finally there is gambling in relationships, allowing others to know you as a person at the risk of their rejection, to know you as a Christian at the risk of their laughter. So often we as Christians hold ourselves in, afraid to let others see us as we are, afraid to be vulnerable. Yet unless we are willing to risk this most precious commodity, our own pride, our relationships will remain flat and superficial.

This is the central question that Jesus Christ is asking of all men, "Are you willing to risk the unknown, putting your pride aside, and move into a relationship with the very creator of the universe?" This involves stepping out on a limb, getting into a situation with unforeseen results, for Paul describes God in his letter to the Ephesians as one "who by his power within us is able to do infinitely more than we ever dare to ask or imagine" (Eph. 3:20). Yet if we play it safe and remain secure in our own little world we stand to miss the greatest thing this world has to offer, a personal relationship with Jesus Christ.

Stepping Out in Faith

Thus, as I considered the whole idea of risk and its relationship to how I am to live my Christian life in our security-conscious culture, I realized I must be willing to risk those things most precious to me—my talents, my money and my pride—and allow myself to get out on a limb, to get out into deep water where I must depend on my Lord or sink. Often we as Christians are afraid to put ourselves into a position where we need to depend solely on Christ for support. We feel that if everything falls through our faith will be jeopardized; yet if we never let ourselves into a situation where our only recourse is to rely on him, we will never experience his power. We try to guard our faith on all sides for fear that if we really test it we will find it to be false. We go through life never being sure that what we believe in is true, hoping it is, and thus never experiencing the strength and wisdom available to us if we would only step out in faith.

Francis Schaeffer in his book *The Church at the End of the 20th Century* asks an important question:

> *Suppose we awoke tomorrow morning and opened our Bibles and found two things had been taken out.... The first item missing was the real empowering of the Holy Spirit and the second item, the reality of prayer. What difference would there be from the way we acted yesterday?*

What is your response to this question? Would it make any real difference in the way you lived that day? When did you last allow yourself to get into a stretching experience where you experienced the power of the Holy Spirit that has been promised? When were you last reminded of the reality and strength available in prayer? Schaeffer goes on to say that if we really believe

God is there we live differently.

In his book *The Meaning of Persons* Paul Tournier states,

This is what living means, jumping over the hedges of the personage that have gradually grown up and hemmed us in. We think that by being cautious we are protecting life whereas we are slowly smothering it.

Jesus emphasizes this point in a statement recorded in John 12:

I tell you truly that unless a grain of wheat falls into the earth and dies, it remains but a single grain of wheat; but if it dies, it brings a good harvest. The man who loves his own life will destroy it, and the man who hates his life in this world will preserve it for eternal life. (Jn. 12:24-25)

It is so easy to live a safe life, never risking what we have been given, afraid like the third servant that we will lose what is precious to us. But, as our Lord so strongly states, this is the surest way to destroy the very thing we are trying to protect.

This is how Jesus spoke to me, a student considering the implications of serving him in Canada: He revealed through the parable of the talents the way to live an exciting, triumphant Christian life. I learned that whether I go overseas to a developing country or remain in Canada, I have a unique role to play in the outreach of the good news of Christ. My mission field is the place where God leads me to be; whether in a suburban practice in Calgary or as a doctor in the deepest jungles of Africa, I am a missionary to the people with whom I am in contact. I have been given a talent to further his kingdom, which may involve financial support or preaching on the front line, and I will be held responsible for what I have been given. As I seek to invest my talent for his kingdom, I also am learning that I must not be quick to judge my success by worldly standards; I have been called into a relationship, and the fruits of that relationship will come in their own season. Finally I discovered that to really live an exciting Christian life, one that involves a day-by-day walk with God, I must be willing to risk everything I hold precious, including my own pride, and depend on his wisdom and strength for my support.

In this parable it is interesting that a fourth servant is not mentioned, the one who invests the talents he has been given only to lose everything. I believe that if we are willing to get into situations where we must truly depend on the power of the Holy Spirit we will never lose. Being out on a limb may be very frightening and lonely at times, but such is the nature of risking. Jesus never promised that the Christian life would be a bed of roses. Yet it is only in such situations that we as Christians discover the truth of the statement, "Those who trust him wholly, find him wholly true."

Thus the question that I must ask, and that each of us must ask personally, is, Which servant do I most resemble? How have I been living my Christian life: safely or with a joyful abandon, looking on each new day as an opportunity to further experience the trustworthiness of our Lord? I would challenge you to allow him to prove his steadfastness to you; ask him to place you in a position where you must rely on him or sink, a stretching experience. Be willing to gamble those things you hold so dearly, like security and pride. Are you willing to take a chance and discover yourself and your Lord? Dare you not risk?

WHERE DO WE GO FROM HERE?

12

RUSSELL WEATHERSPOON

After an experience like we have had this week, perhaps the first reaction of some of us will be to find a global map, look for the spot diametrically opposed to our hometown and, Urbana memorabilia and all, head for it. Now, folks who do this might encounter difficulties, not the least of them being that the charted spot might be in the middle of an ocean—in fact, there might not be any land, just ocean. But I understand the sentiment: "Strike while the iron is hot!"

For the rest of us whose spending money ran out the second day and who are therefore *forced* to go home, I have a few suggestions that should keep us pretty warm with activity between now and the time we pack our bags for that overseas trip.

Preparing to Serve

We should have realized by now that a prerequisite for missions is a real desire to see others introduced to the Lord Jesus; that part of being a missionary is the giving of our professional or vocational abilities to the country in which we are serving. Let us suppose that you have little desire and few abilities. What is to be done? Well, if you are willing to give yourself to your studies back at school, by the time you graduate you will have gained something to give vocationally. That problem is solved. In other words, a little less moonlight and a little more lamplight.

However, vocational ability alone will not enable you or prepare you to be a missionary. A weak desire to share your faith can in reality be an admission that you never have had the opportunity to learn how. Both your Inter-Varsity chapter and your local church can be mini-schools of missionary training. Through a chapter's activities, such as evangelistic Bible studies, booktables and special presentations like TWENTYONE-HUNDRED, you can learn to talk to and exchange ideas with strangers. Over a period of time you will watch some of those strangers become friends and some of those friends become Christians. The chapter will probably also help you get acquainted with foreign students.

At Brooklyn College in New York one experience holds my memory's attention with a tighter grip than all the rest. During a special presentation, which our chapter inoffensively called "Repent," an Oriental girl wandered in. She was a student of the martial arts and of Confucian philosophy. She managed to get the name of our group, its general purposes and the fact that we have a booktable once a week. From that initial encounter blossomed a dialogue and a relationship between this young lady and our club unparalleled in the experience of many of us. After about one year spent mostly in questioning us, visiting our meetings and requestioning us, she gave her life to Christ. I know there are many of you who have had similar experiences. The thrill of watching someone who is earnestly searching for truth find it in Jesus Christ, through the leading of the Holy Spirit, is nothing less than exciting. If there is no formal fellowship of believers on your campus, why not start one?

A second source of training and experience is a local evangelical church, which can help cultivate in you the spirit of cooperation and obedience as you assume responsibilities delegated to you by the leadership. In any fellowship, willingness to serve is desirable, but on the mission field it is indispensable. (Just imagine the shock of the people in your church when you get home and volunteer your services—the Sunday school picnic, anything! Next Urbana they'll probably subsidize the whole young people's group to come.)

At the airports and other points of departure, some of us will be surprised to see that our bags have gained twenty pounds— until we remember all the pamphlets we picked up during the week. When you get home, take these brochures, along with any names supplied by Intercristo, and write to the people concerned. What are their present personnel needs? What is their financial status? What do they consider major goals in the operation of their mission? How do the people where they minister receive them? What do they require educationally, medically and doctrinally of their candidates for the field? How much support will you personally be responsible to raise?

By the way, how many of you have ever had to raise your support from other believers in order to go on a missionary venture? During most of my college life I worked with High School Evangelism Fellowship, an organization which trains Christian young people to evangelize their high schools. Helping the students memorize Scripture and teaching principles of witness was fun. I was soon confronted, however, with the ominous task of raising my support, which, in my mind—although I knew really nothing about it—meant walking from church to church with a cup outstretched, a pitiful look on my face and the hope in my heart that some born-again person would have pity on me. The reality of the situation was totally other: I found that both churches and individual believers took an interest in what I was doing and requested the privilege to give. I soon learned that this was a method, and a biblical one, of inviting others in on the blessing of God (Paul describes it in Phil. 4:10-19). In short, if you have never raised support and are nervous about it, don't be.

Widening Your Experiences
All of these thoughts on support bring another suggestion to

mind. Summer's right around the corner—and down a few blocks judging by the snow outside. Have you made any plans for it yet? How about spending part of it in a foreign culture, sharing Christ and getting a taste of missionary life?

Two summers ago I went to Jamaica, West Indies, with a contingent of thirty or so New York young people to hold street meetings in the towns and camp meetings in the rural sections. If one holds street meetings in New York City, he gets used to competing with hustlers, crap games, prostitutes and anything else for the attention of the passersby; he also gets used to the idea of taking a security guard along to make tract passing a little easier. I'm exaggerating, of course, but sometimes there can be rough days. And in passing out tracts, sandwiches and punch as we did, we had rough days.

When I learned we were going to Kingston, one of Jamaica's principal towns, I got a little bit nervous. You can imagine what I was thinking after doing this in New York. You might say, "Russell, what were you worried about? Don't you remember all those commercials on television that talk about that lovely tropical isle situated like a jewel in the middle of the West Indies and that woman who comes on the screen and says, I love Jamaica!" That's true. That's what the commercial says. But you know what the commercials say about New York? I live there, and they tell me it's a "Summer Festival."

On the other hand, you have to imagine my shock when I saw substantial crowds of Jamaicans stand in the noonday heat for two hours and more to listen to a team of American and Jamaican Christians share the gospel. On that first day alone, over a hundred came to accept Christ as Savior. It was a new day, a new land, a different group of people, a whole different response. As a matter of fact, even the Christians were different.

Pius Wakatama said that when you go to a new country, you need a strong stomach. We held a camp meeting in one of the small hamlets in the backwoods of Jamaica, and I had a meal there with water. It tasted all right, but looks can be deceiving. I came down with a pretty stiff case of dysentery—in case you don't know, that's diarrhea with a side order of abdominal cramps. This lasted several days.

As this small hamlet thing was going on, and I was doing the bends, we had to hold another meeting in a far-off district. I was sitting in a bus that was banging along the roads, and my stomach was cramped up, and my fiancée was trying to hold me up. I'm saying to myself, "I hope we get there, I hope we get there, I hope we get there, 'cause I'm making a beeline for the you-know-what."

When I got there, I jumped out and ran for the door, but it was locked. Some Jamaican Christians who lived next door brought me inside their home, let me use their W.C. as they call it (water closet), gave me a bed to sleep in and handed me some carrot milk, which I'd never seen before in my life. But I can tell you one thing—after I started taking that carrot milk and had a bit of a breather and a rest, I was able to minister.

Do consider seriously the possibility of widening your experiences by going to a foreign culture. If you can get overseas this summer, perhaps to the Overseas Training Camp or to one of the short-term mission projects offered by many mission boards, go.

Combating Racism and Ethnocentrism

In our conversations these days, we have been talking a lot about racism and ethnocentrism. We are living in a country which is racist. What are we going to do? As Pius Wakatama pointed out, racism thrives on ignorance. So does ethnocentrism. I have an idea. It might not work, but I have an idea. How about if some of you folks from the rural towns beat it over to the suburbs this summer and take orders from somebody in a local church there and learn what it's like to live in the suburbs. How about you folks from the suburbs beating your way over to the urban areas and taking orders from a local church there. How about some of you people from urban areas beating your way to a rural section. Mess with the cows and the pigs for a while. I think this will prepare you if not for the foreign field at least to understand that the way you do things is not the only way people do them.

A fellow came from a hick town in New Jersey to New York City. Like many nice white folk that come from hick towns to bust open the deep, dark cities, in which I live, he came with his crew cut, his smile and his gimmicks, which definitely work out in the suburbs but sometimes don't work in the cities. Nevertheless, he came. He had his rural ways about him, and he had his ethnocentrism about him, and to some slight degree he had his racism about him. And he was my staff leader.

But in those days of 1964 to 1967, as I watched on television things like Selma, Alabama, George Wallace and Lester Maddox; as I watched a part of America tell me they still did not consider me a man and as I tried to figure out whether Christianity was part of that statement—whether Christianity was telling me you are not a man, you are not even a person—here was a hick whose life was controlled by the Lord Jesus Christ. As far as I was concerned, and as far as many of the kids of my neighborhood were concerned, he was naive. But we all knew he was controlled by the lordship of Christ.

If you come from a city and God has commanded you to go to a rural area, go. If you come from a rural area and God has commanded you to go to the suburbs or anyplace else, go. Don't try to be a city slicker if you're a hick. And if you're a city slicker, don't try to be a hick. Just go and learn. Elisabeth Elliot Leitch says that for a whole year while she was among the Aucas,

> I watched and learned and kept my mouth shut. I had to keep my mouth shut most of the time because I did not know the Auca language. For once I listened and had nothing to say. It was a valuable exercise, and although the language itself was highly complex, the definition of my task was simple. Learn it.

I stepped into a staff leader's apartment when he came to New York City to minister and found Colonial furniture. In New York you don't do your house in Colonial! There was even a Declaration of Independence on the wall. I said, "Oh, no." I hate Colonial. A couple of months ago, after I had been ministering in New York City for about four years and was planning to spend my whole life ministering to the needs there, the Lord spoke to me emphatically and said, "Out to the suburbs." I couldn't believe it. I said, "Are you sure?" He said, "I'm sure." I'll give you one guess what style of architecture is up there—Colonial. God is beating back my ethnocentrism now. I am beginning to learn what bottle collecting, antiquing and collecting old newspapers is all about. I'm learning how to appreciate what these people know and love. And like Mrs. Leitch I'm keeping my mouth shut.

Where Do We Go from Here?

Where do we go from here? To those who are sympathetic with our desires to share Christ: our parents if possible, our pastor or elders, interested members of our church and our Christian friends. You have to allow others to become a part of the blessing of sharing the responsibility of world evangelism. Ask for their prayers and encouragement.

On the way back home, why don't you pick up a new habit, if you don't have it already. Get a newsweekly, a good one like *Time, Newsweek* or *U. S. News & World Report*, one that has an international scope. Begin to acquaint yourself with the world at large and its present crises. If God has been leading you to consider one country especially, cut out the articles about that nation. Keep a notebook with these articles and pray for the national leaders as well as for the believers there.

Where do we go from here? Back to our stationery and ballpoint pens to write letters to individual missionaries. A believer serving Christ and others abroad can give a valuable perspective on a country, a perspective available nowhere else. And your observations and enthusiasm can buoy him up, giving him the joy of knowing that another shares his particular burden.

Where do we go from here? Back to our chapters and churches for experience in group and personal evangelism, discipleship and development of the spirit of willingness. Back to consult with mission boards, finding out specific information about them. Back to plan a summer that is rich in new lessons—lessons derived from watching others share Christ on their soil, their way. Back to those who feel as we do about missions to get their prayer support and their encouragement. Back to get a subscription to a news magazine that will keep us informed of the world at large. Back to correspond with a missionary and get a unique perspective of the nation to which God is leading us.

Where do we go from here? Back to talk the whole matter over with God some more, cultivating the spirit which says, "Anywhere, Lord, anywhere."

GOD'S WORK IN THE WORLD TODAY

CHUA WEE HIAN AND RENE PADILLA*

Latin America

It was nineteen years ago that I attended my first missionary convention. At that time, I was just beginning my studies in college, and the work of the International Fellowship of Evangelical Students was just starting in Latin America. True, there had been other movements working, but the IFES as such had had little to do with Latin America up to that time. Interestingly enough, at that conference I met a great pioneer in student work—Bob Young. We on the staff in Latin America cannot forget his example. He had been on the staff of IVCF here in the States, had traveled for a number of years and then had taken off for Latin America. A few years after meeting him, when I traveled throughout various countries (especially in northern South

*Chua Wee Hian delivered this world report, asking Rene Padilla to present the section on Latin America.

America), everywhere I went, wherever there was a university, I met people who had known Bob Young. I don't know how he covered so much territory, but the Lord surely had used him to lay a foundation for the work in the future. He was a pioneer.

At the same time, there was an American young lady who was working as a school teacher in Lima. God used her tremendously to help the students. She was not on the staff of the IFES; she was just a teacher. But her home was open to the students, and there they received aid and inspiration. Through her help many of those who attended the meetings became leaders in the student work.

Years afterwards I met a professor at the University of Sao Paulo (he's still there), a man from Canada who is a specialist in physics. I do not think many others have done as much, by God's grace, as he has on behalf of the student work in Brazil.

I mention these examples because I believe that God has different ways of leading. If one is ready to be led, God can use him in a tremendous way as a witness to Jesus Christ.

Things have changed. I remember that when I started on IFES staff I would go to a city and barely meet any Christian students. Today I can visit practically any Latin American country and see representatives of student groups such as yours witnessing to the Lord Jesus Christ. We have been thrilled to see the growth of the work in these years.

At present, three movements in Latin America are completely self-supporting. You may be acquainted with our philosophy in IFES. Each movement is independent. Each works its own program. Each is to follow the Lord's leading. We do not have any "canned" methods of evangelism and do not lay down the program for anybody. We try to help the students by giving them training, especially regarding the study of the Scripture.

One of the main programs we have is the publication of literature, and we have been thrilled to see the growth of the literature program in Latin America. By the way, I want publicly to say thank you to those who contributed toward the buying of a building in Buenos Aires. We now have there both the office of the IFES for Latin America and the office of our publishing program. At present, most of our books are translated. We are trying to find people who will write books in Spanish—we have a few. But it is a thrill to see the way the Latin American students are using literature to reach their fellow students for Christ.

At times we have thought that perhaps the evangelistic impact of the groups is far from what we would like to see, but I can say publicly tonight that we praise the Lord because in the last two or three years we have truly seen a breakthrough, especially in some countries. We never dreamed of having eighty students at a conference, forty of them non-Christians, and of having most of them, if not all, make profession of faith and follow on with the Lord. We are concerned for those students who hardly have had help to grow to maturity, but we thank God for what we see in them of the image of Christ.

Africa

Africa is a continent of striking contrasts. On the one hand, North Africa represents resistance to the gospel. Since the seventh century, Islam has been the dominant force in religion. Christians are few and far-between. The only bridgehead that IFES has is a reading room in Algiers. There students will drop in to borrow books, to read and to talk with IFES associate staff worker Ruth Stewart.

By contrast, when you go to Africa south of the Sahara you find large congregations, packed churches. In Kenya, 65% of the population claim to be Christians. Student work in English-speaking Africa is flourishing. In countries like Ghana, Nigeria, Kenya, Tanzania, Uganda, Zambia and South Africa, you find large groups of Christians meeting for evangelism, prayer and fellowship. The work in West Africa is self-supporting.

Come with me for a few minutes to East Africa. I was there for a few weeks, and this was an exciting experience for me as a Chinese Christian to have fellowship with my African brothers and sisters. In fact, for many of them it was the first time they had seen a Chinese Christian. Some of them even came up to feel me all over to make sure that I was made of flesh and blood and was not a celestial being. They opened their hearts and their rooms to me. It was tremendous to be able to fellowship in the Lord Jesus Christ.

Last month John Stott conducted three evangelistic missions in Nairobi, Kenya, Makerere, Uganda, and Dar-es-Salaam, Tanzania. At Makerere University in Uganda, between 600 and 700 students attended the series of evangelistic lectures. At the end of this series several students committed their lives to Jesus Christ. In Uganda there is spiritual hunger. And at that university the Christian Union has a membership of just over 300. Nairobi also has a strong Christian Union. On Sunday afternoon members of this group go to the quadrangle of four hostels (dormitories) to proclaim the good news of Jesus Christ. They sing and testify, and some of the students explain the way of salvation to their contemporaries. African Christian students are bold in their witness for the Lord Jesus.

I would like to introduce you to Hamisi Chondoma, a Tanzanian who was brought up in a Muslim family. He went to the University of Tanzania, and, during the first year of his studies, he became a Christian. His roommate led him to Jesus Christ. Several months later, he wanted to be baptized openly, so he was baptized in the open-air swimming pool of the university, watched by hundreds of students. Today Hamisi is one of the leading lights in the Christian fellowship of that university.

In 1972 there was a great movement among young people in Ethiopia, and this struck Addis Ababa, the capital city, with tremendous force. Hundreds of students were won for the Lord Jesus Christ. The orthodox church leaders were perplexed and, of course, very anxious because many of the young people became Christians. In fact, most of the leaders of the Christian fellowship in Addis Ababa were imprisoned and sentenced to several months of hard labor. Because of international pressures, however, these students were released on bail. On Friday night you can see 400 of these students packed into a church hall to listen to the gospel. We rejoice at the ways in which God is working in English-speaking Africa. We see large numbers of students coming to know Jesus Christ.

But there is one weakness. There are few regular Bible study groups on these campuses, and the African students need to be taught and trained to handle the Word of God for themselves. So it was exciting during the last few months to be able to invite people from different countries to come to Africa to labor as staff workers, joining African staff in discipling students. The Finnish movement sent Eila Helander, a trained theologian from Helsinki, to teach and to help William Adodoadji, the African staff worker, train Bible study group leaders. In April of 1974 Hank Pott, who is presently the Inter-Varsity staff worker at UCLA, will be going to Zambia. There he will seek to train students to love the Word of God and to grow in the Lord Jesus Christ.

The IFES has a clear mandate for both Eila Helander and Hank Pott. They are to work themselves out of their jobs. I love the way in which Eila has grasped this concept. Writing to her prayer partners, she said, "First, I must make my self necessary. Then after two or three years I must make myself unnecessary." Will you pray for Hank Pott? Let's pray him in: Let's pray that he will get his visa for doing work in Zambia. And after two or three years, let's pray him out, because we want to see him training Africans to be staff workers and to lead their own movement.

We also have work in French-speaking Africa, which is led by a team of Swiss and Scottish workers. The groups are small, but God is empowering his servants alongside French-speaking African students to make Jesus Christ known on the French-speaking campuses.

Europe
I would now like to invite you to fly with me to Europe. Please fasten your seatbelts.

Let us fly first to Britain and the Scandinavian countries. In our brief tour of the universities we see large Christian fellowships with students meeting daily for prayer, and on weekends we see open Bibles as gifted Bible teachers expound the Word of God. Some of these movements, like the ones in Britain and Norway, are over fifty years of age; but God has revitalized these movements, and these groups of students are aggressively witnessing for Jesus Christ on their campuses. Oxford University this year held a series of evangelistic lectures, and over 160 students committed their lives to Jesus Christ during, as well as after, the series of messages.

As you visit these groups, you will find students who are committed to Jesus Christ. You will find high school students at ski camps telling their friends about the Lord Jesus Christ and seeing great conversions of students from nominal Lutheran backgrounds to know and love the living God.

One of the most significant contributions of the British IVF and the Scandinavian IFES-related movements is the large number of graduates who have become pastors of churches. In Britain, about a third of those who are preparing for the Anglican or state-church ministry are Inter-Varsity graduates. All these movements have sent out hundreds and hundreds of missionaries to be disciple makers in all the nations of this world. In a few days' time, IVF of Britain will be holding its annual missionary convention.

Now let us fly to some southern European countries. Two months ago I was walking through the University of Rome. I was told that about 100,000 students are enrolled in this center of higher learning. I asked our associate staff member, Jean Elliot, how many students who love Jesus Christ would be found witnessing for him on this vast campus. Jean answered me, "As far as I know, only one." *One* committed Christian student in a student body of nearly 100,000.

As you leave Rome and travel to other Italian university centers, you find that the GBU (Inter-Varsity) chapters are small. Only a handful of Italian students are involved in these groups. We in IFES are naturally very concerned. We have been working there for nearly twenty-five years but have seen little fruit. I spent thirteen hours with the committee recently, and the GBU leaders, both Italians as well as missionary helpers, have asked me to look out for an Italian-speaking man. If you know someone who can speak Italian, someone who has the vision, the guts, the drive, the enthusiasm for pioneer work in this difficult country, will you please get in touch with me?

In Spain and Portugal we find small groups emerging. God has used workers like Ruth Siemens to pioneer local groups in cities like Barcelona. Today groups are found in the cities of Barcelona, Madrid, Santiago and Zaragoza, and students are coming to know Jesus Christ, especially through evangelistic

Bible studies. Recently students in Barcelona and Valencia were able to distribute questionnaires asking non-Christian students about their attitudes and their purpose in life. Through these questionnaires they were able to invite some of these students to study God's Word together. We thank God for conversions.

I remember being present at a conference in Valencia, where a Roman Catholic girl became a Christian. Her concept of God changed immediately. Formerly she had thought that God was so busy he had no time for her, a young student; but when she discovered that God delighted to meet with her, that she could speak to him in prayer, in the conversational prayer sessions she prayed ten times. Many Roman Catholic students are coming to a vital faith in Christ and expressing the joy of their salvation.

When we go to Portugal, we find ourselves in a difficult situation. What do you do when the times are so unpredictable? when police would disrupt campus life? That is a problem that IFES staff worker Alex Araujo faces. In spite of these problems, groups are growing in places like Porto, Coimbra and Lisbon. The IFES also has work among French-speaking African students in Europe, and Bill Thomas, one of the Urbana 73 speakers, ministers to these students.

In Austria we have introduced an experiment. A team of young graduates from England, Norway and Holland is working to establish a strong Christian fellowship in the University of Vienna. All four are supported by their local fellowships. The Officers Christian Union has increased its missionary giving by 500% because two of its representatives are on this team. According to reports we have received, students are being converted and young ones are growing amazingly. The hall where the students meet on Thursday night is simply too small, and they are looking for larger premises.

Another area of ministry is Eastern Europe. We thank God that during the last four years we have been able to pioneer about twenty to thirty Bible study groups. These have no labels, but God has used IFES special workers and envoys to visit and encourage these students. Our workers are not spies, involved in international intrigue and political espionage. Instead they are

Barnabases encouraging Eastern European students to love and serve the living Lord.

In the Middle East, our work is focused mainly in the cosmopolitan city of Beirut, Lebanon. Here live hundreds and hundreds of Arab students from Cyprus. We have an international team headed by David Penman, a New Zealander, working with men like Al Fairbanks, a black teacher from America, and also teams of Egyptian and British students, seeking to reach out to these 60,000 Arabic-speaking students. And God, through the Holy Spirit, is bringing men and women in that city and that country to know and love him.

Asia

I would like to attempt the impossible and sketch five word portraits of what God is doing among Asian students.

Portrait 1 depicts remarkable growth. If someone were to paint a picture of evangelical student work on the Asian continent fifteen years ago, there would be lots of room on the canvas, because back in 1958 there was only a handful of Christian fellowships. Today several hundred groups, some totaling over 300 members each, are actively discipling their contemporaries on the campuses of Asia.

Consider Taiwan. There in that island republic every summer the Campus Evangelical Fellowship attracts between 3,000 and 4,000 students to their summer conferences. This year over 1,000 students professed faith in Christ Jesus at those conferences. Think of the remarkable indigenous fellowship in Korea, known as the University Bible Fellowship. This started fourteen years ago, and today it has an active membership of 10,000 student members. If you were to go to the University of Singapore, you would find there 100 action groups with five to six members reaching out to several hundred other students. It is also interesting to note that 10% of the faculty of that university are committed Christians.

Portrait 2 illustrates the ongoing task of disciple making. In some fellowships it is mandatory for the young believer to spend at least thirty days studying the Scriptures with an older Christian. In the Philippines and West Malaysia month-long training courses are used to build up and train student leaders. Teaching missions and evening schools of theology are integrated into the training programs of national movements in India, Pakistan and Singapore.

Portrait 3 embodies stewardship and sacrifice. Today in Asia there are thirteen self-supporting national movements, which support over 150 graduates, staff workers and traveling secretaries. Most of these people are medical doctors, engineers, theologians, university professors and teachers, and they are prepared to accept very low salaries and to sacrifice because the Lord Jesus has made the greatest sacrifice of all for them. They travel thousands of miles with their suitcases, visiting campus groups. The staff in India and Pakistan have to cycle and walk in the sweltering heat of 100° in order to meet the students and encourage them to grow in the Lord Jesus Christ. But joy comes when students go on to witness for Jesus Christ and make disciples on their campuses.

Not only do staff make sacrifices; some of the Asian students do the same. The University Bible Fellowship of Korea used to send students onto the streets. The boys would polish shoes and the girls would sell a Korean hot pickle called *kimchi*. The money they earned they gave to student work. This was something revolutionary. The usual Confucian culture of Korea, China or Japan despises menial tasks. The scholar has long fingernails. But these students, when they read that Jesus was a carpenter and that Paul made tents, were willing to dirty their fingers, to go to the streets, polish shoes, sell kimchi and serve God in this task of stewardship. No wonder that group has grown in such great numbers.

Portrait 4 demonstrates missionary responsibility. Some of our groups hold seminars and conferences which seek to stir their students to consider a missionary commitment. The first Asian student missionary convention is being held in Manila at the same time as this Urbana convention. And today over 400 Asian missionaries are serving God across national barriers and frontiers! Asian missionaries have worked in many, many places. I think of the groups in Japan. These are small compared to Korea, Singapore or Hong Kong. But the KGK of Japan has sent over 100 missionaries to different parts of the world—an amazing work of God. I must mention, too, the number of graduates in the various movements who through their profession have maintained a solid witness for Jesus Christ. Some have built up churches in isolated villages and towns. Others have helped existing churches to grow.

Portrait 5 represents unmet needs. I would like to focus on one area, Bangladesh. In that war-torn country there is spiritual hunger. Bengali-speaking Indians have made trips into that country and have asked the IFES family to send a team of two or three people to work among Bangladesh students in the university towns. At the moment, Indians and Americans are not really welcome in that country, but the IFES has many member movements. Canadians in particular would be greatly welcomed. Wouldn't it be wonderful if at the next Urbana we could report a new movement in Bangladesh?

North America

On my journeys to Africa, Asia and soon to Latin America, I have been telling students about what God is doing in North America. I tell them about the high school groups and the lovely camping sites in Canada. I tell them about the number of students who are coming to know the Lord Jesus in both high schools and universities there. I tell students, too, of the way God has been working in the United States through Inter-Varsity Christian Fellowship. During the past few years, thousands of students have come to know and love the Lord Jesus Christ. Training conferences have been well attended, and students are grounded in the Scriptures. There are the Bible and Life courses, which are aimed at building up students in the Word of God, and, of course, there is Urbana, where students in North America and other parts of the world are challenged to consider their place in God's missionary program.

And the students rejoice. In fact, some of them are praying daily for you. The gift you have made during the past days is an expression of our partnership in the gospel. We are workers together with God. The IFES family has national groups in fifty-two countries, and we are pooling our resources, manpower and finances to establish self-supporting national movements. IFES staff, a team of about thirty mobile workers, will go to a country to encourage national leadership. Some of them engage in pioneer ministries. Ruth Siemens, for instance, has been used of God to start student groups in Latin America, and later on in Spain. We in the IFES are glad that we can loan Samuel Escobar to the Canadian movement.

A large number of American staff are serving through IFES. I want to thank God publicly for the lives and ministries of such people. Doug stewart is helping to pioneer the work in Mexico. Bill McConnell has joined the Brazilian team to work among university students in that large country. One staff worker who is a continual headache to me is Ada Lum of Hawaii—a headache because over twenty fields and movements are asking for her services at the same time. She has been going to various movements to train nationals to write Bible study guides in their own language and for their own particular cultural setting. She has also trained hundreds of Bible study leaders and staff who are able to train other nationals. Our newly appointed theological secretary, Bruce Demarest, is also from this country. His job is to encourage theological students, especially in non-evangelical seminaries and faculties, to remain true to their biblical and evangelical convictions.

All over the world throughout the IFES groups I sense a new spirit of partnership. For example, in Thailand there are more Buddhist temples than individual Protestant Christians. But today in Thailand there is an active Christian Fellowship, the Thai Student Christian Fellowship, which has six chapters and over 150 members involved daily in discipling their contemporaries. This work started only about eight years ago. The people who sowed the gospel seed were missionaries from Britain and the United States. I think of a professor from Wheaton who went to teach geography in one of the universities in Bangkok. And God has used these people and Asian missionaries today and many, many others to build up this group. This is a beautiful example of how the Holy Spirit has woven a pattern of partnership, and we give him all the glory.

I challenge and invite you to join with Christian students all over the world in the IFES family to obey the marching orders of Jesus Christ, our Supreme Commander. Let's give him our best. Let's give him our all to make disciples of all nations, to win students to know him, love him and confess him as Lord of the Universe and Lord of their lives. Will you join me and all my colleagues, students around the world, to make Jesus Christ known and to show the world that he is Lord of all?

PART III

THE
BIBLICAL BASIS
OF MISSIONS

THE BASIS OF MISSIONS IN THE OLD TESTAMENT

PHILIP
TENG

The gathering of over 14,000 students here is an indication to the world of Christian students' concern about evangelism and missions as an expression of their obedience to the Lord's Great Commission. This convention is a tremendous encouragement as well as a challenge to Christians all over the world. You have come here to study evangelism and missions, but more important to find out God's will for your life. I pray that this convention will be an instrument in the hands of Almighty God for the reinforcement of the missionary cause in the whole world.

The theme of my messages is "The Biblical Basis of Missions." I divide this theme into four subtitles: first, the basis of missions in the Old Testament; second, the basis of missions in the Gospels (that is, Christ and missions); third, the basis of missions in Acts (that is, the Holy Spirit and missions); and fourth, the basis of missions in the Epistles (that is, the church and missions). Now we take up the first subtitle: The Basis of Missions in the Old Testament.

God's Calling to Abraham

The Bible is the record of a mission: the divine mission of saving the human race carried out by the Triune God and his commissioned people.

The history of the people of Israel is the history of a mission. The record of the corporate mission of the people of Israel began with the fascinating story of a personal mission—the mission of Abraham. The burden of Abraham's mission is clearly stated in God's calling to him: "I will bless thee . . . and thou shalt be a blessing: . . . and in thee shall all families of the earth be blessed" (Gen. 12:2-3). That was a great mission—the mission of blessing the whole world! Abraham became a great missioner, or missionary. God called Abraham and he responded in faith. He left behind his old way of life and started the pilgrimage of a heavenly errand. Abraham is called the father of faith, but his faith was a means to an end and that end was a mission. Faith by itself is without content. In the life of Abraham, faith was required of him because the carrying out of his mission was often met with hindrances and difficulties which could be overcome only by faith in God, the originator of the mission.

God's calling to Abraham also applies to his descendants, for God said to Abraham, "In thy seed shall all the nations of the earth be blessed" (Gen. 22:18). The word *seed* has a threefold reference. In the first place, it refers to the people of Israel, for God said to Abraham, "I will multiply thy seed as the stars of the heaven, and as the sand which is upon the sea shore" (Gen. 22:17). God's purpose in raising up the nation of Israel was to show the world through its history his way of salvation and thereby to bring all the nations of the world to enjoy his blessings. In the second place, the word *seed* refers to Jesus Christ. All heavenly blessings have come to us through Jesus Christ, as Paul tells us in the opening verses of his Epistle to the Ephesians. In the third place, the word *seed* refers to Christians, who are called by Paul the spiritual children of Abraham (Gal. 3:29). The apostle Peter has made it very clear to us that we Christians are called by God to the great task of blessing others (1 Pet. 3:9), which is our mission. *Christians are missionaries.* We cannot be true Christians without being missionaries. We are here at this convention to realize that we are all commissioned by God for the great mission of taking God's blessings to the whole world. None of us can rightfully excuse himself from this important mission.

So Abraham's mission passed on to his descendants. God's calling to Abraham was also given to his son Isaac: "And the LORD appeared unto him [Isaac], and said, . . . I will bless thee . . . and I will perform the oath which I sware unto Abraham thy father . . . and in thy seed shall all the nations of the earth be blessed" (Gen. 26:2-4).

It was also given to Jacob: "And, behold, the LORD stood above it, and said [to Jacob], I am the LORD God of Abraham . . . and in thy seed shall all the families of the earth be blessed" (Gen. 28:13-14).

This line of thought does not stop here. Through the mouth of Jacob, a great blessing was given to Joseph, who was the next link in the line of this mission: "Joseph is a fruitful bough . . . whose branches run over the wall" (Gen. 49:22). What a beautiful metaphor for a vessel of blessing!

We can, therefore, say that the spiritual trademark of the patriarchs, or forefathers, of the Israelites was "Blessed to Bless."

Then this note of mission suddenly disappeared from the time of Moses onward when the people of Israel were engaged in a desperate struggle to survive and to maintain their faith in Jehovah. The general tone of this period naturally and necessarily became one of separation from other nations in order to keep their heads above the water of the influence of heathen corruption and degeneration. They were in great danger of losing their spiritual identities and of being carried away by the flood of conformity to the prevailing lifestyle of their immediate neighbors.

This historical background provides us with the light in which to see the need for both the positive and negative aspects of the Christian life: positive—to be a means of blessing to other people; negative—to be kept from drifting into conformity to the world, which in its principles is opposed to our mission of blessing others. These two aspects make up the divine balance which we must maintain in order to travel on the right path.

The Teaching of the Prophets

Then time came for God to remind his people again of their mission. God did it through the prophets. In the utterances of the prophets we again see the people of Israel in the hand of God as a vessel of blessing for the whole world. Their mission was definitely and clearly to go beyond their national lines and aim at bringing all nations to a true knowledge of God.

The teaching of the prophets tells us at least three things that have to do with missions: first, the universality of God's claim; second, the universality of God's plan of salvation; third, the universality of the Messianic kingdom.

The Universality of God's Claim. The absolute and universal claim of God is most clearly, definitely and fully set forth in one single chapter in the Old Testament—Isaiah 45, one of the most significant chapters of the whole Bible. We find at least eight claims of God in this chapter.

First, Jehovah is the only God. This claim is repeated nine times in Isaiah 45 (see vv. 5-6, 14, 18, 21-22). This God must be proclaimed, acknowledged and worshiped in all the world.

Second, Jehovah is the God of creation: "the LORD that created the heavens ... that formed the earth and made it ..." (v. 18). The whole creation declares the glory of its creator. His universal lordship and ownership should be announced everywhere.

Third, Jehovah is the God of the human race: "I have made the earth, and created man upon it" (v. 12). The whole human race belongs to God by virtue of creation. This fact must be made known to all men.

Fourth, Jehovah is the God of moral order, therefore of judgment: "Let the skies pour down righteousness ... I the LORD have created it" (v. 8). There is only one moral order in the world and that is the order established by God. And he is therefore the only judge.

Fifth, Jehovah is the God of history: "Ask me of things to come" (v. 11). "Who hath declared this from ancient time? Have not I the LORD?" (v. 21). God shapes the history of mankind and directs it toward the final fulfillment of his plan. This is the biblical philosophy of history, which lends great support to world evangelization.

Sixth, Jehovah is the God of revelation: "I have not spoken in secret" (v. 19). God has not left the knowledge of him to the secrecy of the subtle reasonings of the wise, but has manifested it through the prophets for all men.

Seventh, Jehovah is the God of salvation for all men: "Look unto me, and be ye saved, all the ends of the earth" (v. 22).

Eighth, Jehovah is the Lord of all men: "Unto me every knee shall bow" (v. 23).

This is a microscopic presentation of almost the whole of Christian doctrine. All these universal claims of God require worldwide action in evangelism and missions.

The Universality of God's Plan of Salvation. In the minds of many of the prophets, the scope of God's plan of salvation certainly went beyond Israel and included the Gentiles. The prophet Isaiah said, "Neither let the son of the stranger that hath joined himself to the LORD speak, saying, the LORD hath utterly separated me from his people" (Is. 56:3). The prophet Zephaniah prophesied that all nations will call upon the name of God: "I will give to the people purified lips that all of them may call on the name of the LORD" (Zeph. 3:9). The concept of purification was no longer exclusive with the people of Israel. The prophet Malachi made it clear that the right of worshiping God was going to be bestowed upon the Gentiles: "From the rising of the sun even unto the going down of the same my name shall be great among the Gentiles; and in every place incense shall be offered unto my name, and a pure offering, . . . saith the LORD of hosts" (Mal. 1:11).

The development of the concept of the universality of God's plan of salvation in the prophecies of the Old Testament can be arranged in the following order of degree:

First, the title of *the people of God* will be widened in its application to include all nations who were at one time "strangers." The prophet Hosea said, "I will say to them which were not my people, Thou art my people; and they shall say, Thou art my God" (Hos. 2:23).

Second, the once closed house of God will be opened to all nations, who will rejoice with the people of Israel in the praise of God. The house of worship will no longer be the peculiar privilege of the chosen people. It was against this background that the prophet Isaiah said, "His rest [house] shall be glorious" (Is. 11:10).

Third, the Messiah's flag of love and protection will be flung over all nations. He will no longer be a national savior but Savior and King of the whole earth. The prophet Isaiah declared that "there shall be a root of Jesse [Messiah], which shall stand for an ensign of the people; to it shall the Gentiles seek" (Is. 11:10).

Fourth, nations will be partakers of God's forgiveness of sin. The grace of purification will be granted to the Gentiles as much as to the people of Israel. The prophet Isaiah said, "And he will destroy in this mountain the face of the covering cast over all the people, and the vail that is spread over all nations. He will swallow up death in victory; and the Lord GOD will wipe away tears from off all faces. And the rebuke of his people shall be taken away from off all the earth. . . . for the LORD hath spoken it" (Is. 25:7-8). The redeemed people of all nations will commune with God with clean lips.

Fifth, the Gentiles will turn away from their ways of iniquity and glorify God (Is. 66:19).

Sixth, people of the ends of the earth will be taught of God's truth: "And the isles shall wait for his law" (Is. 42:4).

Seventh, the redeemed of God in the whole world will walk in the light of God: "I will make my judgment to rest for a light of the people [Gentiles]" (Is. 51:4).

Eighth, not only will the Gentiles join the people of God but they also will be found in the leadership of the people of God: They will be priests and Levites. "I will also take of them [Gentiles] for priests and for Levites, saith the LORD" (Is. 66:21). This concept was far too advanced for the average Israelite to understand.

All this was going to be done through the instrumentality of the people of God. It was the prophet Zechariah who used the clearest words to delineate the mission of Israel. He said, "It shall come to pass, that as ye were a curse among the heathen, O house of Judah, and house of Israel; so will I save you, and ye shall be a blessing" (Zech. 8:13). Zechariah pointed out the failure of Israel: They were a curse. How miserably they failed in their mission! But God did not give them up; he was going to save them and help them carry out their mission—to be a blessing to the whole world.

The Universality of the Messianic Kingdom. The concept of the Messianic kingdom is essential and central in the Old Testament prophecies. Again, the scope of this kingdom far transcends the boundaries of Israel. The idea of mission is intrinsically present in the universality of the Messianic kingdom.

I am going to mention three things about the Messianic kingdom: the King, the capital and the dominion.

The Messianic King. There are two different ideas of the Servant of God in Isaiah: the corporate idea and the individual idea. The former refers to the people of Israel and the latter refers to the Messianic King. The latter is hidden in the former, but the two are clearly distinct from each other. The Jews only recognize the former. They emphasize the former at the expense of the latter. That is why they did not recognize Christ when he came to the world. Both are inseparably bound up with the concept of missions. The Servant of God was entrusted with the mission of bringing the nations to know God and enjoy his blessings. On the other hand, the Messianic King as the servant and missioner is a most significant and profound concept in the sublime prophecies of Isaiah, and it is one of the wonders of God's plan of salvation. The Messianic King had a mission the fulfillment of which involves suffering and sacrifice on his part. As the Servant, the King's "visage was so marred more than any man, and his form more than the sons of men" (Is. 52:14). The prophet Isaiah also emphatically pointed out that the sufferings of this Servant-King "sprinkle many nations," which means that the efficacy of his sacrifice reaches the whole world.

The Messiah is King-Servant-Prophet. His role as prophet is by no means the slightest of his offices: "He shall be exalted and extolled, and be very high. . . . Kings shall shut their mouths at him: for that which had not been told them shall they see; and that which they had not heard shall they consider" (Is. 52:13-15). To the Gentiles the Messiah will be their light—the light of truth, wisdom and judgment. This light was to be sent to the ends of the earth by the people of God.

The Messiah will be ruler of all nations. His kingdom will cover the whole earth. God said, "Behold, I have given him [the Davidic King] for a witness to the people, a leader and commander to the people. Behold, thou shalt call a nation that thou knowest now, and nations that knew not thee shall run unto thee because of the LORD thy God" (Is. 55:4-5). It is clearly pointed out here that the Messiah will be King of Nations, not merely King of Israel. The lordship of this King should be proclaimed throughout the width and breadth of the globe through evangelism and missions.

The Capital of the Messianic Kingdom. Jerusalem as the capital of the Messianic kingdom will be the center of blessing for the whole world. Psalm 87 presents to us a precious and beautiful picture of the world significance of Jerusalem: "The LORD loveth the gates of Zion more than all the dwellings of Jacob. . . . I will make mention of Rahab and Babylon to them that know me: behold Philistia, and Tyre, with Ethiopia; this man was born there [in Jerusalem]. And of Zion it shall be said, This and that man was born in her" (Ps. 87:2-5). This means that Zion, or Jerusalem, is the spiritual fatherland of many Gentile peoples. Then the psalmist goes on to describe the joy and blessings of the sons and daughters of Jerusalem: "As well the singers as the players on instruments shall be there [and they shall say]: all my springs [of joy] are in thee [Jerusalem]" (Ps. 87:7). The prophet Isaiah sings of Jerusalem as the center of Messianic blessings: The Gentiles shall come to thy light, and kings to the brightness of thy rising" (Is. 60:3).

The Dominion of the Messianic Kingdom. The prophet Zechariah cries in prophecy, "Behold, thy King cometh unto thee: he is just, and having salvation; lowly, and riding upon an ass, and upon a colt the foal of an ass. . . . His dominion shall be from sea even to sea, and from the river even to the ends of the earth" (Zech. 9:9-10). Evidently this wonderful prophecy has been fulfilled in Jesus Christ, who entered Jerusalem on a colt and whose spiritual dominion is from sea to sea, even to the ends of the earth. All this has been brought about by God through missions. Even as God has done it in the past, he is doing it at the present time.

The Prophets' Missionary Visions

In the prophetic books of the Old Testament, we find eschatological images of the final fulfillment of God's plan of salvation. These images are wonderful missionary visions: (1) the vision of a sea filled with the water of the knowledge of the glory of God (Hab. 2:14); (2) the vision of tamed wild beasts living together in peace—the wolf with the lamb, the leopard with the kid, the calf with the lion (Is. 11:6); (3) the vision of a rich feast on top of the mountain of the Lord (Is. 25:6); (4) the vision of the house of God raised above all mountains with people of all nations flowing to it (Is. 2:2).

These four visions represent four precious ideas: the knowledge of the truth of God spreading to the ends of the earth; the peace and love of God prevailing in the whole world over hatred and war; all nations invited to the feast of the rich grace of God; the presence of God in all races of mankind. This is the inspired ideal of the prophets, which will one day be fulfilled when the King comes back. But before the leading to the coming of the King, you and I have the privilege of carrying out the mission of blessing to the ends of the world.

Crises in the History of Israel Regarding Israel's Mission

The First Crisis: Abraham's Haran. Let us begin with Abraham. Abraham, as great as he was in faith, had his failure. He stopped short of God's calling when he discontinued his journey at Haran, halfway between his native country and the land where God wanted him to go. But, thanks to God, he only stopped there for a limited period of time. God called him again and he rose and pressed on.

In regard to Abraham's experience, let us notice two things which are of special importance.

In the first place, God asked him to get out of his own country, and from his kindred, and from his father's house, to a land he would show him (Gen. 12:1). That was an absolute condition which Abraham had to fulfill before he could reach a place where he was blessed and became a blessing to others. We are reminded here that we must be willing to make a radical departure from our accustomed way of life (which is so natural and so easy on our self-centeredness) and move on to a new path of life which is rightly called "the land of milk and honey" because it is spiritually fruitful.

Abraham was faced with a tremendous choice—a choice on which hung not only his destiny but also the destiny of a nation and, indeed, the destiny of the whole world. It was a most serious crisis. Abraham made the right choice and obeyed the call of God.

The change of his name from *Abram* to *Abraham* is a beautiful symbol of the transformation that took place in his life. Abram means "exalted father," but Abraham means "father of nations." This change of name indicates that the center of Abraham's life moved from himself to his relationship with others.

Abraham's offering of his only beloved son as a sacrifice to God was the peak of his life of self-negation. Immediately following this selfless act, God reiterated his great promise to him: "In thy seed shall all the nations of the earth be blessed" (Gen. 22:16-18).

In the second place, there were at least two conditions which Abraham had to fulfill before he could accept the call of God and become a vessel of blessing.

The first condition was that Abraham must understand that his own blessing and the blessing of other people are linked together as one thing. They can never be separated; he could not take the one and leave the other. The two form one organic whole. Abraham did understand this twofold nature of the call of God, and he obeyed. God always hides his blessings for us in our willingness to be a blessing to others. God hides his love in his commandment. God hides his rich rewards in our obedience. God hides his best treasures in a self-denying life. God's ways are higher than our ways. Christ says, "Give, and it shall be given unto you; good measure, pressed down, and shaken together, and running over, shall men give into your bosom" (Lk. 6:38).

The second condition was that Abraham must have faith before he could accept the call of God to be a blessing because trial and hardship are involved in such a life. Many times in his life things seemed to go against the promises of God. God's promises to him had to do with three things: his seed, the promised land and the nations. But he was greatly tried in all these three aspects. God promised to give him the land of Canaan, but he arrived there only to find it already occupied by others; God promised to give him a son, but he had to wait for twenty-five years; God promised that he would be a blessing to nations, but he actually brought trouble to the land of Gerar (Gen. 20:1). In view of all this, he simply had to have faith before he could stand firm in the face of all these trials. Today we, too, must have faith before we can have victory over all the forces that assemble to drive us away from the path of blessing.

The Second Crisis: Wandering in the Wilderness. The second great crisis in the history of Israel rose when the Israelites began their wandering in the wilderness. They had crossed the Red Sea and had been delivered from the land of slavery. But that was only the beginning of their salvation. They were saved, but saved for what? Certainly they were not saved in order to wander in the wilderness. They were wandering away their lives. What a tragedy! Unless they stopped wandering and crossed the River Jordan, their salvation from Egypt would be contentless. They would never inherit the Land of Promise and fulfill God's plan. They wandered for forty years in the wilderness; they squandered away most of the years of their lives in barrenness of life. What a heartache! The wandering life is a life without goal and purpose. It never gets anywhere. It will end in bitter emptiness.

But the grace of God did not fail. There were Joshua and Caleb and those who followed them in crossing the River Jordan, and they inherited the Land of Promise.

The Third Crisis: The Election of Man as King in Place of God. The third crisis in the history of Israel took place when the people faced the issue of choosing between Jehovah and man as their king. At this most critical hour, they made the tragic decision of enthroning man instead of God. Man taking the place of God always results in self-centeredness, which is the root of all sin and miseries. When man rebels against God, he in fact rebels against his own good. In rejecting the rule of God, man takes the only alternative left for him—the alternative of falling under the tyranny of self. The situation of man today is essentially the same as 3,000 years ago when the people of Israel made their tragic mistake. Modern man is trying his best to get rid of God, and he has indeed set up his own kings under whose reign he suffers merciless slavery. There is the king of sex, the king of drugs, the king of violence, the king of meaninglessness of life. Man has become a curse and a burden to himself as well as to others, instead of a blessing. Today, under the cloak of freedom, man is suffering slavery. One of the popular slogans today is that man has come of age and no longer needs God. Yes, God is dead and man is free—free to fall under the yoke of standardless subjectivism and self-centeredness, which promises to become the worst tyranny known yet.

The Fourth Crisis: Fleeing from the Errand of Peace. God in his grace planned to save the people of the Gentile city of Nineveh, and he revealed his mind to Jonah. God commissioned Jonah as a missionary to take the message of reconciliation to Nineveh, but, being preoccupied by a narrow and misled patriotism, Jonah fled away from his mission and went to Tarshish instead of Nineveh. This attitude on the part of Jonah shows how ignorant the people of Israel were about their mission. It seems that by this time in the history of the chosen people, the significance of God's calling to Abraham had more or less completely gone out of their minds. It is a great tragedy that Jonah as a prophet should have lost sight of the main purpose of all God's plan.

Jonah was a man of contradictions: His name Jonah means a dove, which is symbolic of peace, yet he refused to be a messenger of peace; he was a prophet who should understand the will of God, obey it and help others obey it, yet he acted contrary to the explicit commandment of God; he told the people on board the boat that he knew Jehovah, who was the Lord of heaven and earth, yet he would not allow Jehovah to be the Lord of his own life; he said that he knew the love of God, yet he acted as if the love of God were nonexistent.

God graciously intervened, and Jonah learned a great lesson

through suffering. But he did not really learn the lesson well until he saw the heart of God as recorded in the fourth chapter of Jonah. In this light, we can easily see that the book of Jonah is one of the greatest books of the Bible because it picked up the lost thread of Israel's mission. It seems that suffering is almost indispensable in the hand of God as a corrective measure for his constantly erring people both in the Old Testament and in the New. As we all well remember, the early church began to spread the gospel outside Jerusalem when it was persecuted. Does outreach have to come in that way? Do we have to suffer before we obey the will of God?

The Fifth Crisis: Tower-building instead of Bridge-building. In the minds of David and Solomon the building of the Temple was meant to be a bridge—a bridge for making known the grace and truth of God to the whole world. Solomon, in his dedication prayer for the Temple, definitely included the Gentiles in the recipients of blessings from the house of God (2 Chron. 6:32-33).

But to the people of Israel this bridge became a tower—the tower of national pride. The Bible tells us that following man's estrangement from God, he began to be interested in tower-building, of which the Tower of Babel was the prototype. Man wants to exalt and glorify himself by building himself towers of fame. As a result, there are so many high towers that the view of Calvary is completely blocked out. There are so many tower-builders and so few bridge-builders that God has a hard time in finding people who are willing to be blessing-bearers. In the history of Israel, the Temple became more of a symbol of national self-centeredness than of blessing to others. Are we tower-builders or bridge-builders?

The Sixth Crisis: Dissociation of Election from Its Purpose. The people of Israel were proud of their election as the chosen people of God, but they forgot they were elected for a purpose—the purpose of blessing the whole world through them. They took the privilege of election and laid aside its purpose. This was a fatal dissociation which hindered the plan of God. As a matter of fact, the people of Israel were laid aside by God because they laid aside their mission.

The apostle Paul has made it clear to us in Romans 11 that the people of Israel lost their privilege exactly because of this failure and that God, in his infinite wisdom, made use of their failure to bless the whole world by putting the church in their place. Shall we commit the same fatal mistake? If we believe that we as Christians are the elect people of God, shall we, too, take the privilege and lay aside the responsibility?

When the apostle Paul talked about predestination, he did so against a background of active evangelism. The biblical doctrine of predestination is not merely the statement that some people are preordained by God to eternal life, but it is that statement plus active evangelism which is its living context. Truth taken out of its living context is no longer truth. The doctrine of election as related to the people of Israel and the doctrine of predestination as related to Christians have one basic thing in common, namely, both of them mean election and mission.

The Seventh Crisis: Esther's Great Decision. The destiny of the Israelite people hinged on Esther's decision—whether she chose to care for her own privilege and pleasure in the Persian palace or preferred risking her life for the good of her people. It was only too easy for her to decide on the former, as we often do, but the strong and resolute voice of one man of God influenced her and guided her thinking, and she made the right decision. Her soul was shaken by the challenge of Mordecai: "And who knowest whether thou art come to the kingdom for such a time as this" (Esther 4:14)? She began to think of her responsibility in the light of her privileged position as queen of the empire, and that altered the whole fate of the people of Israel. Yes, it is not exaggerating to say that the average Christian's having a right understanding of the balance between privilege and responsibility and acting thereupon will change the whole course of the church of Christ today. Thank God for having graciously raised up a Mordecian voice of warning and challenge for every generation so that all Christians may be reminded of their mission.

I think I am justified in saying that this convention is a major force in the movings of God along the line of carrying out his worldwide mission. May God raise up many missioners in this convention to further his mission of blessing near and far.

THE BASIS OF MISSIONS IN THE GOSPELS: CHRIST AND MISSIONS

PHILIP
TENG

This morning we have come to the second subtitle: The Basis of Missions in the Gospels, that is, Christ and Missions. My talk is divided into three parts: (1) Christ as a missionary, (2) the kingdom of God and missions and (3) the Great Commission and missions.

Christ as a Missionary

The Gospels are records of the redeeming love of God through Christ. Love is always a mission because it reaches out for its own fulfillment. The divine mission of God has a Missionary and he is Christ. A missionary is "one who is sent" to accomplish a mission. Does Christ think of himself as a missionary? Yes, he mentions 39 times in the Gospel of John alone that he is sent by God. But this Divine Missionary also sends us to be missionaries. He says, "As my Father has sent me, even so send I you" (Jn. 20:21). He is the Proto-missionary, and as such he has set an example for us to follow. It is therefore very important for us to find out how he acted as a missionary. Our findings will point out the right path for us to follow.

I wish to discuss six points regarding Christ as a missionary: (1) Christ's goals, (2) Christ's missionary methods, (3) Christ's missionary attitude, (4) Christ's missionary spirit, (5) Christ's missionary commitment and (6) Christ's missionary field.

What Were Christ's Goals? First, he came to seek and save the lost: "The Son of Man came to seek and to save that which was lost" (Lk. 19:10). Christ came to the world to bring the lost back to God and heal the estrangement between man and God. This is the task of reconciliation. In effecting this reconciliation, "He gave his life a ransom for many" (Mk. 10:45).

Second, he came to give the abundant life: "I am come that they might have life, and that they might have it more abundantly" (Jn. 10:10). This is the task of imparting and vigorizing spiritual life in believers. Christ did not come just to settle the legal aspect, so to speak, of our salvation but also to give us a new life which is united with his own. Christ did not come just to teach us what is good and what is bad. His is not merely a teaching mission but essentially a life-giving mission. The life that he gives has all its native properties for fruit-bearing. Moral goodness and excellence are fruits of this new life. Mankind has had many excellent teachers of morality but only one redeemer and life-giver.

Third, he came to show the Father: "He that hath seen me hath seen the Father" (Jn. 14:9). "No one hath seen God at any time; the only begotten Son, which is in the bosom of the Father, he hath declared him" (Jn. 1:18). In the incarnation of Christ, the God of eternity entered into time and the infinite intersected the finite, which is a great mystery to our minds.

But more important to us is that the incarnation of Christ shows us in concrete terms the ineffable majesty, beauty and perfection of God. The life and work of Christ reveal to us the true image of God—so much so that Christ said to Thomas, "He that hath seen me hath seen the Father." We see the light of the knowledge of the glory of God in the face of Christ (2 Cor. 4:6). Christ's was the great mission of reflecting the glorious image of

God. It is not only Christ's mission but also ours. We Christians are to bear the likeness of Christ which is the express image of God. Paul says in Romans 8:29, "Whom God did foreknow, he also did predestinate to be conformed to the image of his Son." Our conformity to the likeness of Christ is so important that it is called by Paul the predestinated will of God.

Fourth, he came to fulfill the law: "Think not that I am come to destroy the law, or the prophets: I am not come to destroy, but to fulfil" (Mt. 5:17). Christ came to fulfill the law in two ways: First, he obeyed the law in all his earthly life; second, he bore our failure in keeping the law and paid our debt to the law on the cross. He did not pay our debt to Satan as some people think, because we do not owe Satan anything. But we do owe the debt of obeying the law of God. So Paul says, "Christ hath redeemed us from the curse of the law, being made a curse for us" (Gal. 3:13). Christ has also given us power to keep the spirit, not the letter, of the law.

Fifth, he came to set people free from sin: Jesus said, "If the Son shall make you free, ye shall be free indeed" (Jn. 8:36). "For this purpose the Son of God was manifested, that he might destroy the works of the devil" (1 Jn. 3:8). Since the work of Satan is sin, Christ came to destroy sin and save us from sin.

Christ as prophet saves us from the ignorance of sin; Christ as priest saves us from the guilt of sin as well as from the root of sin; Christ as king saves us from the power of sin.

Christ's remedy for sin is therefore the cross, which means identification: a twofold identification—objective identification and subjective identification. *Objective identification* means that Christ identified himself with us on the cross, that is, he died on the cross for us. This is the doctrine of the substitutional death of Christ. *Subjective identification* means that we identify ourselves with Christ on the cross, that is, we die with Christ on the cross which means self-crucifixion or self-negation. Self-negation deals with self-centeredness, which is the root of all sin. In a word, objective identification, which is the substitutional death of Christ, saves us from the guilt of sin, and subjective identification, which means self-negation, saves us from the root of sin.

Sixth, he came to reveal truth: "For this cause came I into the world, that I should bear witness unto the truth" (Jn. 18:37). Christ not only revealed truth to us, he is truth. Christ is truth in two senses: First, he is truth because his life is the perfect embodiment of truth; second, he is truth not because he conforms to truth as something independent of him and normative to him, but because truth emanates from him.

Moreover, the fact that Christ is truth indicates that truth is not merely something intellectual in nature, but something living—living relationship with God, with people, with things and with oneself. Christians are not students of truth as theories, but they are disciples of the living Word of God which is Christ A student studies books, but a disciple learns of his master and teacher.

The above are the goals of the mission of Christ as explicitly stated by himself. Christ's mission is, in a secondary sense, our mission. Christ said to his disciples, "He that believeth on me, the works that I do shall he do also" (Jn. 14:12). Our mission, therefore, is primarily the tasks of reconciliation, of bringing others into new life and into discipleship of the living Word of God, of showing the likeness of Christ, of witnessing to the grace of forgiveness of sin and to the power over sin which we can possess through faith, of leading people into a self-denying and thereby a fruit-bearing life.

What Were Christ's Missionary Methods? I am going to mention two. First, identification: Christ became man, living among men, and as Son of Man he fulfilled his mission. He did not use a substitute, but he came to the world himself. He did not abhor the womb of a virgin, the manger, the hard life of a carpenter, the sickening association with degraded sinners, the hatred and insult of men, and finally the agony of Gethsemane and the suffering of Calvary. He went through all this in order to save us. Paul sums up all this in three beautiful verses:

[Jesus Christ] who, being in the form of God, thought it not robbery to be equal with God: but made himself of no reputation, and took upon him the form of a servant, and was made in the likeness of men: And being found in fashion as a man, he humbled himself, and became obedient unto death, even

the death of the cross. (Phil. 2:6-8)

We notice five things in these verses which Christ did in his identification with us: (1) He willingly gave up rights and privileges which belonged to him. (2) He humbled himself in spirit. (3) He identified himself entirely with those whom he wanted to serve. (4) He obeyed the will of God. (5) He died to himself and lived for others.

These five points are the secret of Christ's success in his mission, and they are also the secret of the success of any missionary of Christ.

Second, exemplification: Christ lived his teaching. The uniqueness of Christ as a teacher lies in the fact that he practiced his words. He taught his disciples to humble themselves and serve one another, and he washed their feet. He taught them the lesson of prayerfulness, and he prayed at dawn and at night, in company and in solitude. He taught them the lesson of forgiving enemies, and he prayed for those who nailed him to the cross. Yes, he is the greatest teacher in human history.

What Was Christ's Missionary Attitude? He said, "The Son of man came not to be ministered unto, but to minister" (Mk. 10:45). Christ did not come to the world with a scepter in his hand, but with a yoke on his neck. When the Son of Man under a yoke calls us to come to him and share his yoke, we are moved, and we readily accept his calling and count it a great privilege to serve with him.

It was in connection with service that Christ gave his teaching on true greatness which has five significant points for our edification: (1) Christians should have a totally different attitude in life from other people. Christ said, "Ye know that they which are accounted to rule over the Gentiles exercise lordship over them; and their great ones exercise authority upon them. But so shall it not be among you" (Mk. 10:42-43). (2) True greatness is measured by service (Mk. 10:43). (3) God honors humility which produces service (Mt. 23:12). (4) A price must be paid for true greatness (Mk. 10:38). (5) Christ is the best example for our service (Mk. 10:45).

What Was Christ's Missionary Spirit? "Not as I will, but as thou wilt," Jesus said (Mt. 26:39). There was a great agony in the heart of Christ, the agony of struggling between the will of God and his own will. Out of this struggle came his glorious resolution: "Not as I will but as Thou wilt!" Christ did not seek self-fulfillment, but the fulfillment of the will of God.

This is also a real and continual struggle in the life of every missionary. A successful and fruitful missionary comes out of it with the battle cry: "Not as I will but as Thou wilt!"

What Was Christ's Missionary Commitment? He was "obedient unto death" (Phil. 2:8). It is recorded in Mark that when Jesus went up to Jerusalem for the last time, there was something in his face that made his disciples "amazed" and "afraid" (Mk. 10:32). What was it? The Bible does not tell us what it was, but, gathering from the context, I believe it is quite clear that there was an extraordinary air of determinedness and firmness in the expression of the face of Christ which deeply impressed his disciples and created a sense of awe in their minds. The Bible says here that Jesus went ahead of his disciples on their way to Jerusalem. Evidently there was something unusual about Jesus walking before them, and the logical explanation for it is that the pace of Jesus was unconsciously quickened by his resolute decision to accept suffering and death in obedience to the will of God.

Finally, What Was Christ's Mission Field? "And other sheep I have, which are not of this fold; them also I must bring, and they shall hear my voice; and there shall be one fold, and one shepherd" (Jn. 10:16). Christ did not limit his mission to the Jews; his fold is open to all nations. He said, "I, if I be lifted up from the earth, will draw all men unto me" (Jn. 12:32).

The Kingdom of God and Missions

A large portion of Christ's teaching is about the kingdom of God. He made it clear that the scope of the kingdom of God is worldwide and not limited to the Jews.

First, Christ teaches that many people shall come from the east, and from the west, and from the north, and from the south and shall sit down feasting in the kingdom of God (Lk. 13:29). The blessings of the kingdom of God are for all the people of the world. The picture of the kingdom of God as a feast is very precious. But evidently an invitation has to be sent out to the nations and the guests must be brought to the feast. This sending and gathering constitutes our mission. The missioners of the king are ordered to go to the east and to the west and to the north and to the south to proclaim the good news of the feast of his kingdom, and gather those who respond to the Great Invitation of the King. Those guests who were "in time past Gentiles in the flesh, who are called Uncircumcision . . . without Christ, being aliens from the commonwealth of Israel, and strangers from the covenants of promise, having no hope, and without God in the world" are now made nigh to God by the blood of Christ (Eph. 2:11-13). The far-off are made nigh; the strangers have become sons; the outsiders are now recipients of the covenants of promise; the hopeless and godless now constitute the feasters in the kingdom of God. What a glorious transformation!

Second, Christ teaches that the Gentiles will not only be among the feasters in the kingdom of God but also will, together with the believing Jews, inherit the kingdom of God (Mt. 21:43). Christ said to Paul in a vision,

> I have appeared unto thee for this purpose: to make thee a minister and a witness both of these things which thou hast seen, and of those things in the which I will appear unto thee; delivering thee from the people, and from the Gentiles, unto whom now I send thee, to open their eyes, and to turn them from darkness to light, and from the power of Satan unto God, that they may receive forgiveness of sins, and inheritance among them which are sanctified by faith that is in me. (Acts 26:16-18)

Christ sent Paul as a missioner to gather the Gentile believers into the inheritance of his kingdom, and today he sends us to do the same thing for all nations.

Third, Christ teaches that "this gospel of the kingdom shall be preached in all the world" (Mt. 24:14). By whom? By missionaries who are gospel-bearers to the ends of the earth. Christ pointed out clearly that the gospel of this kingdom must be preached in all the world before his second coming. We can, therefore, say that the missionaries, or the gospel-bearers, are also heralds of his coming.

The Great Commission and Missions

Missions is the task of carrying out the Great Commission. If all other bases of missions fail, surely the Great Commission alone establishes the logic of missions:

> Go ye therefore, and teach all nations, baptizing them in the name of the Father, and of the Son, and of the Holy Ghost: Teaching them to observe all things whatsoever I have commanded you: and, lo, I am with you alway, even unto the end of the world. (Mt. 28:18-20)

The Recipients of the Great Commission—"Go Ye." Who are the "Ye"? Some Christians say that the Great Commission was given to the apostles alone. That this is not true is readily demonstrated by the following points:

First, the apostles could not possibly accomplish the task of preaching to "every creature" or "all nations" in their lifetime.

Second, if we say that the Great Commission is only meant for the apostles because it was addressed to them, then we must follow by asserting that all of Christ's teaching was only meant for one generation of believers because it was addressed to them! That is evidently not the truth.

Third, we must also remember that the same commission was given for the second time, in different words, to a larger group of disciples than the apostles (Acts 1:8). This fact clearly indicates that the Great Commission was meant for all the followers of Christ.

The inevitable conclusion is that the Great Commission is meant for the apostles as well as for all believers of all generations, including you and me. All of us must have a share in it no matter in what way.

The Nature of the Great Commission—A Commandment to Be Obeyed. The Great Commission is not merely exhortation or advice; it is a commandment. If we are under authority, we simply have to obey. Christians are soldiers, and as soldiers we are expected to obey orders from Christ, our commander-in-chief. We do not treat orders as options and act at our own impulses. Every one of us must in one way or another have a share in passing on the blessing of the gospel to others near and far. It is a test of our obedience to Christ.

The idea of Christ as the Invisible Visitor in our homes is very beautiful and has been popularized by a decorative plate which hangs on the walls of many Christian homes. On the plate are painted these words: "Christ is the invisible visitor in this house and silent listener to every conversation." Many Christians want Christ, but they only want him as a visitor and nothing more. A visitor has to be very careful in what he says and does; he must not say anything or do anything that displeases the host or hostess. Christ as an occasional visitor does not have a say in the managing of the house and he is easily disposed of. But Christ demands lordship in our homes and in our lives: He must take over and have control in everything. It is interesting and significant that the word *savior* is used in relation to Jesus only twenty some times in the New Testament whereas the word *Lord* is used in relation to Jesus over 500 times! The ratio is 1:20, which is surely significant.

If we acknowledge the lordship of Jesus Christ, we must obey his commandments, and one of his most important commandments is the Great Commission.

The Scope of the Great Commission—"Every Creature," "All Nations." Christ commanded his followers to go "into all the world, and preach the gospel to every creature" (Mk. 16:15). They were to be his witnesses "unto the uttermost part of the earth" (Acts 1:8).

We praise God for those messengers of the gospel who, in obedience to the Great Commission, have across the centuries gone into the "regions beyond" with the torch of the love of God at the price of their lives. Today, we in the seventies of the twentieth century, still have our "ends of the earth" where the gospel of Christ has not reached. Today we have the last mile to run in the race of world evangelization, and it is a hard mile which presents a tough challenge to the faithful followers of Christ. The best in us rises to meet this challenge with faith and dedication. Under the grace of God our generation may be the one that has the honor and privilege of crowning the long run of world evangelization.

As the Chairman of the Continuation Committee of the First All-Asia Mission Consultation, I am glad to be able to report to you that more and more churches in Asian countries have been awakened to their missionary responsibilities and wish to join their Western brethren in carrying out the Great Commission. Our goal is to send 200 new missionaries to our mission fields in 1974.

Let us listen to the missionary cry of the prophet Isaiah: "Enlarge the place of thy tent, and let them stretch forth the curtains of thine habitations: spare not, lengthen thy cords, and strengthen thy stakes; for thou shalt break forth on the right hand and on the left" (Is. 54:2-3). Let the chorus of this cry resound in our minds and hearts: "Lengthen thy cords! Lengthen thy cords!"

The Task of the Great Commission. The first task in the Great Commission is to proclaim. The Lord said to his disciples, "Go ye into all the world and preach. . . ." To preach is to proclaim to the world what God has done through Christ. Proclamation is an essential part of the Great Commission. There could be no biblical evangelism without proclamation. "Witness by presence" is good, but it is not enough. Proclamation can take different forms, but it must be there.

The second task in the Great Commission is to convert. The Lord said to his disciples, "Go ye therefore . . . baptising them in the name of the Father, and of the Son, and of the Holy Spirit." Baptism indicates conversion. We are commissioned by Christ to convert people to him—not to the church as an institution. Evangelism without conversion is not biblical evangelism.

The third task in the Great Commission is to disciple. The Lord said to his disciples, "Go ye therefore . . . teach all nations . . . teaching them to observe all things whatsoever I have commanded you." The task of the Great Commission does not end with baptism, but it continues with the ministry of teaching. The Lord has made it very clear in the Great Commission that the purpose of teaching is "to observe all things whatsoever I have commanded you." There is a legitimate distinction between teaching to know and teaching to do. The former is studying while the latter is discipling. The true Christian is a disciple rather than a student. Teaching without discipling is a great failure. The Great Commission moves from proclaiming to converting and then to discipling. Any one of the three links missing is a breach of the Great Commission.

The Procedure of the Great Commission. Acts 1:8 is an integral part of the Great Commission. It teaches us that Jerusalem does have a part in the Great Commission. If Jerusalem is removed, then the Great Commission does not have a start. But we must not end with Jerusalem. There are many Christians and churches that make Jerusalem both the start and the end of their program. They never move beyond Jerusalem. Jerusalem has become their uttermost part of the world. What a small map, what a small vision and what a small heart!

On the other hand, there are those Christians and churches that have neglected their Jerusalem. They think all the time of the uttermost part of the earth and overlook the immediate need around them. The Great Commission commands us to attend to the foreign mission field as well as to the mission field that lies at our threshold.

The Assurance for the Great Commission. The assurance for the Great Commission consists in two factors. First, promise: The Lord promised his disciples that he was going to be with them always. They enjoy his presence most when they are engaged in carrying out the Great Commission. What a precious comfort and encouragement!

Second, authority: The Lord has all power in heaven and in earth, and it was on the basis of this power and authority that he gave the Great Commission to his disciples. This authority guarantees the final success of the Great Commission.

The power and authority of Christ constituted the assurance that the apostles had in their minds about evangelism and missions. They had faith in the person and power of Christ. They knew in whom they believed. For instance, in reading through the First Epistle of John, no one can escape the impression of John's sureness of the Person of Christ. He begins the letter by saying,

That which was from the beginning, which we have heard, which we have seen with our eyes, which we have looked upon, and our hands have handled, of the Word of life; for the life was manifested, and we have seen it, and bear witness . . . that which we have seen and heard declare we unto

you. (1 Jn. 1:1-3)

These accumulated repetitions indicate the absolute sureness that John had in his mind and heart in regard to the Person of Christ, who is the center of his proclamation.

In the case of the apostle Peter, he testified to the reality and truth of his message to the Christians of his day by a vivid reference to his experience with Jesus on the Mount of Transfiguration (2 Pet. 1:18). This blessed memory and assurance made him zealous in evangelism in his efforts to edify the saints of his time.

When we think of the apostles as a group, we are reminded of the scene of their first meeting with the risen Lord (Jn. 20:19-21). The first thing the risen Lord did when he appeared to them was to show them his pierced hands and side. And the Bible says, "Then were the disciples glad." Why glad? Those were marks of great tragedy and terrible suffering that had befallen Jesus, their beloved Master. Why glad? They were glad because when they saw his pierced hands and side, they became assured of the reality of the risen Lord. How can you help being glad if you know for sure that your Jesus is the Lord that rose from the dead, victorious over sin, death and Satan?

Please note a very important sequence here: The Lord showed his pierced hands and side to his disciples before he commissioned them for world evangelization. "As my Father hath sent me, even so send I you." Assurance precedes commission. No one wants to be commissioned for a hopeless task. But the disciples gladly accepted the Lord's commission because they knew who gave it to them. I am sure whenever they suffered trials, difficulties and persecution later on in their task of evangelism, they recalled the pierced hands and side which they had seen with their own eyes and were comforted and strengthened. This indelible memory meant two things to them: They were assured of the reality of their message about the risen Lord, and they were constrained by the great love represented by those marks of unspeakable suffering. That is enough for them and enough for us.

The risen Lord said to the disciples, "Peace be unto you." It is interesting to notice that these precious words were repeated in the following verse. I am sure that this repetition is significant.

In these three verses we find three things which happened in immediate succession: the first "peace be unto you," the showing of the pierced hands and side, and the second "peace be unto you." Evidently, the second "peace be unto you" has specially to do with the assurance that came with the showing of the pierced hands and side. Objectively, only the risen Lord can give us real peace; subjectively, only our assurance of the reality of the resurrection of the Lord can produce real peace in our hearts. Who can have peace of heart if he has given his whole life to a cause in which he has only a shaky confidence? But all of us can dedicate our lives with rejoicing to the cause of Christ whose final victory is absolutely assured.

The apostle John had an interesting and significant experience which is recorded in Revelation. He was shown the vision of the final victory of Christ. In chapter 4 he sees God on his throne with the whole plan of salvation unfolded before him, and in this glorious vision, a cry of victory pealed in the sky, "Behold, the Lion of the tribe of Juda, the Root of David, hath prevailed" (Rev. 5:5). What a glorious proclamation! John looked around expecting to see a strong lion, but instead he saw a lamb that was slain. Two opposite images are united in God's wonderful plan: a lion and a lamb. The lion is the lamb; the lamb is the lion! The power of God's lion lies exactly in the weakness of God's lamb that was slain. The New English Bible talks in Revelation 5:6 of "a lamb with the marks of slaughter upon him." Evidently, these marks refer to the marks in his pierced hands and feet. John saw the lamb take over the scroll with his pierced hand. It is the pierced hand that can open the sealed scroll of the plan of God and bring it to pass; it is the pierced hand that touched John when he fell on the ground as dead and raised him up; it is the pierced hand that holds the key of hell and death (1:17b); it is the pierced hand that holds the key of David, which opens and no man shuts (3:7); it is the pierced hand that holds the seven stars which are the leaders of the seven churches. In a word, it is the pierced hand that can carry through the whole plan of God.

When John saw this vision, I am sure, his whole outlook was changed. He took heart in face of terrible persecution; all the things that he had suffered for Christ began to take on a new meaning and became precious to him.

It is interesting to notice in Revelation 1:12 that John "turned around" and saw a vision of the Lord in glory. Indeed, we have to turn from our outward situation and look to the Lord before we can have a new vision, and this vision will turn everything around. It always does us good to turn away from our immediate circumstances and take a look at the victorious Lord who holds everything in his hand.

We all remember that after the apostles were threatened by the authorities of the city of Jerusalem, they went back to their own company and lifted their voices to God with one accord and said,

> Lord, thou art God, which hast made heaven, and earth, and the sea, and all that in them is: who by the mouth of thy servant David hast said, Why did the heathen rage, and the people imagine vain things? The kings of the earth stood up, and the rulers gathered together against the Lord, and against his Christ. For of a truth against thy holy child Jesus, whom thou hast anointed, both Herod, and Pontius Pilate, with the Gentiles, and the people of Israel, were gathered together, for to do whatsoever thy hand and thy counsel determined before to be done. And now, Lord, behold their threatenings: and grant unto thy servants that with all boldness they may speak thy word. . . . And when they had prayed, the place was shaken where they were assembled together; and they were all filled with the Holy Spirit, and they spake the word of God with boldness. (Acts 4:24-31)

Here the apostles were sure of three things: First, God is the Maker of heaven and earth, and everything is in his control; second, God foretold what was going to happen, and it happened; and third, God is going to carry through his plan. This threefold assurance resulted in joy and boldness. As they prayed with this assurance, God echoed their faith by shaking the place where they were assembled.

Boldness is what we need today—boldness to proclaim the gospel of the all-sufficiency of Christ in a cynical and humanistic age; boldness to ask for greater things to be done for God;

boldness to make large plans for God; boldness to make greater sacrifice for his kingdom.

But this boldness comes from assurance. The Lord called his disciples "a little flock." This little flock of the apostles were naturally afraid of the formidable task before them, but they took courage when they heard the Lord say to them, "Fear not, little flock; for it is your Father's good pleasure to give you the kingdom" (Lk. 12:32). They were comforted and emboldened because they knew what was going to happen: They were going to inherit the kingdom of God.

The apostle Paul, writing to Timothy from a prison in Rome, said, "I suffer trouble . . . even unto bonds; but the word of God is not bound" (2 Tim. 2:9). Paul looked beyond his bonds and saw the spread wings of the gospel. He was sure of the expansion of the church under the power of God. Then he went on to say, "If we suffer, we shall also reign with him" (v. 12). It sounds strange to talk about reigning in a prison, but all this becomes normal when seen in the light of his assurance. Paul expresses the same assurance in Philippians,

> But I would ye should understand, brethren, that the things which happened unto me have fallen out rather unto the furtherance of the gospel; so that my bonds in Christ are manifest in all the palace, and in all other places; and many of the brethren in the Lord, waxing confident by my bonds, are much more bold to speak the word without fear. (Phil. 1:12-14)

Even as all things work together for good for those who love God so do all things work together for good for the furtherance of the gospel. Paul was faced with persecution and trials at Corinth, but God said to him, "Be not afraid, but speak, and hold not thy peace: for I am with thee, and no man shall set on thee to hurt thee: for I have much people in this city" (Acts 18:9-10). Paul was assured of the presence of God in his ministry at Corinth, and he knew that God had many people in that city and that they were going to be saved. So he took heart and continued his faithful work to the end.

In regard to world evangelization, the Lord said to his disciples that his gospel would be preached in all the world (Mt.

24:14). These words all sounded incredible at the time when they were spoken, but they have been wonderfully fulfilled today before our own eyes. God has seen to it that it is done. He has raised up faithful Christians as his instruments to carry out his plan. Even our faithfulness is a work of his faithfulness in fulfilling his promises.

The assurance of the apostles is also ours. Jesus Christ our risen Lord stands behind the Great Commission which he has given us. Let us march on with assurance and dedication from victory to victory until the dawning of the glorious day of consummation of God's plan of salvation.

THE BASIS OF MISSIONS IN ACTS: THE HOLY SPIRIT AND MISSIONS

PHILIP
TENG

This morning we have come to the third subtitle: The Basis of Missions in Acts, that is, The Holy Spirit and Missions. My message is arranged under five headings: (1) The Holy Spirit as author and finisher of missions, (2) the Holy Spirit as promoter of missions, (3) the Holy Spirit as power for missions, (4) the Holy Spirit as strategist for missions and (5) the Holy Spirit as supplier for missions.

The Holy Spirit as Author and Finisher of Missions

The Lord committed to his followers the task of evangelizing the world. But clearly and emphatically he told them that they had power to fulfill this Great Commission only when they had received the Holy Spirit: "Ye shall receive power, after that the Holy Ghost is come upon you: and ye shall be witnesses unto me both in Jerusalem, and in all Judaea, and in Samaria, and unto the uttermost part of the earth" (Acts 1:8).

Power is, in every sphere of work, the one all-important requisite. Even more this is true with the church's mission, for we "wrestle not against flesh and blood, but against principalities, against powers, against the rulers of the darkness of this world, against spiritual wickedness in high places" (Eph. 6:12). We need a supernatural power against a supernatural enemy, and only the Holy Spirit can supply this power. It is interesting to note that of all the "armor of God" which Paul speaks of in Ephesians 6, the "sword of the Spirit" is the only offensive piece without which you can never win a battle. Faith without work is dead, as the body without the spirit is dead. The form of godliness without power is dead; worship without spirit and truth is dead; giving without love is dead; oratory without unction is dead; the letter without the spirit is dead; and a missionary apparatus without the power of the Holy Spirit is dead. The Lord thought so much of this "power from on high" that he even forbade his disciples to begin their mission before they were equipped with this Divine Supply. How can we afford to think differently from the Lord?

In speaking of the Holy Spirit the Lord said something which was too much for the disciples to take in, something they thought hardly sensible. He actually said, "Verily, verily, I say unto you, He that believeth on me, the works that I do shall he do also; and greater works than these shall he do; because I go unto my Father" (Jn. 14:12). They could not understand these amazing words at the time, but later they all learned to know that they were true. The Holy Spirit was going to mean greater efficiency than even Christ's presence in the flesh had meant to them before. Christ called the Holy Spirit "another comforter" (Jn. 14:16). The word *another* indicates that the Holy Spirit was going to be to the disciples all that the Lord Jesus had been to them previously. Not only that, but also through this "another comforter" they would be enabled to do greater works than Jesus himself had done! There is no "going away" with him, and there is no limit to his presence. Another All-Sufficiency for them!

We can never overestimate the importance of the Holy Spirit. He was the center of the Lord's last discourse (Jn. 14—16), and it was none other than the Holy Spirit concerning whom Jesus gave his "last commandment" to his disciples just before his ascension: "Tarry ye in the city of Jerusalem, until ye be endued with power from on high" (Lk. 24:49). We simply cannot brush aside something on which the Lord has laid so much emphasis.

It is, therefore, logical for us to say that missions began with the Holy Spirit. But the significance of the Holy Spirit in regard to missions does not stop here. He is also the finisher of missions.

The supernatural sign of speaking with tongues which accompanied the coming of the Holy Spirit at Pentecost was itself a clear and divinely appointed indication that the power of the Holy Spirit was going to send the gospel to all races and nations where different "tongues" are spoken. We can, therefore, also say that the Holy Spirit is the guarantor of the success of world missions. We clearly see today that this divinely appointed indication has come true: The gospel has been preached in almost all tongues.

The Holy Spirit as Promoter of Missions

The Book of the Acts of the Apostles is really "The Book of the Acts of Jesus through the Apostles by the Holy Spirit." The Holy Spirit took a leading part in every move of the early Church. We see him explicitly at work in all the works of the early church: when the church first broke out in power with 3,000 and 5,000 people convicted and converted on a single occasion; when Peter and the other disciples witnessed boldly in the face of persecution; when the early Christians overcame selfishness and gave more than liberally to the Lord's work (Acts 4:32-37); when the first martyrdom took place, showing glorious victory over persecution and vengeance; when the gospel of salvation reached the first Gentile family in the city of Caesarea (Acts 11:12); when the message of the forgiveness of sin began to spread to Ethiopia and Africa through Philip speaking to the powerful eunuch (Acts 8:29); when the churches in Judea, Galilee and Samaria came to be firmly established (Acts 9:31); when that wonderful missionary-minded church at Antioch began to be prosperous as a preparation for foreign missions (Acts 11:24); when the mutual love of the first churches was manifested by collecting a love offering through the inspired prophecy of Agabus (Acts 11:28-29); when the Antioch church launched its missionary program (Acts 13:2); when Paul overcame his first enemy of influence in the person of Elymas on the isle of Cyprus (Acts 13:9); when the Apostolic Gospel Team rejoiced over persecution at Antioch of Pisidia (Acts 13:52); when the apostles recognized work among the Gentiles and announced the great Proclamation of Freedom from Law for Gentile Christians at the First Council of Jerusalem (Acts 15:28); when Paul was forbidden to continue his work in Asia Minor and was led into Europe, an act of far-reaching significance (Acts 16:6-10); when leaders were chosen to look after an indigenous church at Ephesus (Acts 20:26).

Behind all these important events and movements of the early church, the Holy Spirit was the real promoting and sustaining power. Moreover, no one can fail to observe that most of the events on this list have to do with missions. Are we, therefore, not justified in saying that the chief concern of the Holy Spirit in the early churches was the promotion and empowerment of missions?

The Holy Spirit as Power for Missions

Outpourings of the Holy Spirit on Missionary Work. There is an important distinction between the infilling of the Holy Spirit and the onfalling, or oncoming, or outpouring, of the Holy Spirit. The former has mainly to do with depth of spiritual quality and character and with power in service, whereas the latter is a sovereign act of God to indicate the ushering in of a new era or the beginning of a new movement or expansion. The outpouring of the Holy Spirit happened only four times in the book of Acts—with 2:3 compare 2:18; 8:15-18; 10:44-45; 19:6. Each of these was accompanied by supernatural signs.

It is most revealing that all four times were related to missions: The first time was the coming of the Holy Spirit at Pentecost, and the Lord referred to it as the empowering for world missions (Acts 1:8); the second time was when the gospel reached the first non-Jewish city of Samaria; the third took place when Peter was sent by the Holy Spirit to preach to the first Gentile family, that of Cornelius in the city of Caesarea; and finally, the fourth time came about when Paul broke into new ground, showing clearly the distinction between the gospel of Jesus and the teaching of John the Baptist (Acts 19:1-6). These are facts which show how concerned about and how related the Holy Spirit is to missions.

The Empowerment of the Holy Spirit for Fruitfulness in Missions. When Peter was filled with the Holy Spirit, he preached and 3,000 souls were converted. It was not the number of decisions that counted, for we are all familiar with the notorious fact that there is a shocking discrepancy between the number of decisions made at campaigns and real conversions. It was the quality of such a large number of new converts that showed the power of the Holy Spirit: "And they continued steadfastly in the apostles' doctrine and fellowship, and in breaking of bread, and in prayers" (Acts 2:42).

Barnabas was filled with the Holy Spirit, and "much people was added unto the Lord" (Acts 11:24). Not unto the church, but unto the Lord. That must mean true conversions. There were both Jews and Gentiles among them. As a result, a prosperous and spiritually minded church was established.

Down through the centuries there have been amazing instances of the rapidity of results under the power of the Holy Spirit. Let us take a few examples. In the ninety-six years following 1811, there were over a million converts in West Polynesia. In Burma, during the first eighty years of evangelistic work, an average of one new convert was baptized every three hours around the clock, and one in ten of such converts became an active worker for the Lord. In the Fiji Islands, James Calvert, who went there in time to bury the remains of eighty human victims of a cannibal feast, lived to see crowds of converted savages around the Lord's table for Holy Communion. At the end of the fifty years between 1835 and 1885, 1,300 churches could be counted. In Formosa, Mackay had 1,200 converts at the Lord's table after twelve years' work. Instances like these could be multiplied again and again.

The Empowerment of the Holy Spirit for Missionary Expansion. The Spirit-filled church at Jerusalem expanded along three main routes: by the converted "devout Jews" who were present at the Pentecostal scene and who went back to their own places with the gospel; by the Christians who scattered after the martyrdom of Spirit-filled Stephen and the persecution that followed, and then in turn by the Spirit-filled, Spirit-led ministry of Philip, advancing to Samaria and Ethiopia; by other scattered Christians who took the northern route to Phoenicia, Cyprus and Antioch, and in turn from the Spirit-filled church at Antioch to Asia Minor and Europe. We see the Holy Spirit at work in all these directions.

Church history abounds with illustrations of the empowering of the Spirit. At significant turns in the history of the church, which we may call *hours of travail* before or during the birth of new life or new expansion, we see special phenomena of the manifestation of the power of the Holy Spirit. For instance, at the beginning of the Wesleyan Revival, which influenced the history of England to such a remarkable extent and which, through men like Whitefield, contributed to the Great Awakening in New England under the leadership of Jonathan Edwards, we see a visitation of the power of the Holy Spirit which is sometimes called the Methodist Pentecost. We find these words in John Wesley's Journal:

> *Jan. 1, 1739. Mr. Hall, Kinchin, Ingham, Whitefield, Butchins, and my brother Charles, were present at our love-feast in Fetter Lane, with about sixty brethren. About three in the morning, as we were continuing instant in prayer, the power of God came mightily upon us. . . . As soon as we were recovered a little from that awe and amazement at the presence of His Majesty, we broke out with one voice, "We praise Thee, O God, we acknowledge Thee to be the Lord."*

George Whitefield recalled this occasion and remarked, "It was a Pentecostal time indeed!" One month later he preached to 20,000 colliers at Kingswood, Bristol, with marvelous results. The great movement expanded to all England, to all Great Britain, to America and to many other countries. Many scholars agree with Prof. A. M. Renick of Edinburgh in saying that even William Carey, the London Missionary Society and the strong evangelical wing in the Church of England are all fruits of this mighty revival.

The Empowerment of the Holy Spirit for Victory over Satan.
On his first mission field, Paul met with a formidable enemy in a
sorcerer by the name of Elymas, who had great influence with
the deputy of the country against the Christian faith. Paul,
"filled with the Holy Spirit," rebuked him and made him tempo-
rarily blind by a miracle, and thereby broke the cast of the power
of darkness over the island of Cyprus. Paul pointed out in his
rebuke that Elymas was a tool of Satan to hinder the cause of the
gospel, and he was enabled by the Holy Spirit to bring about
victory over him.

The power of darkness reigns through superstition and sin,
which results in moral corruption. But the transformation of individual lives and communities, wherever the gospel is
preached, is an undeniable proof of the power of the Holy
Spirit. Dr. J. H. Bavinck of Holland has pointed out in his book
The Science of Missions that the conviction of sin which is
necessary for salvation cannot be brought about by a philosophical approach alone, based on natural theology, using reason as
a common premise for arguing against the falsity of heathen
ways of life and faith. Neither will the psychological or dialec-
tical approach be sufficient. "The Holy Spirit alone," says Dr.
Bavinck, "can call to repentance, and we are only means in
his hand." He goes on to say, "If elenctics [or the conviction of
sin] were a human activity, the situation would be nearly hopeless." That is only too true.

The Holy Spirit and Prayer Power. The working of the Holy
Spirit is so interwoven with prayer that sometimes they are
taken as one thing. They are mutually causative. In Acts nothing
else is so closely linked together with the power of the Holy
Spirit as prayer.

St. Patrick, known as the apostle of Ireland, spent forty days
on top of Croagh Patrick in meditation and prayer for the opening up of West Ireland to the gospel, and it did open.

There is consensus among church historians that William
Carey was the true herald of modern missions. The movement
which he started was born of a special monthly prayer meeting
for worldwide outpouring of power from on high, which Dr.

Arthur T. Pierson calls a "stated monthly season of such united, organized pleading with God for a lost world." Some historians have traced this prayer movement back to the trumpet call to prayer for a new and worldwide Pentecost blown by Jonathan Edwards from New England and echoed in England across the ocean. Edwards himself led in a mighty revival in New England and had great impact on the preachers and churches of his own time as well as of generations to follow. His ministry was marked by evident manifestations of the power of the Holy Spirit.

When the pioneering messengers of the gospel began to labor on the island of Tahiti, the power of darkness so prevailed that the efforts of the first fourteen years seemed to be wholly in vain. The tireless toil and unsparing self-denial of the early missionaries were not rewarded by a single convert. The directors of the London Missionary Society seriously proposed abandoning this fruitless field. But there were a few who felt that this was the very hour when God was about to rebuke unbelief and reward faith. Finally, instead of abandoning the field, a special season of united prayer was appointed. Many confessed unbelief and prayed fervently. A miracle happened just at this crucial hour. Unknown to each other, two vessels started from two opposite ports, one from Tahiti bound for London, the other from the Thames bound for Tahiti, and they crossed each other's tracks at mid-ocean. The latter carried letters of encouragement to the missionaries. The former bore letters from the missionaries in Tahiti, announcing such a mighty work of God that idolatry was entirely overthrown. What a wonderful and amazing coincidence between prayer and the power of the Holy Spirit!

The Holy Spirit as Strategist of Missions

Acts affords us guidance in regard to the strategy of missions. It reveals to us principles of missionary work which have to do with the leading of the Holy Spirit.

Occupation of Key Cities. Philip was led to Samaria; Peter to Caesarea; Paul started work in many key cities in Asia Minor. Today, the metropolitan areas are the strategic centers for evangelism, since this is indeed a "Metropolitan age."

Capture of Key Persons and Classes for Christ. When Paul

went to Cyprus, he dealt with the deputy of the country in the power of the Holy Spirit, won him for the Lord and thereby created a favorable influence on the island. At Athens, Paul engaged the intelligentsia of the city in disputation and roused their interest in the Christian faith, which resulted in the conversion of some intellectuals, among whom was a man of position by the name of Dionysius (Acts 17:18, 34). Again, at Ephesus he worked among scholars of the school of Tyrannus for two years. Paul never worked so long in one place among any other class of people. What was the result? "All they which dwelt in Asia heard the word of the Lord Jesus, both Jews and Greeks" (Acts 19:10).

Philip was led by the Holy Spirit to speak to the Ethiopian eunuch, who was a leader in his country, and this was the first step towards the christianization of that land.

Of course, this does not mean that the gospel is meant only for a certain class of people, but it does teach us that there is real wisdom in laboring patiently among intellectual people on the mission fields. We should never neglect them. Many missionaries or missionary societies skip over the educated class and leaders because work among them requires a greater price to be paid.

Movement into New Areas. Paul moved on to new areas every time after he had established a local church. If missionaries today follow this principle, the strength of the great missionary army will not be taken up by working in churches already established, but will break out to new areas in every direction. This will start a mighty expansion in this generation. Every missionary should be trained to be willing to move on to new places and start all over again. It is hard, but by doing this missionary work as a whole will be much more effective.

Establishing and Sustaining Indigenous Churches. In the farewell exhortation to the elders of the Ephesian church on his mission field, Paul said, "The Holy Spirit hath made you overseers, to feed the church of God" (Acts 20:28). Evidently, it is the will of the Holy Spirit that the churches on the mission fields should be self-governing, self-propagating and self-supporting. If you do not go with the Holy Spirit, you will never raise up strong churches. "When they had ordained them elders in every church, and had prayed with fasting, they commended them to the Lord, on whom they believed" (Acts 14:23). Having ordained leaders in his mission churches, Paul commended them to the Lord, for the Lord is able to take care of them. So one of the most important jobs of missionaries is to train national leaders.

Another point of supreme importance is that national churches must be trained to be missionary-minded. The apostle Paul could speak of the churches which he started as having "fellowship [with him] in the gospel from the first day until now" (Phil. 1:5); and as sounding "out the word of the Lord not only in Macedonia and Achaia, but also in every place" (1 Thess. 1:8).

Love Service in Missions. "And there stood up one of them named Agabus, and signified by the Spirit that there should be great dearth throughout all the world" (Acts 11:28). Evidently the purpose of the Holy Spirit in announcing the coming famine through Agabus was that Christians should manifest their love to one another by action at such a time. The Christians at Antioch understood the significance of this prophecy and "sent relief" to the brethren in Judea. It was a beautiful expression of brotherhood in the love of Christ.

It is true that the primary task of the church is to evangelize the world, but the Holy Spirit reveals to us here that love services have their own place in missions. Do schools, hospitals and other welfare services come under this category? Certainly they do serve a twofold purpose: means of evangelism and channels of love.

Mass Evangelism in Missions. As soon as the curtain is drawn on the Pentecostal spectacle, we have a scene of mass evangelism presented to us: Peter, with the Apostolic Team, full of the Holy Spirit, preached to thousands of amazed people with wonderful result. A short time later, at the gate called Beautiful, Peter again testified to gospel truth before a crowd of 5,000, counting only the men. Even the hostile rulers were overwhelmed by this huge crowd (Acts 4:21).

Crowds at evangelistic meetings are nothing new, but, as an

organized means of evangelism, mass campaigns are an upsurg-
ing power in this generation. They have sound scriptural basis
if they have the Holy Spirit as their main power source. We will
do well to remember that ours is an age of mass action. United
campaigns, run on a spiritual line, are greatly needed on the mission fields today.

Unity as Power for Missions. The Spirit-filled church at Jerusalem showed a wonderful spirit of unity (Acts 2:41-47). Paul
speaks of "unity of the Spirit" (Eph. 4:3). Our Lord said in his
prayer for his disciples, "And now I am no more in the world,
but these are in the world, and I come to thee. Holy Father, keep
through thine own name those whom thou hast given me, that
they may be one as we are. . . . that the world may believe that
thou hast sent me" (Jn. 17:11, 21).

Our Lord teaches us here an important truth: The unity of believers produces a power which convinces the world of the
reality of the gospel. The Lord laid repeated emphasis on the
oneness of believers in this great prayer. The words *that they
may be one* are used four times in this chapter, and every time
they take on a new meaning. In verse 11, oneness of believers
has to do with the name of God; in verse 23, it is spoken of as a
power to draw people to Christ; in verse 22, it is related to the
glory of God; in verse 23, it has the added significance of the
manifestation of the love of God. In view of these words of our
Lord, we can never speak too much of the importance of the
unity of believers.

While there are lines and methods of uniting the church of
God which are not scriptural and therefore unacceptable to bib-
lically oriented Christians, we evangelical churches must un-
reservedly start a decisive movement for unity based on biblical
terms. There must be combined action on the mission fields if
we really want more effective evangelism. We should set up
committees to study the best ways for unity with as many evangelical groups as possible taking part. There is only one path for
us to tread, and that is to unite and evangelize the world before
the Lord comes back. We must not only speak negatively of an
unbiblical unification, but we must also act positively for a biblical one.

The Holy Spirit as Supplier for Mission

The Holy Spirit and the Supply of Recruits for Missions. "The Holy Spirit said, Separate me Barnabas and Saul for the work whereunto I have called them" (Acts 13:2). The Holy Spirit called Barnabas and Paul for missionary service, and they went. He calls and recruits volunteers for mission fields.

Please note four things in this verse: (1) It is the Holy Spirit who does the calling. (2) He calls workers for a definite service. (3) He calls the best—Barnabas and Paul. (4) They obeyed.

Let me enlarge a bit on these four points. First, it is the Holy Spirit who does the calling. None of us should be discouraged about missionary work, since the Holy Spirit is the recruiter. The Holy Spirit moved in the latter part of the nineteenth century, and the student world of America and England was roused to join in missionary action. Through the instrumentality of men like D. L. Moody, the Student Volunteer Movement was formed, and in twenty-five years' time over 9,000 volunteered for the mission field.

Second, he calls workers for a definite service. The history of missions teaches us a very important lesson: The greatest majority of successful and great missionaries have been those who go toward a definite goal which the Lord has prepared for them.

Third, he calls the best. The Antioch church had every reason to keep Barnabas and Paul at home. They were needed more than anyone else. Yet the Holy Spirit sent them away. Many gifted Christian workers disobey the Holy Spirit because they are persuaded to believe that their gifts are meant for the churches at home. No workers who have failed in the homeland can be expected to be successful on the mission field. Facts have proved beyond doubt that missionaries who have done great things on the mission fields can be as greatly used of God at home. Yes, the mission fields demand and deserve our best men and women.

Fourth, they obeyed. I think I am justified in saying that a good measure of the weakness of missionary work today is attributable to the unwillingness of gifted workers to obey the call of the Holy Spirit to go to the mission field. They prefer to stay at home. The inner call of the Holy Spirit can be drowned by the tide of general opinion. The Christian public at home should encourage their best men and women, whom they think they cannot spare, to go to the mission field.

The Holy Spirit and Sacrificial Giving for Missions. Immediately following the record of Pentecost, we read of sacrificial giving in the apostolic church (Acts 2:44). Ananias and Sapphira "sold a possession, and kept back part of the price" (5:1-2). Peter referred to it as "lying to the Holy Spirit" (5:3). Two things are clear in this verse: First, the Holy Spirit moved Christians to give sacrifically; second, many followed the prompting of the Holy Spirit, but some tried to cheat with clever designs.

The Macedonian churches showed "abundance of joy" in "great trial of affliction," as well as "riches of liberality" in "deep poverty" (2 Cor. 8:2). What a precious contrast between outward conditions and inward grace!

The church at Thessalonica is a good example of the Macedonian churches, and Paul speaks of it as a church in which the Holy Spirit has moved in power: "For our gospel came not unto you in word only, but also in power, and in the Holy Ghost" (1 Thess. 1:5). Again this proves that a Spirit-filled church is a giving one.

The "Macedonian giving" is not only giving of money but is basically giving of oneself—they "first gave their own selves to the Lord" (2 Cor. 8:5). The giving of money and the giving of lives have constituted the great "Missionary Giving," all prompted by the Holy Spirit.

The Pietist Movement rose in the seventeenth century and gave birth to a missionary thrust of which the Moravian mission was a part. The Holy Spirit moved so clearly at Herrnhut that the tide of the spirit of giving rose high, and consequently out of a small congregation of six hundred grew a mission which sent out 2,170 missionaries in 120 years to many of the most difficult places in the world. In 1930, after 200 years of work, the ratio of missionaries to the total membership of this group was, according to Dr. Robert Glover, one to ninety-two, which is probably an unsurpassed record.

In conclusion, let us remind ourselves of Paul's words to the Galatians: "Are ye so foolish? having begun in the Spirit, are ye now made perfect by the flesh?" (Gal. 3:3). Since it was by the power of the Holy Spirit that missions were started, are we to finish it by human efforts? Even as the Galatian Christians fell prey to legalism, so the church of this age has fallen prey to "technique-ism," which has been allowed to take the place of the Holy Spirit, who is the real source of power for missions. When missionary effort has become devoid of the Holy Spirit, it is rendered a human affair and as such is a hopeless situation. But if it remains in the control of the Holy Spirit, he will be the author and finisher of missions. The task will be accomplished!

There should be a renewed call to a revival of utter dependence on the Holy Spirit and a diligent seeking after the fullness of the Holy Spirit in our individual lives as well as in the lives of missionary societies. Then a true missionary revival will be realized.

THE BASIS OF MISSIONS IN THE EPISTLES: THE CHURCH AND MISSIONS

17

PHILIP
TENG

This morning we conclude our study on the biblical basis of missions by taking up the fourth and last subtitle: The Basis of Missions in the Epistles, that is, the church and missions. My message again has three sections: (1) the nature of the church, (2) the urgency of the church's mission and (3) the consummation of the church.

The Nature of the Church
In Ephesians, the apostle Paul uses eight illustrations to explain the nature of the church. We find the missionary responsibility of the church in all these illustrations.

The Church as the Body of Christ. The apostle Paul calls the church *the body of Christ* (Eph. 1:23). And in this metaphor, he points out something which has an important bearing on missions. He says in Ephesians 2:16 that the Jews and the Gentiles have become one body, the body of Christ which is the church.

The "middle wall of partition" (2:14) no longer exists in the church of Christ. Since God has included the Gentiles in his church, it follows logically that the church has a universal mission through which the body of Christ continues to grow in all parts of the world. Paul also says in Colossians that in the church "there is neither Greek nor Jew, circumcision nor uncircumcision, Barbarian, Scythian, bond nor free: but Christ is all, and in all" (Col. 3:11). This glorious vision is being realized through missions.

Every member of the human body is expected to fulfill its function, and all members of the body are expected to work in perfect unity. That is the only way for the body to keep healthy and growing. Christ expects the same thing from his body. Paul, speaking the mind of Christ, says that "the whole body fitly joined together and compacted by that which every joint supplieth, according to the effectual working in the measure of every part, maketh increase of the body" (Eph. 4:16). It is when every member of the church of Jesus Christ understands his duties as a missioner and joins together with other Christians in harmonious action that the church will grow. Here we have the two basic principles of church growth: unity and total mobilization.

The Church as New Man. First, corporately: The whole church is called by Paul *a new man* (Eph. 2:15) consisting of two parties—the Jews and the Gentiles.

Second, individually: Every member of the body of Christ is called *a new man*, who is created according to the image of God consisting in righteousness and true holiness (Eph. 4:24). All true believers have become new creatures in Christ regardless of their nationalities.

This teaching sheds an important light on the task of missions. The aim of missionary work is not to swell church membership, but to increase the number of new creatures in Christ. If we mainly think of membership, we easily fall under the curse of creedalism. There is an important distinction between *creed* and *creedalism.* Creed is absolutely necessary because it is the crystallization of what we believe. We cannot really believe without knowing clearly what we believe. Creed is a concrete statement of our faith. But creedalism is different. Creedalism means the conscious or unconscious attitude that as long as we have brought people to a position where they can say yes to our creeds, we have done our job. Wherever creedalism prevails, churches are satisfied with formal membership and show no real concern for lack of signs of spiritual life in the lives of church members. A spiritually healthy church is less impressed with numbers than spiritual vitality. I do not belittle the significance of numbers. They do tell something, and sometimes they are even indispensable. What I do mean is this: Numbers are meaningless unless they indicate spiritual reality or unless they lead somewhere. In fact, churches that lay emphasis on spiritual reality are usually churches that grow statistically.

The Church as the Household of God. Paul says in Ephesians 2:19 that the Gentile believers are brought into the household of God, which is virtually identical with the church. The word *household* (or *home* or *family*) suggests the idea of love and fellowship. The church as the household of God is a place where the love of God is manifested and where the children of God enjoy fellowship with one another. One of the responsibilities of a local church is to provide opportunities for fellowship between its members. The church exists for a fivefold purpose: worship, teaching, evangelism, service and fellowship. The Christian life is essentially a life of fellowship: It has its roots in fellowship with God vertically, and it expresses itself in fellowship with Christians horizontally. When the Christian life is devoid of fellowship, it is substantially short of reality. It has been said that one Christian is no Christian. This may be overstated, but there is surely truth in it. It tells us that the real Christian life is a fellowship life. Fellowship is the context of the Christian life. You cannot live a life without context.

This illustration of the church teaches us something important which relates to missions. The Christian fellowship is glorious because it is a family fellowship of all the redeemed of God from all over the world. The church of Christ is a universal family consisting of people of all races and nationalities. Missionary service, therefore, means the effort of extending this glorious international family of Christ—a family in which there is true equality, acceptance and love between all its members. This is in fact the fulfillment of Confucius' audacious idea of "one brotherhood of all people within the four seas."

The Church as the Kingdom of God. Paul calls the Gentile Christians "fellow-citizens with the saints" (Eph. 2:19). The word citizen implies a nation or a kingdom. The apostle Peter calls the church a "holy nation" (1 Pet. 2:9), and the apostle Paul calls her the "kingdom of God's dear Son" (Col. 1:13). We can, therefore, use either nation or kingdom for the church.

The first basic idea behind the concept of a kingdom is authority or power. Paul says, "The kingdom of God is not in word, but in power" (1 Cor. 4:20). This power is manifested in two things: first, in the obedience of the citizens of the kingdom to the will of the king; second, in the citizens' victory over sin and Satan.

The second basic idea behind the concept of a kingdom is found in Romans 14:17: "The kingdom of God is . . . righteousness, and peace, and joy in the Holy Spirit." This means that the kingdom of God expresses itself in a specific type of life in which righteousness, peace and joy are the predominant characteristics. The translation from the power of darkness into the kingdom of God's dear Son (Col. 1:13) is a glorious experience. This translation is as concrete, definite and real as the birth of a new baby. Everyone who has been thus translated finds in his heart and life obedience, righteousness, peace and joy. It is a great privilege and joy to have a share in the mission of furthering this kingdom in the whole world by bringing people into its glorious blessedness.

The Church as Spiritual Temple. The church is, as Paul puts it,

> built upon the foundation of the apostles and prophets, Jesus Christ himself being the chief corner stone; in whom all the building fitly framed together groweth unto an holy temple in the Lord: in whom ye also are builded together for an habitation of God through the Spirit. (Eph. 2:20-21)

The church is depicted here as a holy temple which is a habitation of God through the Holy Spirit. Or, as Peter puts it, the church is a "spiritual house" built with living stones (1 Pet. 2:5).

This illustration of the church teaches us at least two important lessons:

First, the church is spiritual. She is a place where spiritual
laws and principles are employed; a place where spiritual sacrifices are offered and spiritual fruits are borne; a place where
spiritual gifts are exercised in service; a place where the Holy
Spirit moves freely.

Second, the church is living. She is built on the living Word
of God as revealed through three channels: the prophets, the
apostles and above all Jesus Christ. Her building materials are
all living: the Living Stone which is Christ as the corner stone;
the living stones which are born-again Christians; and the living
Word. She is inhabited by the living God. Every activity in the
church should aim at building up the members' living relationship with God.

Here again we see something important regarding missions:
The goal of missions is not merely to reproduce on the mission
fields all the denominations which we have in the homelands
with all their dividedness, but to establish churches that are
built on the pattern of the living Word of God, where sound
spiritual principles are employed in a lively way in worship,
government and program.

The Church as Bride of Christ. The apostle Paul calls the
union of the church with Christ a great mystery. It is indeed a
great mystery of love of which the union of husband and wife is
a symbol. This illustration of the relationship between the
church and Christ is true both corporately and individually: Corporately, the church as a whole is the bride of Christ; individually, every born-again Christian is a bride of Christ (2 Cor. 11:2).

The central point of this illustration is union in love. Love is
more of the heart than the mind. And it follows that the Christian life is more of the heart than the mind. Mind is very important, and it is far from me to belittle the significance of the mind.
But I do want to point out that in an age that glorifies the mind, it
is important for us Christians to keep our faith a matter of the
heart rather than the head. Of course, the either-or approach is
not ideal, the best is both—we need both a heart relationship
with God and an understanding of the mind. That is exactly the

230 of the universe, hope of the world

answer we find in the Bible. I used to appreciate a question posed by a certain scholar: "Which of the two would you prefer —the seraphim, which means fire, or the cherabim, which means knowledge?" But later it dawned on me when I was reading my Bible one day that there was fire right in the center of the cherabim. So knowledge and fire are beautifully united together in the revealed Word of God. We need both the fire of the heart and the wisdom of the mind.

Evangelicals today need more training of the mind before they can meet the needs of today, but this is done not at the expense of a deep experience of the heart. Every missionary going out to another land must have a deep heart-experience of gospel truths before he can pass on a living message. The mind is often localized, but the heart is a universal language which everybody understands. Missionaries who go to the mission fields with degrees but without a deep heart-experience with Christ will fail and come home shattered and disillusioned.

The Church as a Candlestick. Paul speaks of Christians as "children of light" (Eph. 5:8), which reminds us of the apostle John's vision of the seven churches as seven candlesticks. The church is meant by God to be a light in the world. The light of the gospel is to shine through the church in all the world. "Send the light" is still the motto of all missionary-minded churches; it is still the chorus of the hymn of missions.

Light is always outreaching, never ingrown. The Christians and churches that are torch-bearers are always aggressive in evangelism and missions.

On the other hand, when Paul speaks of Christians as children of light, he is thinking of their Christ-like character. This leads us to another side of our task as light-bearers, which is sometimes called *non-verbal witness.* Verbal and non-verbal witness constitute the Christian light.

The Church as the Army of Christ. The picture of the church as an army is vividly painted by Paul in Ephesians 6. The armor of this army consists of both defensive and offensive equipment and weapons. The church is to be both defensive and offensive; she is both conservative and progressive. She defends and conserves purity of doctrine and purity of character, but she also moves ahead in offensive attack on Satan and sin as well as in active and agressive evangelism to bring people to God's side of the battle.

Where does the church of Christ stand in an antitraditional age like ours? She is *anti* all things that are antiChrist, and she is most conservative in keeping the true Christian heritage. What is the true Christian heritage? It is found in the Lord's letters to the seven churches in Asia Minor (Rev. 2—3). The Lord commended the victorious Christians in these churches for a number of things which constitute the precious Christian heritage. It is a sevenfold heritage: purity of doctrine and the first love, as exemplified by the Ephesian Church; boldness and firmness in face of persecution, as expressed by the church at Smyrna; good works as found in the church at Thyatira; emphasis on spirituality rather than form, as exhibited by the victorious members of the church at Sardis; purity of character, as represented by the white garments worn by the remnant in the church at Sardis; obedience and faith in evangelism and missions, as shown by the church at Philadelphia. This sevenfold heritage is the true mainstream of Christianity, and it is behind this holy tradition that we firmly stand. We have noticed that one of the seven points is taking hold of every open door and entering into it with evangelism and missions. This is part of our great heritage, and we must uphold it.

As the army of Christ, let us march on with believing and bold evangelism and missions to the uttermost part of the world.

The Urgency of the Church's Mission

The Only Way of Salvation. The apostle Paul says in his first Epistle to Timothy, "There is one God, and one mediator between God and men, the man Christ Jesus; who gave himself a ransom for all" (1 Tim. 2:5). This is in keeping with Peter's preaching when he said, "There is none other name under heaven given among men, whereby we must be saved" (Acts 4:12). The claim of the gospel of Christ as the only way of salvation is clearly stated in the Gospels and the Epistles. This is what we believe and proclaim.

In this age of relativism and syncretism, the voice of universalism and self-salvation is strong. Probably the two strongest philosophies or thought-forms in universities all over the world are logical positivism and relativism, as some well-known scholars have pointed out. The former denies the possibility of knowing things as they really are; if anything is considered to be known, it is only known in the laboratory; there is no knowledge beside scientific knowledge. Relativism tries to make everything relative.

When relativism has been carried into theology, it has given birth to four forms of thought: a new conception of God, new morality, new evangelism and new secularism. In the new concept of God, God himself is made relative—instead of the great *I Am*, he has become the God of Becoming. In the new morality, morals are made relative: No standard is absolute except love, which in turn is left to relative and subjective interpretations. In the new evangelism, the absolute finality of Christ in salvation is made relative. In the new secularism, the sacred is made relative, and, as a result, we are left with "religionless Christianity."

Over against this relativism we have the biblical claim of the gospel of Christ as the only way of salvation. If we really believe in this absolute claim of the gospel, we have to act in accordance with it. True faith always involves action. Conviction in faith and indifference in action are never compatible with each other. The logic of the urgency of evangelism and missions is readily established by the absolute claim of the gospel. It is becoming more and more evident that only Bible-believing Christians are really concerned with carrying out the Great Commission.

We all agree with Paul when he says, "For whosoever shall call upon the name of the Lord shall be saved" (Rom. 10:13). But how do we react when we hear Paul continue to say, "How then shall they call on him in whom they have not believed? and how shall they believe in him of whom they have not heard? and how shall they hear without a preacher? and how shall they preach, except they be sent?" (Rom. 10:14-15). Shall we add here, How can we send except there are those who are willing to go?

Loyalty and Faithfulness to the Lord's Commission. We find a good example for loyalty and faithfulness to the Lord's commission in the life of Paul. Paul was very clear about the Lord's commission to him which he received at his conversion. He mentions this commission many times in his epistles as well as in his testimonies recorded in Acts.

How did he carry out this commission? He said to the Colossian Christians that he rejoiced in his sufferings as a commissioned minister of the gospel among the Gentiles (Col. 1:24); he said to the Corinthian Christians that in his ministry as a commissioner of the gospel he did not faint:

> We are troubled on every side, yet not distressed; we are perplexed, but not in despair; persecuted, but not forsaken; cast down, but not destroyed; always bearing about in the body the dying of the Lord Jesus, that the life also of Jesus might be made manifest in our body. (2 Cor. 4:8-10)

He said to Timothy,

> I am appointed a preacher, and an apostle, and a teacher of the Gentiles, for the which cause I also suffer these things, nevertheless I am not ashamed. (2 Tim. 1:11-12)

He said to the elders of the Ephesian church,

> The Holy Spirit witnesseth in every city, saying that bonds and afflictions abide me. But none of these things move me, neither count I my life dear unto myself, so that I might finish my course with joy, and the ministry, which I have received of the Lord Jesus, to testify the gospel of the grace of God. (Acts 20:23-24)

What wonderful words from the lips of a dedicated missionary! Probably the best two illustrations of Paul's tremendous spirit of commitment to his commission are found in Acts. We find in Acts 14:19-21 that Paul was stoned by the people of the city of Lystra. They took Paul for dead and pulled him out of the city. It is possible that Paul was dead, but God raised him to life again. What did he do after he came to himself? He went back into the very city where he had been treated so brutally. What for? Just to boast of his wonderful recovery? There could be only one reason and that is that Paul was deeply concerned about the spiritual need of those people and wanted to preach the gospel to them.

We read in the following verse that Paul was back in the city of Lystra for the third time a short time later. What bravery and what spirit of commitment!

The other illustration is recorded in Acts 24:24-25. When he was brought before the Roman Governor Felix for trial, Paul took this opportunity to witness to gospel truth. What did Paul say? "He reasoned of righteousness, temperance, and judgment to come." Paul knew that Felix was a governor who was used to receiving large bribes, yet he talked about righteousness; he knew that Felix was living with a Jewish woman who was not his wife, yet he talked about temperance; he knew that his life was in the hand of Felix, yet he talked about the judgment of God. What bravery! Paul knew very well that it was dangerous for him to talk about these things before a man like Felix. But out of a sense of faithfulness to his commission as well as out of a desire to awaken Felix to his spiritual need, he ignored the danger and rose up to his duty. What faithfulness and commitment! The governor trembled before this spiritual giant!

Paul tells us that we as Christians are also commissioned by God: "God was in Christ, reconciling the world unto himself, not imputing their trespasses unto them; and hath committed unto us the word of reconciliation" (2 Cor. 5:19). All Christians are commissioned ambassadors for the great task of reconciliation—the task of bringing people back to God through evangelism and missions.

The Sure Judgment of God. The apostle Paul had a sense of urgency in his mission which stemmed from his sureness of the judgment of God. "Knowing the terror of the Lord, we persuade men" (2 Cor. 5:11), he said. Paul's concept of his mission was universal: "Now we know that what things soever the law saith, it saith to them who are under the law: that every mouth may be stopped, and all the world may become guilty before God. Therefore by the deeds of the law there shall no flesh be justified in his sight" (Rom. 3:19-20). The whole world lies under the judgment of God, so the whole world needs the gospel of grace through Christ.

Paul experienced great stirring of his spirit at Athens and said to the people gathered at the Areopagus, "Now [God] commandeth all men every where to repent: because he hath appointed a day, in the which he will judge the world in righteousness by that man whom he hath ordained" (Acts 17:30-31).

Evangelism is often linked together with the judgment of God in the epistles of Paul. For instance, Paul says in 2 Timothy 4:1, "I charge thee therefore before God and the Lord Jesus Christ, who shall judge the quick and the dead at his appearing and his kingdom; preach the word; be instant in season, out of season." Here we have evangelism, judgment and a sense of urgency.

If we really believe that all men will be judged by Christ according to their relationship with him, we will be serious about evangelism and missions, seizing every opportunity to preach the gospel.

Ardent Desire to Glorify God. Deep down in his heart Paul had a strong desire to glorify God by bringing more people to God to sing God's praise. He said to the Romans, "That the Gentiles might glorify God for his mercy; as it is written, For this cause I will confess to thee among the Gentiles, and sing unto thy name" (Rom. 15:9-11).

Again, Paul says to the Corinthians, "All things are for your sakes, that the abundant grace might through the thanksgiving of many people redound to the glory of God" (2 Cor. 4:15). This verse means that the more Christians there are the more God will be glorified. This desire in the heart of Paul is a good illustration of the Lord's teaching on prayer. The foremost thought in our prayer should be, according to the Lord's Prayer, "hallowed be thy name." The only way to realize this desire is to bring more and more people to God because the name of God is hallowed only among those who know him, worship and praise him. When Paul saw the city of Athens full of idols, his spirit was greatly stirred because the glory of God was robbed. This ardent desire to glorify God is a strong impetus for evangelism and missions in the life of Paul. So with us.

Constrained by the Love of Christ to Share. Paul says in 2 Corinthians 5:14, "The love of Christ constraineth us; because we thus judge, that if one died for all, then were all dead; and that he died for all that they which live should not henceforth live unto themselves, but unto him which died for them, and rose again."

Paul says here that we are constrained by the love of Christ not to live for ourselves, but to live for him who died for us. But how do we live for him? Paul tells us in the following verse that we live for him by engaging ourselves in the task of reconciliation, bringing people into peace with God.

Greek scholars tell us that the Greek word for the English word *constrain* is a strong word, suggesting the idea of a flood. Paul's heart was, as it were, flooded by the love of Christ, and he was moved away from himself and began to live for Christ, engaging himself in the task of sharing the love of Christ with others through evangelism and missions. It is impossible for us to engage in missions without this constraint.

R. A. Jaffery, the co-founder of the Alliance Bible Seminary where I am now teaching, went to South China as a missionary over seventy years ago. He suffered from a weak heart from his youth and he had diabetes, but his day began at 4 a.m. After his personal devotional time, he would begin writing articles in Chinese for the Bible magazine of which he was the editor. He designed a special kind of desk which could be pulled over his bed so that he could write lying down in order to conserve his strength. After thirty years of service in South China, God called him to go to Vietnam for pioneering work. He went and began a work which has now grown to a membership of 60,000 Christians. God then called him to go to Indonesia where he had to start all over again. He obeyed and started a rapidly growing work until his death in a Japanese concentration camp. He was constrained by the love of Christ.

The Second Coming of Christ. In the epistles, evangelism and missions are closely associated with the second coming of Christ. To the evangelical mind, the second coming of Christ is always an incentive to evangelism and missions. This concept has a sound basis in the teaching of the epistles, which in turn has its origin in the teaching of Christ. The apostle Peter speaks in the same sentence of the second coming of Christ and God's desire to save more people (2 Pet. 3:9). God wants to have his plan of salvation completed before the second coming of Christ. The apostle Paul speaks of the "fulness of the Gentiles" against the background of the second coming of Christ (Rom. 11:25). All this is in keeping with the teaching of Christ, who said, "This gospel of the kingdom shall be preached in all the world for a witness unto all nations; and then shall the end come" (Mt. 24:14). In the light of this verse, missions has to do with hastening the second coming of Christ.

Many signs indicate that the second coming of Christ is getting nearer and nearer. But instead of reaching the climax of world missions, we are experiencing an anticlimax. The evil one is getting busier and busier in putting up hindrances to God's plan. His tactics are twofold: without the church and within the church. Without the church, Satan is hardening and blinding the inner eyes of more people against the light of the gospel of Christ; within the church, he is setting up mechanisms that create in the minds of Christians the impression that the day of missions is over and that there is not much that they can do. As a result of all this, there are signs of a slackening of pace in the missionary efforts in the Western countries.

But over against this, the Lord is organizing a double counterattack. On the one hand, he is rallying together all Bible-believing Christians for a renewed missionary movement; on the other, he is awakening the younger churches in the so-called Third World to realize their missionary responsibilities. Probably the fact that you find names from the Third World in the list of speakers at this convention is a prophetic indication that the East and the West are going to join forces for the great task of missions. We are running the last mile in the world missionary enterprise. It is a hard mile, but it is a challenge to our loyalty, faithfulness and commitment to the Great Commission.

The Consummation of the Church
God is a God of perfect plan. All his plans will be fulfilled. The word *fullness* used in connection with the plans of God is very precious. God accomplishes all his plans at the fullness of time. For instance, the incarnation of Christ took place "when the fulness of the time was come" (Gal. 4:4). It did not happen by chance. God had made perfect plans for it in history.

Paul uses this word in regard to God's plan for the people of Israel. He says in Romans 11:25, "Blindness in part is happened to Israel until the fulness of the Gentiles be come in. And so all Israel shall be saved." God has not forsaken his chosen people but has a wonderful plan of salvation for them. There is perfect timing. Even as God delivered his people from the Babylonian captivity at the fullness of the prophesied seventy years, which looked impossible at the time because of adverse circumstances, so will God save them at the fullness of the Gentiles.

Christ himself used this word *fullness* in regard to his second coming. He said, "They shall fall by the edge of the sword, and shall be led away captive into all nations: and Jerusalem shall be trodden down of the Gentiles, until the times of the Gentiles be fulfilled" (Lk. 21:24). The Lord said this in the context of his prophecies about his second coming.

Even as God made plans for the first coming of Christ, so God has made perfect plans for his second coming, which is the hope of the church. Everything is leading to that glorious event in history. The prophets foretold it; the Lord himself confirmed it; the apostles proclaimed it; all signs today are pointing to it. Biblical evangelism and missions are filled with significance in view of the second coming of Christ.

Missions are not doomed to failure but to a glorious consummation:

Lo, a great multitude, which no man could number, of all nations and kindreds, and people, and tongues, stood before the throne, and before the Lamb, clothed with white robes, and palms in their hands, and cried with a loud voice, saying, Salvation to our God which sitteth upon the throne, and unto the Lamb! (Rev. 7:9-10)

This is the vision of the apostle John, and it is also ours. But before and leading to the realization of this glorious vision, you and I have the task of evangelism and missions on our shoulders.

PART IV

**COMMUNION
MESSAGE**

THE KEY TO MISSIONARY ADVANCE

18

JOHN R. W. STOTT

Now among those who went up to worship at the feast were some Greeks. So these came to Philip, who was from Bethsaida in Galilee, and said to him, "Sir, we wish to see Jesus." Philip went and told Andrew; Andrew went with Philip and they told Jesus. And Jesus answered them, "The hour has come for the Son of man to be glorified. Truly, truly, I say to you, unless a grain of wheat falls into the earth and dies, it remains alone; but if it dies, it bears much fruit. He who loves his life loses it, and he who hates his life in this world will keep it for eternal life. If any one serves me, he must follow me; and where I am, there shall my servant be also; if any one serves me, the Father will honor him. (Jn. 12:20-26)

Here John tells a little story in which there is an encounter between four people or four groups of people. The first are some Greeks who had come to Jerusalem and who wanted to see Jesus. The second is Philip and Andrew, who came to tell Jesus

about the Greeks. The third is the Lord Jesus himself, who explained how the Greeks could see and meet him because he was
going to die for them. Fourth, there is the servant of Jesus. This
is where *we* come into the story—as the servant of Jesus who
must follow Jesus so closely that he too must die to himself. The
theme, then, of this passage is that death is the key to missionary
advance, which seems an appropriate subject at the conclusion
of a missionary convention as we gather at the Lord's table to remember his death.

The People

First, then, the Greeks. John sees in them a symbol of the unsatis-
fied and hungry world, both Gentile and Jewish. He tells us that
they were Greeks, with a rich background of Greek philosophy
and all that that implied, but that they had come up to Jerusalem
for the Feast of the Passover, which indicates their interest in
Judaism. Yet all the philosophy of Greece and all the religion of
Judaism had failed to satisfy them, for they said, "Sir, we want to
see Jesus." It was not just that they wanted to catch a glimpse of
him—everybody could do that—but they wanted to see him and
meet him and talk to him that he might satisfy their hunger.

Those Greeks stand for the paradoxical condition of the world
as it still is today: religious—most of the world is religious—but
not Christian; paying pilgrimages to their Jerusalems but still
hungry for Jesus. The whole world is saying to this convention,
now articulately and now in a mute appeal, "Sir, we want to see
Jesus."

Second, we turn from the Greeks to Philip and Andrew. If the
Greeks stand for the world, Philip and Andrew stand for the
church, the visible church, confused, unsure of itself, diffident
about Jesus and embarrassed by the needs of the appeals of the
world. It was some credit to Philip that the Greeks came to him
at all. Would that non-Christians came to us as readily as those
Greeks turned to Philip! Yet Philip was evidently very uncer-
tain about what to do. The Greeks wanted to see Jesus, that was
clear, but would Jesus want to see the Greeks? That was not so
clear in Philip's mind. Wasn't Jesus preoccupied with other
things? Weren't these Greeks beyond the pale anyway? Philip

was in his customary condition of theological bewilderment.

In his dilemma, Philip went and told Andrew. Very sad that he needed to. Very sad that he could not have led these Greeks to Jesus directly. But one can at least be thankful that he had a friend with whom he could share his dilemma. Andrew had already gotten a bit of a reputation as an evangelist. It was he who had led his brother Simon to Jesus. It was he who had told Jesus about the boy in the crowd with his loaves and fishes. So these two men, Philip and Andrew, plucked up courage to go to Jesus together. Philip went and told Andrew, Andrew went with Philip, and they both went and told Jesus. You will note that two Christians can often do together what they may be too shy or too weak to do apart.

Third, we come to Jesus himself. I want you to notice how Jesus responded to Philip and Andrew. He answered them, "The hour has come for the Son of man to be glorified." In other words, if the Greeks want to see me, they *shall* see me. They are asking to see me at exactly the right moment because the hour has struck in which the Son of man will be glorified, that is, manifested in all his glory to the world. And that hour that has come for his glorification was the hour of his death, as we know from other references to this hour in the Gospels and from what he immediately goes on to say.

If the world wants to see Jesus glorified, they have to see him crucified. It was on the cross that the full glory of Jesus was revealed: his hatred for sin and his love for the sinner, his justice and his mercy, his reconciliation of man to God, of Jew to Gentile.

This great truth, of all these blessings that come from the cross, Jesus went on to illustrate in his little parable of the seed: "Unless a grain of wheat falls into the earth and dies, it remains alone; but if it dies, it bears much fruit." And the fruit could not come to the Greeks and the Gentile world unless he were willing to die. If a seed remains in the warm security of the granary, it will never reproduce itself. It has to be buried alive in the cold, dark grave of the earth, and there it has to die. When it dies, it multiplies, and out of its death new life is born. And out of that wintery grave the springtime corn emerges—some thirty, some

sixty, some a hundred fold. What dies, you see, is a single grain.
But from the death of the one many come to life. You could sum
it up in a simple rhyme: If it clings to its own life, it stays alone.
But if it dies, it multiplies.

Of that great principle, the cross of Jesus is history's supreme
example. If Jesus had clung to his life and refused to die, the
world would have died in its lostness. But because Jesus died
physically on the cross and spiritually in the God-forsaken darkness, there is life for the world, and multitudes have found life
through the death of Jesus. The seed that died has been abundantly fruitful. So when anybody asks us about Jesus as the
Greeks asked Philip, we have to reply as Jesus did in terms of his
death and resurrection. It is at the cross that men see Jesus, meet
Jesus, find Jesus. The new life that he offers is life through death
—through his death.

That brings me, fourth, to the servant of Jesus. This is where
you and I come into the story. Jesus moved in his conversation
from himself and the death that he was going to die to his servants and the death that we too must die: "If one any says he
wants to be my servant, let him follow me, that where I am, there
shall my servant be also." It is obvious that a servant must follow his master, but it is not quite so obvious where following
Jesus will lead.

Jesus made it plainer in another passage when he said, "If anybody will come after me, let him deny himself and take up his
cross and follow me." There is only one place to which you can
follow Jesus when you are bearing a cross, and that is to the
place of execution. And it is the same here. Jesus said, "Where
I am, there shall my servant be also," namely, on a cross. The
servant is not above his master. If the master died, the servant
must be ready to die as well.

Not, of course, that we can die for the sins of the world as he
did, nor even that all of us must die physically, let alone by crucifixion, but rather that we must die to ourselves, to our own
self-centered ambitions, to our materialism and our love of comfort, luxury and ease—die to our pride, our vainglory and our
hunger for the praise of men. Bonhoeffer was right when he said,
"When Christ calls a man, he bids him to die." Yes, but we do not

want to die. We love life, especially if we can live it for ourselves. We want to stay in the warm granary. We do not want to drop into the cold, dark earth.

Reasons for Dying

So let us notice now that Jesus gives reasons with which to support his call to die. I am anxious that we consider these carefully.

First, to die is the way to find ourselves—amazing paradox but absolutely true. "He who loves his life loses it, and he who hates his life in this world will keep it for eternal life." Tens of thousands of young people today are caught up in an identity crisis, wondering who they are and looking for themselves. They take it for granted that in order to find ourselves, we must at all costs lay hold of ourselves and live for ourselves and keep ourselves. Jesus says the very opposite is the truth. He says if we love our life, if we cling to our own life and refuse to let it go, that is a sure way to lose ourselves. Whereas if you hate your life, in the sense of being willing to lose it, giving it away in the service of God and the world, in the very act of abandoning yourself when you think everything is lost, in that very moment you will find yourself.

"He who loses his life finds it." This is the great Christian truth. The way of Jesus is self-discovery through self-sacrifice. Freedom through service, and life through death. To die is the way to find ourselves.

Second, to die is the way to follow Jesus. "If anyone serves me, let him follow me. And where I am, there shall my servant be also." Every authentic Christian bears or wears the cross, not necessarily as a decoration on a pendant or necklace or badge or broach, but as an indelible mark of his lifestyle. I do not hesitate to say that if there is no cross in our lives, no denying ourselves, no dying to ourselves, we cannot be recognized as the followers of Jesus.

The death we die may take one of a thousand different forms. Basically, we die to ourselves. In our career, we may be called to die to some cherished academic ambition in order to give our lives in practical service. Or it may be the exact opposite: that

Christ may call us to die to an activist role in order to qualify academically to do research, to teach or to write. Again, it may be that we are called to die to a social life in order to occupy some lonely outpost for Jesus. Or it may be the exact opposite: that we are called to die to the love of our own company in order to serve in the hurly-burly of the city, factory or hospital. It may be that we are called to die to the freedom of a single life in order to marry. Or it may be the exact opposite: that we are called to die to marriage in order to live a single life. There is no Christian stereotype in this or in any other aspect of the Christian life. Only the principle is clear: In order to follow Jesus we have to die to self.

To die is the way to find ourselves, the way to follow Jesus, and, third, it is the way to win others—not only the way to find ourselves, but the way to find other people. This seed metaphor, about dropping into the ground and dying, Jesus applies to ourselves as well as to him. If we cling to our own life, we will stay all alone. But if we die, we shall multiply. We hear a lot about the glamor of evangelism and not enough about the cost. Souls are not normally won for Jesus by slick, easy, superficial methods, but by sweat, blood, tears and death. The history of missions is full of examples. Sometimes the death has been literal, as in the early persecutions of the Roman Empire, in communist lands, among the Aucas. The blood of the martyrs is still the seed of the church. Sometimes the death is metaphorical. A man buries himself in a Muslim land, in the ghetto of the inner city, in a refugee camp, among a small tribe still in a stone-age culture, in the secular city. In effect, he buries himself, unrecognized, despised, misrepresented, rejected. He may labor patiently for years without recognition in a kind of living death until the fruit appears. When it dies, it multiplies. To die is the way to win others.

Then, fourth, to die is the way to be honored by the Father. Notice the phrase, "If any man serve me [in walking the way of the cross] him will my Father honor." What honors are you looking for? We are too eager for worldly honors, for the awards and the accolades and the decorations of men. Have we so lost our sense of proportion that we prefer the honors of men to receiving honor from God? God the Father honors those who serve his Son by following him even to death.

So there are four arguments with which Jesus buttresses his summons to die. Being willing to die is the way to find yourself, the way to win others, the way to follow Jesus and the way to be honored by the Father.

The Lord's Supper

In conclusion, this great truth on which we have been meditating is dramatized in the Lord's Supper. The broken bread and the outpoured wine symbolize Christ's body broken, Christ's blood shed in order that we might live. And it may be that Jesus intended that these further should be symbols of our own lives, broken, given, poured out in the service of Christ and others, like Mary's box of ointment. She broke the box; she poured out the ointment in her love for the Lord Jesus.

We come together to the table tonight and first thank Jesus for his death in order that we might live. Then let us go on to die to ourselves and to offer ourselves without reluctance or reserve in his service and the service of the world. I tell you such death is the way of life for ourselves and for others.

CONVENTION
SPEAKERS

John W. Alexander is President of Inter-Varsity Christian Fellowship—USA, Madison, Wisconsin. Previously he served as Chairman of the Department of Geography at the University of Wisconsin. His publications include *Fire in My Bones*, *Managing Our Work* and *Economic Geography*.

Chua Wee Hian is General Secretary of the International Fellowship of Evangelical Students. Born and raised in Singapore, he has studied in London and the USA. He served as Associate Secretary of IFES for East Asia before assuming his present position and also has been Editor of *The Way*, a quarterly magazine for Asian students.

Edmund P. Clowney is President of Westminster Theological Seminary, Philadelphia, and Professor of Practical Theology. He has been a pastor and former moderator of the General Assembly of the Orthodox Presbyterian Church. He is the author of *Called to the Ministry* and *The Doctrine of the Church*.

Donald J. Curry is a student in the Faculty of Medicine, University of Calgary, and the international students coordinator for the VCF club there.

Samuel J. Escobar is General Director of Inter-Varsity Christian Fellowship—Canada. Formerly he was Editor of *Certeza* and all Spanish publications of the International Fellowship of Evangelical Students for Latin America. He served on IFES staff in Argentina, Brazil and Spain.

David M. Howard is the Director of Urbana 73. He is Missions Director of Inter-Varsity Christian Fellowship, on loan from the Latin America Mission of which he was Assistant General Director, serving for fifteen years in Colombia and Costa Rica. He is the author of *By the Power of the Holy Spirit, Student Power in World Evangelism, Hammered as Gold* and *How Come, God?*

Gregorio Landero is President of Accion Unida (United Action), a program of evangelism and social concern in Northern Colombia. He has served as a pastor and as church coordinator of the Evangelical Churches of the Caribbean.

Elisabeth Elliot Leitch served in Ecuador among Colorado, Quichua and Auca Indians from 1952 to 1963. She is the widow of Jim Elliot, martyred by Aucas in 1956, and has recently been widowed again upon the death of her husband Dr. Addison Leitch, professor at Gordon-Conwell Theological Seminary. She is the author of seven books, including *Shadow of the Almighty, Through Gates of Splendor, Liberty of Obedience* and *A Slow and Certain Light*.

Paul E. Little is Assistant to the President of Inter-Varsity Christian Fellowship and Associate Professor of Evangelism, Trinity Evangelical Divinity School, Deerfield, Ill. He is currently on the staff of the Billy Graham Evangelistic Association as Associate Director for Program of the World Congress on Evangelism—1974. He is the author of *How to Give Away Your Faith, Know*

Why You Believe and *Know What You Believe.*

Samuel H. Moffett is Dean of the Graduate School, Theological Seminary of the Presbyterian Church of Korea, Seoul. Born in Korea of Presbyterian missionary parents, he served as a missionary in China from 1947 to 1949 and in Korea from 1955 until the present.

Rene Padilla is Associate General Secretary of the International Fellowship of Evangelical Students in Latin America, and the Editor of *Certeza,* a magazine for Latin American students. He has been heavily involved in literature work and has written numerous articles, including "Revolution and Revelation" in *Is Revolution Change?*

John R. W. Stott is Rector of All Souls Church, London, and honorary chaplain to Her Majesty, the Queen of England. He is President of the Evangelical Alliance of England in 1973-74. He has written many books, including *Basic Christianity, Understanding the Bible* and *Christ the Controversialist,* and he has participated in three previous Urbana Conventions.

Philip Teng is the pastor of a Christian and Missionary Alliance Church in Hong Kong and the Vice President of Alliance Bible Seminary. He also is Chairman of the C&MA Church Union and Foreign Missionary Society of C&MA, Hong Kong, and Chairman of the Continuation Committee of the First All-Asia Mission Consultation.

Bill Thomas is an IFES staff member in Brussels, Belgium, reaching Third World students in Europe. He was formerly a member of the East Harlem Protestant Parish, a missionary to Zaire, and a teacher and church worker in France.

Pius Wakatama is a student at Wheaton College. He has been an editor, writer and translator for Word of Life Publications, Rhodesia. He has recently been appointed a professor in the Christian College of Southern Africa.

Russell Weatherspoon is a student at Brooklyn College and president of the local Inter-Varsity Christian Fellowship chapter. He has been active in High School Evangelism Fellowship.

J. Christy Wilson, Jr. is the former pastor of the Community Church in Kabul, Afghanistan. Born in Iran of missionary parents and holding a Ph.D. in Arabic studies, he has served since 1951 as teacher, linguist and pastor to the international community in Afghanistan. Dr. Wilson directed the first IVCF Missionary Convention in Toronto in 1946.